Praise and Petition in the Old Testament

Praise and Petition in the Old Testament

Essays on the Psalms—Volume 2

Erhard S. Gerstenberger

EDITED BY
K. C. Hanson

CASCADE Books • Eugene, Oregon

PRAISE AND PETITION IN THE OLD TESTAMENT
Essays on the Psalms, Volume 2

Copyright © 2024 Erhard S. Gerstenberger. All rights reserved. Except for brief quotations in critical publications or reviews, no part of this book may be reproduced in any manner without prior written permission from the publisher. Write: Permissions, Wipf and Stock Publishers, 199 W. 8th Ave., Suite 3, Eugene, OR 97401.

Cascade Books
An Imprint of Wipf and Stock Publishers
199 W. 8th Ave., Suite 3
Eugene, OR 97401

www.wipfandstock.com

PAPERBACK ISBN: 978-1-6667-4081-3
HARDCOVER ISBN: 978-1-6667-4082-0
EBOOK ISBN: 978-1-6667-4083-7

Cataloguing-in-Publication data:

Names: Gerstenberger, Erhard S., 1932–2023, author. | Hanson, K. C. (Kenneth Charles), 1951–, editor.

Title: Praise and petition in the Old Testament : essays on the Psalms, volume 2 / Erhard S. Gerstenberger ; edited by K. C. Hanson.

Description: Eugene, OR: Cascade Books, 2024. | Includes bibliographical references and indexes.

Identifiers: ISBN 978-1-6667-4081-3 (paperback). | ISBN 978-1-6667-4082-0 (hardcover). | ISBN 978-1-6667-4083-7 (ebook).

Subjects: LCSH: Bible. O.T. Psalms—Criticism, interpretation, etc. | Bible. O.T. Jeremiah—Criticism, interpretation, etc. | Bible. O.T. Lamentations—Criticism, interpretation, etc.

Classification: BS1430.2 G47 2024 (print). | BS1430.2 (epub).

05/31/24

Unless otherwise noted, Scripture quotations are from the New Revised Standard Version of the Bible, copyright 1989 by the Division of Christian Education of the National Council of Churches of Christ in the USA and used by permission.

Contents

Editor's Foreword by K. C. Hanson | vii

Acknowledgments | ix

Abbreviations | xi

1 Petition and Praise: Basic Forms of Prayer in the Babylonian and Hebrew Traditions | 1

2 Where Is God? The Cry of the Psalmists | 15

3 Complaint and Confession: Psalm 69 | 27

4 Form Criticism in Action: Psalm 22 | 44

5 New Form Criticism: Psalm 55 | 78

6 Jeremiah's Complaint: Observations on Jer 15:10–21 | 91

7 Elusive Lamentations: What Are They About? | 103

Bibliography | 123

Author Index | 137

Scripture Index | 141

Editor's Foreword

THIS VOLUME IS THE second of three essay collections on the book of Psalms and related literature by Erhard S. Gerstenberger. It draws together essays that focus on the forms and themes of praise and petition—in Psalms, Jeremiah, and Lamentations.

Gerstenberger has been known since his earliest book, which began as his *Habilitationschrift—Der bittende Mensch: Bittritual und Klagelied des Einzelnen im Alten Testament* (The Petitioning Person: Petition Ritual and Complaint Song of the Individual in the Old Testament) Neukirchener Verlag (1980, reprint, Wipf & Stock, 2009)—as a leader in the analysis of complaint songs and petitionary rituals. What was so distinctive, from that earliest work, was his integration of form-critical analysis with comparative anthropology and ritual studies. His longstanding interest and expertise in the Sumerian hymns and complaint literature shows itself here as well.

As editor, I have selected the essays and organized the volume, and I edited it primarily in standardizing the format and notes as well as creating the comprehensive bibliography and indexes. I have also added to the notes and bibliography the recent English translations of two important works: Gunkel and Begrich, *Introduction to Psalms* (1998; reprint 2002), and Mowinckel, *Psalm Studies* (2014), in additional to more recent translations of other German works by Westermann, Zimmerli, etc.

It is sad that this volume and the one that will follow see the light of day only after the death of Prof. Gerstenberger on April 15, 2023, at the age of ninety. He was sharp and active to the end of his very fruitful life. I am grateful to the author's son, Dr. Björn Gerstenberger, for his assistance in looking through the proofs and his encouragement in completing the project.

K. C. Hanson
May 30, 2024

Acknowledgments

THE AUTHOR AND PUBLISHER gratefully acknowledge the earlier publications of these essays and permissions from the original publishers.

Chapter 1 "Petition and Praise: Basic Forms of Prayer in the Babylonian and Hebrew Traditions" first appeared in *Die Welt des Orients* 49 (2019) 81–94

Chapter 2 "'Where Is God?' The Cry of the Psalmist" first appeared in *Concilium* 28 (1992) 11–22.

Chapter 3 "Complaint and Confession: Psalm 69" first appeared as "Psalm 69: Complaint and Confession" in *To Hear and to Obey: Essays in Honor of Frederick C. Holmgren*, edited by Bradley J. Bergfalk et al., 3–19. Chicago: Covenant Publications, 1997.

Chapter 4 "Form Criticism in Action: Psalm 22" has not previously been published.

Chapter 5 "New Form Criticism: Psalm 55" first appeared as "Psalm 55 and New Form Criticism" in *Methodik im Diskurs: Neue Perspektiven für die alttestamentliche Exegese*, edited by Raik Heckl and Thomas Wagner, 26–43. Biblisch-theologische Studien 156. Neukirchen-Vluyn: Neukirchener, 2019.

Chapter 6 "Jeremiah's Complaints: Observations on Jer 15:1–21" first appeared in *Journal of Biblical Literature* 81 (1962) 249–63.

Chapter 7 Elusive Lamentations: What Are They About?" first appeared in *Interpretation* 67 (2013) 121–32.

Abbreviations

AOAT	Alter Orient und Altes Testament
BH	Biblia Hebraica
Bib	*Biblica*
BWANT	Beiträge zur Wissenschaft vom Alten und Neuen Testament
BZAW	Beihefte zur Zeitschrift für die alttestamentliche Wissenschaft
DN	divine name
ET	English translation
ETCSL	The Electronic Text Corpus of Sumerian Literature. Edited by Jeremy Black. Oxford, 1996–2007
FOTL	The Forms of the Old Testament Literature
FRLANT	Forschungen zur Religion und Literatur des Alten und Neuen Testaments
HBS	Herders biblische Studien
Heb.	Hebrew
hiph.	hiphil (Hebrew stem)
HKAT	Handkommentar zum Alten Testament
HKATErg	Handkommentar zum Alten Testament, Ergänzungsband
JBL	*Journal of Biblical Literature*
JSOTSup	Journal for the Study of the Old Testament Supplement Series

KJV	King James Version
LHBOTS	Library of Hebrew Bible/Old Testament Studies
LXX	Septuagint
MS/S	manuscript/s
MT	Masoretic text
SBS	Stuttgarter Bibelstudien
Sum.	Sumerian
TDOT	*Theological Dictionary of the Old Testament.* Edited by G. Johannes Botterweck, Helmer Ringgren, and Heinz-Josef Fabray. Translated by David E. Green et al. 17 vols. Grand Rapids: Eerdmans, 1974–2021
trans.	translated / translation
TWAT	*Theologisches Wörterbuch zum Alten Testament.* Edited by G. Johannes Botterweck, Helmer Ringgren, and Heinz-Josef Fabray. 10 vols. Stuttgart: Kohlhammer, 1973–2015
VTSup	Vetus Testamentum Supplements
WMANT	Wissenschaftliche Monographien zum Alten und Neuen Testament
ZAW	*Zeitschrift für die alttestamentliche Wissenschaft*

1

Petition and Praise

Basic Forms of Prayer in the Babylonian and Hebrew Traditions

Preliminaries

PRAYER IS A CENTRAL element of religion. We should define it broadly, as any human communication with the divine, or with being, goodness, life, self, and so on, as far as the entity addressed is potentially juxtaposed to the meditating or reflecting ego or community. Taken this way, prayer should be a common experience of all humanity, because inherently, humans cannot avoid relating themselves to the outside world nor searching for place and meaning within the theater they find themselves in. (Most western definitions seem to narrow down the concept of prayer to, for example, addressing a "benevolent supra-human entity").[1]

Prayer may be studied under quite a number of perspectives because it becomes manifest in various contexts or situations. It may be performed, thought out, meditated, intoned, written down, etc. It does occur in individual and collective variants. Prayer-words line up with gestures, rites, and symbolic actions, and become ingredients of liturgies, narrations, discourses, literature. Therefore we should not limit prayer to verbal utterances. Paraphernalia may well take on metaphorical values of the spoken word. Last but not least, formulated, written prayer does occur in determined social contexts and liturgical settings.[2]

---

1. Lenzi, *Prayers*, 56.
2. Reichard, *Prayer*.

Prayer does express a wide range of human sentiments serving different purposes in given situations vis à vis environmental challenges, wondrous or threatening encounters, feelings of forlornness, guilt or bliss. There is little use trying to establish a hierarchic or evolutionary order of motivations for praying as if prayer first has grown out of need for help, or alternatively from awe and admiration, then unfolding from either root (or countless other facets and modalities).[3] The developmental model of "prayer" is hardly adequate to explain the phenomenon in its variability. Yet, human spiritual experience does provide a common ground for plea and praise.

Therefore we may focus on two familiar forms of prayer which seemingly are opposed to each other, yet may be related in an overarching way. They possibly constitute, on different social levels, human means to participate in keeping life's balance. In fact, many pertinent written texts, the only access to antique prayers, e. g. from the ancient Near East, do belong to our categories "petition" or "praise." They also can be observed in living cultures and religions of present-day worlds, including our own. Focusing on but two types or moods of prayer certainly constitutes an encroachment on Mesopotamian more diversified categorizations (e.g., *šuilla*; *eršahuĝa*; *eršemma*; *namburbi*; *diĝiršadabba*; *ikribu* etc. and *adab*; *tigi*; *malgatum*; *širgida*; *balbale*; *zamzam*; etc.; as well as petitions and incantations in rituals like *Namburbi, Šurpu, Maqlu*).[4] But they really do not fit our own categories and vice versa, so we are unable to grasp the essence of those concepts. Biblical designations of psalms are equally incompatible with our patterns (e.g., *mizmor*; *šir*; *šiggayon*; *maskil*; *miktam*; etc.).[5] So we have to use our own modes of thinking and rubrics, always being mindful of their inadequacy over against ancient models.

It may well be opportune to mark loosely the theoretical starting point (working hypothesis) of this investigation: Ancient texts to my mind have not been composed and written down in order to serve a wide educated readership in our understanding. Rather, documented texts very likely undergirded oral communication often assuming important roles in public hearings or ceremonies. This assumption may well be connected with a general understanding of speech (oral or written) being intimately connected with communicative action, also in modern times. Even most idiosyncratic writers in ultimate analysis live from their interaction with the public.

3. Heiler, *Gebet*.

4. Cf. Wilcke, "Gebet"; Wilcke, "Hymne"; Falkenstein and von Soden, *Sumerische und akkadische Hymnen*.

5. Gerstenberger, *Psalms, Part 1* and *Part 2*.

Pleading for Help and Salvation

Numerous Sumerian and Akkadian as well as some thirty prayers of the Old Testament Psalter may be classified—in our own frame of thinking—as petitions or supplications. They presuppose situations of human (also divine?) need, endangerment, frustration, anxieties in which the person threatened addresses some potentially helpful power to deliver him or her from danger, pain, and death. In fact, many of these calls for salvation are stylized as "cries from the abyss" (Pss 69; 88; 130).[6] Other typical topics include deliverance from bad omens,[7] demons of sickness, bad luck, social discrimination, etc.[8] Prayers from the Mesopotamian tradition, having originated probably in the Old and Middle Babylonian periods and reworked or newly composed in the first millennium BCE, bear structural, thematic, and theological semblances to the Hebrew Psalms of individual complaint. They both expose liturgical elements like invocation, eulogy, complaint, confession of guilt, affirmation of confidence, petition, imprecation, vow, apparently all serving the same end: To gain the support of the divine being mostly addressed by name. They both also include typical "shamanistic" (to use a modern designation) features of exorcism and magic.[9] Slight differences in wording, topics, structure, outlook of these ritually identifiable "psalms," generated precisely for ceremonial use, cannot undo their provenance from and alignment to analogous life-situations: the curing of sick or endangered persons.[10]

To sketch a few lines of Babylonian evidence: Cuneiform prayers of supplication, in our case, very fortunately, quite often have been transmitted embedded in more or less elaborate ritual instructions for the ceremonial expert. They are nothing less than guidelines to the correct execution of intricate ritual procedures. Matters touched in such professional advice range from selecting and purifying an adequate local for the healing ceremony, preparing and "sanctifying" the patient, arranging proper material and implements for incense-burning and sacrifices, reciting adequate blessings, magical formulas, prayers (perhaps also mythical stories) at ceremonial junctures, taking care of "contaminated" residues of the performance, etc.[11]

---

6. Barth, *Die Errettung vom Tode*; Cunningham, *Deliver Me from Evil*.
7. Maul, "Herzberuhigungsklagen."
8. Jaques, *Mon dieu qu'ai-je fait?*
9. Gerstenberger, *Der bittende Mensch*.
10. Ambos, "Ritual Healing."
11. Cf. the detailed description of the expert's task in namburbi rituals by Maul, *Zukunftsbewältigung*, 27–156; Borger, "Šurpu"; Hallo, *The World's Oldest Literature*, 645–58; Abusch and Schwemer, *Corpus of Mesopotamian Anti-Witchcraft Rituals*, 1–24; Frechette, *Mesopotamian Ritual-Prayers*, 143–224.

Most extant Babylonian rituals use similar ceremonial elements, but there is at the same time a great variety of details, a certain amount of mingling of rites, and some particularities belonging to only one of the determined types of healing procedures. Thus the making and elimination of substitute figurines and the burning of effigies seems to have been restricted to specific rituals or purposes.[12]

Furthermore: Ceremonial healing practice to a large extent was determined by initial diagnosis. Recognizing causes of illness was essential then as it is today for choosing adequate ritual medication. Therefore observation of ominous signs and their correct analysis were necessary first steps for preparing a cure. The healer or an independent diagnostician took over this responsibility.[13] All in all, the treatment of ills, misfortunes, bad omens in the ancient Near East was a very intricate science set into practice by a gamut of sophisticated rites handed down and cultivated by generations of experts. The great variety of incantations is an indication of long study and practice of medical matters, initiated by the deities themselves as in ETCSL 4.22.1 Ninisina A, especially lines 27–35. The healing goddess speaks to her son Damu, investing him with her knowledge:

> "My son, pay attention to everything medical! Damu, pay attention to everything medical! You will be praised for your diagnoses." Holy Ninisina performs for him her role as incantation priest, which Enki bestowed on her from the princely abzu. Because of the anxiety and intestinal disease which pursue mankind, this person writhes like a snake on scorching ground, hissing like a snake in waste ground, always calling out anew: "My heart! My stomach!"

The patient's prayer, according to a multitude of Babylonian documents, belonged into the center of a full-fledged healing ceremony involving many actions, words, music, implements, psychic experiences, professional knowledge, participation of kinfolks, leadership of a curing expert. The importance of the patient's prayer is, among other things, sometimes highlighted in Babylonian ritual instructions by the introductory formula: "let him (i.e. the patient) recite/speak like this" (*kīam tušaqbâššu*, alternatively *kīam tušadbabšu* "let him recite thus").[14] The actions of the ritual expert and the very structure, wording, emotional content, theological outlook of the prayer do support the hypothesis that handed-down/written entreaties for cure and salvation never were idiosyncratic or biographical texts. Rather,

---

12. Maul, *Zukunftsbewältigung*, 46–47, 85–93; Reiner, *Šurpu*.
13. Heeßel, *Babylonisch-assyrische Diagnostik*.
14. Maul, *Zukunftsbewältigung*, 68.

they have been formulated by the experienced liturgical expert in order to cover countless cases of determined calamities. They represent condensed knowledge of generations of practitioners and cannot be read or interpreted biographically. Patients' prayers have been selected and prescribed by the healer. Occasionally, however, the old documents hint at the possibility that the sufferer was allowed to articulate his own feelings within the ceremony (cf. 1 Sam 2:15; Ps 102:1),[15] like in Christian worship services, when moments of silence are offered for everyone to formulate his or her private concerns. In daily affairs, of course, everyone was free to pray spontaneously (cf. Judg 6:22; 15:18). Prayer was not restricted to liturgical agendas, but ritual prayer certainly was considered the more powerful means of communication.[16]

Comparable rituals for restitution of health and fortune can be observed throughout many cultures and periods all around the world, including our own times and places.[17] A concrete example could be the proliferated and well documented ceremonial practice of the Navajo tribe in Arizona/New Mexico with the patient's prayer as a central concern of the medicine man.[18] Such references should legitimize attempts to read ancient prayers of supplication in a reconstructed performative or ritual context. Needless to say, that a perspective like this does not preclude the possibility of a mere literary origin and use of prayer-texts. Akkadian "God-Letters" or "Letter-Prayers"[19] seem to be a germinal point for exclusively written communications with the divine. Each antique individual prayer needs a scrutiny in regard to its provenance and use.

Preserved ritual frameworks of cuneiform prayers of petition give valuable insights not only into individual acts of performance but also the general purpose and the ceremonial structure of petitionary prayer.

First of all, those ritual instructions are directed in the first place not to the supplicant, but to the master of ceremonies, the *mašmaššu* or *āšipu* (exorcist), or the *kalû* (cult singer). He has received the contents of the sacred performance, ritual instructions and his expertise from the deities; he leads the liturgy as a whole, conducts purifications, songs, exorcisms, magical rites, offerings and sacrifices. And, at determined points, he has the patient or supplicant recite the prayer, which apparently was pivotal for the purpose of the ritual. This fact reveals some fundamental dimensions of prayer in

15. Maul, *Zukunftsbewältigung*, 69–70.
16. Reichard, *Prayer*.
17. Bell, *Ritual*, 115–20.
18. Reichard, *Prayer*.
19. Hallo, *The World's Oldest Literature*, 255–70.

antiquity (and among tribal societies until this day): Individual supplication may be part and parcel of a professional curing ceremony and in that case must be property of the expert who administers rites and words. He (or she) was the owner and author of the prayer texts to be spoken by the suppliant. Theological conceptions as well as individual traits of supplication were due to the professional knowledge of the spiritual leader.

Second: Ritual prayers are integral parts of dramatic, magic and musical enactment. Words and rites belong together. We are accustomed to look at texts in isolation. For the ancients the ceremony of supplication worked in conjunction. Right words and correct execution of rites in all their details were considered a unified force to be presented to the holy beings.[20] The ritual and all its parts do exercise a coercive power, which does have magical dimensions but surely has to be distinguished from "black," that is "destructive" magic. Right words of prayer are in a lenient way compelling. They make divine powers willing to intervene for the supplicant. The notion of magic power or witchcraft, a pejorative concept in Jewish-Christian tradition (cf. Exod 22:17; Deut 18:9–14; 1 Sam 28:7–25), really pervaded all the elements of ritual ceremonies, including prayer.[21] The sometimes hotly debated borderline between prayer and magic formula, therefore, in antiquity was not that incisive as it is for modern thinking. There sure have been in all ancient cultures spells, working by their own inherent power, in determined situations and against certain malevolent beings. But prayer was equally supposed to develop its own stamina and coercion, rationally and mystically and along interpersonal communication.

Purely literary prayers (e.g., god-letters, prayers in epic or other narrative contexts, supplications in exclusively scribal- or school-environments, etc.) need to be identified on their own. Are the Old Testament specimens of individual complaints (e.g., Pss 3–7; 11; 13; 17; 22; 31; 35; 38; 51; 55; 59; 69; 88; 102; 109; 130; 140; 141; 143; etc.)[22] truly liturgical compositions or merely literary imitations? My suggestion is: The majority of preserved cuneiform petitionary prayers belongs to the performative type, has been written down not as scribal exercise, nor as wisdom and school tradition but in order to serve as a commemorative aid for the acting leader of ceremonies in small scale rituals (for individuals and their primary groups) of cure and rehabilitation. Likewise, the Old Testament complaint psalms belong to the performative kind of prayers, collected in the Psalter to be used in early

---

20. Reichard, *Prayer*; Zgoll, *Die Kunst des Betens*; Cunningham, *Deliver Me from Evil*.

21. Abusch and Schwemer, *Corpus of Mesopotamian Anti-Witchcraft Rituals*, 3–4, 8–9, esp. 8 n14.

22. Gerstenberger, *Psalms, Part 1*, 11–14.

Jewish curing rites. Ancient Israel, in a way, became a late heir of the millennial tradition of supplication, drawing into her treasure of sacred poetry some thirty to forty specimens of individual complaint and petition[23] that had originated in pre-Yahwistic curing ceremonies of old.

A good number of questions need to be resolved in regard to the Old Testament situation. Why do neither the book of Psalms nor the Hebrew Scriptures offer ritual instructions for the performance of individual complaints (there are plenty of sacrificial regulations, cf. Lev 1–9, and some other archaic rites, cf. Lev 13–16; Num 5:11-28; 19:1-10; Deut 21:1-9)? Are we able to find evidence in the Psalter or without of ritual experts who administered the patient's prayer? Do the Psalms in themselves betray traces of liturgical recitation? To try some concise answers or suggestions: Possibly, ritual regulations for curing petitions were left behind in the Old Testament because they were under suspicion to carry too much apostate magical art (cf. Deut 18:9-13; 1 Sam 28:3-9) although those cited exceptions would advise against this argument. Still, we would have to consider new, Torah-oriented liturgical settings as an orthodox replacement of magic-contaminated activities. Unfortunately, the headlines of the Psalms are of little help. They partially refer to cultic activities (e.g., music, instruments, choir-masters [?], etc.), but their exact meaning remains unclear. Ritual experts are dimly recognizable in the Hebrew Scriptures. Most notably "men of God" like Elijah and Elisha, in the older strata of tradition, before they turned Yahwistic antagonists of the kings, are prototypes of shamanist healers who also apply a little ritual action to their clients (cf. 1 Kgs 17:19-22; 2 Kgs 4:32-35; 5:9-14). But the testimony stays vague. Among the internal evidence of the individual complaints themselves one could point out references to sacrifice and purifications (cf. Ps 5:4; 51:9), waiting for a divine oracle (Ps 35:3), confinement to agonies in one's own home (Ps 6:7; 38:4-9), etc. Outside the Psalter a prophet does visit the sick person, bring to him a message of Yahweh, and treat him with a lump of figs (Isa 38:1, 4-8, 21; cf. Job 33:14-28). All this is scanty evidence for ritual curing. So, we have to depend most of all on the plausibility of analogy: Curing serious illness of bad fortune in so many cultures is a professional task. Babylonian curers among other means used compelling patient's prayers to counteract evil. Complaint of individuals in the Psalter are very similar to the Babylonian incantational prayers. Therefore we may assume that also Hebrew petitionary psalms belonged into some sort of curing ritual.

What, then, has been the spiritual function and finality of performative supplication in ancient Near Eastern cultures? Ancient Near Eastern

---

23. Gerstenberger, *Psalms, Part 1*; Hallo, *The World's Oldest Literature*.

literatures give the overall impression, that people of the time strongly believed in a created, but continuously threatened wholesome order. The chaos-battle and flood motives as well as historical and legal traditions from Sumerian times onward witness to the gravity of the divine and human task to maintain the good harmony between all participant powers. At stake is nothing less than taming and limiting destructive forces which were present in all beings and the world at large. Life and history were known not to develop in eternal predetermined inflexible molds, but needed constant readjustments. Mesopotamian beliefs in the "fixing of destinies" (Sum. *nam-tar*) culminated in the New Year's rites of Babylon and other religious centers and subsequent struggles with altered situations, new challenges, individual exemptions.

Focusing on prayer we learn from the mass of performed supplications that they were used whenever something disruptive either did threaten or had already occurred and needed to be repaired. The balance of good and evil was considered tilted towards the negative as experienced by some person who suffered the onslaught of evil, the wrath of the gods or some inscrutable fate. Careful diagnostics of each individual case was obligatory.[24] To combat evil and to remedy the situation one needed to know the exact causes and instigators of the ills at hand. Ritual experts, then, decided about which healing rites to perform. Headlines of supplicatory prayers or pertinent rituals quite often indicate the exact range of application. The rituals celebrated presumably were rather successful, judging from similar undertakings observable all over the world not only in still existing tribal societies. (As the internet tells us, there do exist, even in today's industrialized scientific societies, hosts of shamanistic circles and communities.) In effect, the small scale combat of evil in favor of suffering persons and their familial groups was part of the ongoing battle between good and evil, growth and destruction.

Praise of Higher Powers

Praise, in terms of ceremonial performance, seems to be quite a different thing from petition. Eulogizing the deities, for example, as a rule, requires a crowd of people.[25] It does not occur so often within a small group, viz. the kinship circle which may take care of the individual sufferer. As may be gathered from an extensive Sumerian hymnic literature (cf. below, and

24. Heeßel, *Babylonisch-assyrische Diagnostik*.
25. Gerstenberger, *Theologien* (ET: *Theologies*); Westermann, *Das Loben Gottes* (ET: *The Praise of God*)

the corpus ETCSL)[26] the social level of praise, normally, in the ancient Near East is from neighborhood communities upward to the appropriate city and state institutions. Praising literature, in fact, mostly can be linked with royal courts, city and state temples and the appropriate personnel. Vivid descriptions of hymn-genesis and performance have been preserved in some Šulgi-poems, e.g., Šulgi E (ETCSL 2.4.2.05):

> I, Šulgi, the king whose name is very suitable for songs, intend to be praised in my prayers and hymns. At the command of my sister Ĝeštin-ana, my scholars and composers of ... have composed adab, tigi and malgatum hymns about my being the Nintur of all, that is, about how wise I am in attending upon the gods, about how the god of intercession has given me favourable signs that years of abundance will elapse for me in due course. They have composed *šir-gida* songs, royal praise poetry, *šumunša*, *kunĝar*, and *balbale* compositions about how I carried warfare across the sea to the south (lines 14–30) [lines 24–28 left out] ...
> They composed for me *gigid* and *zamzam* songs about my manual skill, ever reliable for the finest task of the scribal art; about my ability to unravel the calculating and reckoning of the waxing of the new moon; about my causing joy and happiness; about how I know exactly at what point to raise and lower the *tigi* and *zamzam* instruments, and how I have complete control of the plectra of the great stringed instruments; how I cannot be stopped by anything insurmountable, about my being a runner tireless when emerging from the race. (lines 31–38) ...
> [lines 39–239 left out]
> May my hymns be in everyone's mouth; let the songs about me not pass from memory. So that the fame of my praise, the words which Enki composed about me, and which Ĝeštin-ana joyously speaks from the heart and broadcasts far and wide, shall never be forgotten, I have had them written down line by line in the House of the Wisdom of Nisaba in holy heavenly writing, as great works of scholarship. No one shall ever let any of it pass from memory ... It shall not be forgotten, since indestructible heavenly writing has a lasting renown. The scribe should bring it to the singer, and can let him look at it, and with the wisdom and intelligence of Nisaba, let him read it to him as if from a lapis-lazuli tablet. Let my songs sparkle like silver in the lode! Let them be performed in all the cult-places, and let no one neglect them in the Shrine of the New Moon. In the music-rooms of Enlil and Ninlil and at the

---

26. Römer, *Hymnen und Klagelieder*; Wilcke, "Hymne."

morning and evening meals of Nanna, let the sweet praise of me, Šulgi, be never-ending. (lines 240–257)

Exact prescriptions as to the ritual performance[27] of the great variety of compositions apparently have not been written down. We do not have, in Sumerian hymns, the minutiae of Babylonian ritual instructions. But the above text does emphasize the careful handling of sacred hymns and music, and the urgency of their proper and sustained performance. Hymns seem to be the basis of dynastic power,[28] comparable in their significance to military force and economic strength.

A broader look at ancient Near Eastern prayers should relativize, however, the high-level use of hymnic forms a little. Supplicatory prayers, far from being hymnic events for themselves, often hail the addressed helper for his or her supreme capacities and benevolence.[29] Presupposed, as it were, was a miserable condition of the supplicant. Praise in this context can only signify an effort to activate those forces and sentiments which might trigger divine saving acts. More about it below. Looking at Sumerian literary texts from the third/second millennium (cf. ETCSL) it becomes obvious that praise-poems may adopt different forms and may be voiced by and addressed to a variety of entities. Instead of venturing into a discussion of genres of eulogies I shall follow the lead of a small expression denoting "praise, blessing."

One particular word or formula may betray a lot about the dynamics of hymn-singing in Sumerian/Akkadian times: DN + *zà-mí* (e.g., Enki, Inana, Enlil, etc.: "praise be to DN" or "hail to DN")[30] which is found often at the very end of a Sumerian poem, but quite frequently also in the body of such texts. In the end-position and without any morphological or syntactic accretion its function comes close to the Heb. *halleluyah*, an exhortation to some audience or group. Shouting "hails" echoes living outbursts of enthusiasm, even if the *zà-mí*-formula may have become a literary device. The inner mechanism of praise would be to bring about that very power and glory to which the addressee is entitled.

Many more mentions of *zà-mí* in the body of hymnic compositions explain further the scope and meaning of this mysterious term. There is a foundational and inauguration effect of *zà-mí* singing or reciting: in the primordial beginning Enlil confers *zà-mí* upon the holy city and temple of Keš (ETCSL 4.80.2, lines 3–9: *den-lil-le keški za-mi am-ma-ab-be*). So

27. Zgoll, "Für Sinne, Geist und Seele."
28. Steible, *Rimsin*.
29. Abusch, "The Promise to Praise the God"; Zgoll, "Audienz."
30. Gerstenberger, *Theologies in the Old Testament* (*Theologien*, 46–85).

the prehistorical sanctuary can become the "house in whose interior is the power of the land, and behind which is the life of Sumer." (lines 29–30).

Enlil-bani, tenth ruler of Isin, receives support and authority from a number of anuna-deities on the occasion of his enthronement or at a New Year's decreeing of destinies; the hymn is recited in direct address by a liturgist, and its overboard praise comes to a close in the phrase: "may the wise scribe in the scribal academy ... not allow your praise to cease" (ETCSL 2.5.8.1, lines 178–184: *zà-mí-zu ĝa-la nam-ba-an-dag-ge*, lines 182–184). The whole poem, a solid eulogy of divine authority, is summarized by the term *za-mi-zu*, "your empowering song." It is, in reality, the backbone of Enlil-bani's reign, and should last beyond his life-time. The preserving (beyond the inaugurating) aspect of praise comes to the fore in various other royal hymns, especially in Šulgi E, which offers the most elaborate exposition of hymn-making and hymn-use (ETCSL 2.4.2.05, lines 14–38, 240–257, quoted above). Poets, scribes, and singers are involved in creating and performing the essential, life- and memory-saving hymns. Obviously, reference is to cultic commemoration after the deified ruler's demise. "His" *zà-mí*-compositions will persist, and with them his name, personality, in commemoration.

Other functions of *zà-mí*-praise are the consoling, restoring, perhaps even resurrecting life. Ur-Namma A (ETCSL 2.4.1.1) is the lament over the untimely death of the first king of the Ur III-dynasty. The final praise goes to Ninĝišzida (line 240) who reverted the fate of the king (a similar motif is found in ETCSL 1.7.3: Ereškigal is lauded). In another famous poem, "nin me šara," political conflicts of the Akkad empire quite naturally affect involved deities. Inana, in order to defend the cause of Enheduana, chief priestess and Akkad-governor of Ur, needs the support of her constituents (ETCSL 4.07.2). The priestess declares: (line 63): "Your portentous song ["holy song": *šir kug*] I now shall intone"; (line 65): "I shall enumerate your divine powers [ME]; (line 138–140): "With 'It is enough for me, it is too much for me!' I have given birth, oh exalted lady, to (this song) for you. That which I recited to you at (mid)night, may the singer repeat it to you at noon!"[31] All these affirmations prove the central importance of praise. They imply a *zà-mí* quality to be communicated to the addressee. Inana wins the battle against Akkad's opponents. Even deities need support and restorations, now and then, of their strength, cf. Enki when bereft of the ME by tricky Inana (ETCSL 1.3.1).

---

31. Translation of Zgoll: "Da (das Herz mir) voll, ja übervoll geworden ist, gewaltige Herrin, habe ich es [das Lied] für dich geboren. Was dir zur Mitternacht gesagt wurde, soll der Kultsänger dir zur Mittagszeit wiederholen."

A good number of self-glorifications voiced by deities or kings, can be adduced as further evidence for the role of praise in the grand scenery of power-balance. "My za-mi" [zà-mí-ĝu] occurs nine times in ETCSL 1.1.3, line 101; 2.4.1.3, line 115; 2.4.2.02, lines 130 and 384; 2.4.2.05, lines 15 and 257; 2.5.4.01, lines A330 and 377; 2.5.5.1, line 108 (self-praises of Enki, Ur-Namma, Šulgi, Išme-Dagan, Lipit-Eštar). These testimonies may be complemented by ca. sixty specimens of zà-mí with suffix of second person singular ("your zà-mí," in direct address). The weight of such personal praises was enormous. They were true treasures of sustenance.

In short, zà-mí was, in the Sumerian tradition, a special, creative power probably originating in acclamative or "hailing" shouts. The term soon came to be sort of a quality-stamp on many kinds of laudatory expressions like meteš i-i (to utter praise), ar de$_6$ (to laud), šir tud (create a song), šir áĝ (perform a song), šir dug$_4$ (recite/sing a song), šir du$_{12}$ (chant a song; šir may, of course, also signify "lament," "dirge," etc.). zà-mí did never become a genre designation. Neither was it a liturgical rubric. It rather indicated the inner power which kept up all realms of life, politics, religious spirituality. Synonymous expressions could probably also represent the power of praising. But only zà-mí really lets perspire the notion of transferring to the eulogized one the life-supporting force. Like in Ps 29:1: "Ascribe to the LORD, O heavenly beings (literally: sons of God), ascribe to the LORD glory and strength" (literally: "bring, give to him" instead: "ascribe"). Comparison with "good me"(divine powers) is instructive.

Where and how were the potent za-mi songs performed? What was their "life-situation"? Judging from the mass of royal involvement in the Sumerian and Old Babylonian hymnic texts it may be suggested that the prime local of performance was the palace and/or the temples of a city's major deities.[32] Hymns thus gain a political dimension. Fostering dynastic power hymn singing was essential for its persistence and the survival of the monarch's memory, that is, dynastic continuity. Some king's—like Šulgi, Naramsin, Išmedagan, Lipeteštar, etc.—explicitly called for continued liturgical presentation of their personal hymns. Climactically, gods and kings in the ancient Near East had their auto-eulogy performed, in the first person of the singer. There are plenty of examples in the Sumerian corpus, but also some analogies in Old Testament prophetic literature (cf. Isa 42:14–17; 43:1–7, 10–13, 14–21; 44:6–8; etc.).

Old Testament hymns were composed and performed under historical and cultural conditions quite different from those of the Mesopotamian

---

32. Anderson, "The Praise of God."

royal administrations.[33] Granted, that ancient Israel in exilic and post-exilic times did have memories of past royal Judahite and Israelite kingdoms. Psalm 89:2–30 or Ps 2 may be remote remembrances of bygone glory, and the messianic twist in Pss 2; 45; 72; 96; 99; 110 may well be actualizations of such old memories. The reality of Israel after the exile was different, however. For one thing, royalty in the religious community which lacked a sovereign ordained by her god, Yahweh, was transferred to the deity himself. Thus the Yahweh-kingship and the related Zion-Hymns made up for authentic dynastic eulogies. On the other hand, Israel's new organization which amounted to an acephalic, religious society or a theocratic organization in theological terms was a "covenant-relationship." Hymnic texts, astonishingly, quite often appear in the "We-form" (cf. Pss 8; 46; 48; 65; 95; 99; 100; 124; 144; etc.), as affirmations of a chanting congregation. On the other hand, first person plural songs are extremely rare in Sumerian and Akkadian hymns. Old Testament hymns count with a participation of the *qahal*, "gathered congregation," while royal ceremonies, apart from religious state festivities, may have been enacted under seclusion.

There are no "professional" prescriptions of hymnic performance to be found in biblical writings. Old Testament narrations, however, clearly reveal the communal character of hymn-singing (cf. 1 Chr 16; 25; 2 Chr 20:18–30; 29:27–30; 30:21; 35:15; Neh 12:27–43). All these passages portray big festive events, expert singers and instrumentalists in charge of praise and ordained by the administration, people responding loudly and joyfully, processions and dedications, sacrifices and exhortations. Hymn-singing was embedded in congregational worship service. Partially, praise-songs themselves refer to these liturgical features (cf. Exod 15; Pss 15; 24; 46; 68; 132; etc.). Private praise of God certainly had a legitimate place in ritual, most of all in thanksgiving offices after successful supplication (cf. Pss 7:18; 22:23–27; 30; 32; 35:27–28; 52:11; 54:8–9; etc.).

Conclusion

The apparent antagonism between (literary!) petition and praise in ancient texts was due to different life-situations and social settings. Supplication and praise do have something in common: They are engaged modes of human discourse in full responsibility for life's good order. Their ceremonial contexts are special, however, in that individual supplication normally occurred in a limited social environment, while singing praises as a rule was a public, political, even national or imperial affair. Small wonder that Sumerian praise

---

33. Gerstenberger, *Psalms, Part 1* and *Part 2*.

compositions encompass larger and official groups, predominantly the figure of the king, the royal court, temple, city and "academic" organizations.

We may well speak of different theological perspectives in ancient Near Eastern supplication and hymn-singing. But the two basic forms of prayer are committed to creating and maintaining that harmonic order intended by the great deities and inherent in all being. Humans on all social levels take co-responsibility to ward off destructive forces and strengthen the beneficial ones. Their prayers in petitionary and laudatory modes (and they do intersect to some extent) are in themselves powerful tools in the efforts to achieve a peaceful, opportune, future-oriented, global earth to live on.

In contrast to western, Christian dogmatic narrowness (reduction of the divine to one personal will, revelation through chosen leaders and historical events, focus on an exclusive metaphysical plan of forlornness and salvation, hierarchic world order copied from royal and imperial structures, etc.) Near Eastern theology implicitly acknowledges the unfathomable depth of being which cannot be harmonized into a human, rational system of government.

2

Where Is God?

The Cry of the Psalmists[1]

God's Absence Today

IS THERE SUCH A thing as "modern" man, who simply wants to be his own master? Who right to the depths of his being indifferently contemplates an empty universe with which he can enter only into a technical relationship? Or is "modern" man someone who has denied God and who—tormented by guilt feelings and inferiority complexes—has to live out his delusion of omnipotence in compensation?[2] Who is this enlightened, modern man?

Seeking to define present-day people does not get us very far. Our world society is too multifarious; the traditions of faith are too different, as are the experiences of millions of people on all the continents. There is no one type of person. However, one thing can be said quite definitely: there are experiences of God in all the cultures and religions of this earth. And where God is present, there can also be the shock of God's absence. Can anything be said today about this remoteness of God?

People experience God mediated by their environment. The mystical ways of the knowledge of God are a communion with being; as such, they also presuppose the world. As always, in the midst of the technological world as in the hinterland, the "absence of God" is produced by circumstances and effects.

Need teaches us not only to pray but also to curse. Where people vegetate in extreme poverty and under the pressure of unspeakable suffering,

---

1. Translated by John Bowden.
2. Richter, *Der Gotteskomplex*.

as in Third World countries and at the socially weakest levels of industrial countries, the elemental experience of godforsakenness also breaks through. The miracle takes place, and believing communities come into being in shanty towns and slum settlements. And the natural, human thing also happens: despair advances. An Argentinian song goes:

> One day I asked, 'Grandfather, where is God?'
> My grandfather became sad and did not give me an answer.
> My grandfather died in the fields, without prayer or confession.
> The Indios buried him, to the music of flute and drum.[3]

In the following verses the question is put to the father: he, too, knows no answer and dies a godforsaken death. The singer is reluctant to ask his brother, of the same generation, for God is certainly not with the oppressed forester in the mountains, but is sitting at the businessman's table. God is concerned with the possibilities of life, with basic welfare on this earth. If the means of survival are chronically lacking, generation by generation, then belief in God's providence must go astray. Or a process of purging must be devised to explain the deprivations and the impossibility of living a full span of life, interpreting it as the pledge of betterment in another life. Or the result must simply become apathy, without speech or thought, at most an attitude still capable of finding somewhere the crumbs which allow the light of life to flicker on. I can picture the Brazilian *nordestinos* (day-laborers in the sugar-cane growing areas of the northeast), dried up by sun and hunger, living signs of the absence of God. It is not hunger alone which makes people despair. Loss of rights, violation of human dignity and persecution weigh at least as heavily. In our supposedly enlightened twentieth century, contempt for human beings has swelled like an avalanche. As a German I think first of all of the annihilation of the Jewish people in Europe, of labor camps and crematorium ovens during Hitler's rule. Millions of victims had to nurse their doubts about God's righteousness in the horror of the ghetto and the machinery of killing. Anyone who could still sing hymns in Auschwitz, which people actually did, needed more than human strength. Even those with the strongest faith experienced God's absence at least temporarily in the senseless hatred and murder. Izabela Gelbard put experiences from the Warsaw ghetto into poetry:

> Mother and old woman and defenseless girl,
> protected by the holy hands of our fathers,
> who during the slaughter, in blood and cursing,
> called to their God, 'LORD You are our protection . . .'

---

3. Yupanqui, in *Cantaré*, 21–22.

> But he did not protect—he was not in the ghetto,
> probably the shame of it choked him.
> Even Szaja Judkiewicz perished. Who was he,
> Judkiewicz? An old, pious Jewish man.[4]

The poet sets the unshakable faith of the ninety-four-year-old man against despair in God.

> O Adonai! Without shroud, without tefillin (prayer thong),
> forgive me, forgive me, YOU are great, LORD OF GRACE.
> YOUR mercy embraces me, YOUR mercy surrounds me,
> although I am without tallis (prayer shawl), which the enemy trampled on.[5]

Quite apart from the indescribable Holocaust of the Hitler period, there have been countless victims around the earth. On the Indian reserves, in labor camps and countless torture chambers and prisons, among enslaved women workers, in the theaters of war and among the endless streams of refugees in our times, cries have been uttered for the God who has disappeared, cries full of bitterness and despair.

Where else does the question of God arise in our time? We would be ill-advised to see only the material and social occasions. The spiritual, enlightened legacy of the past century which has now brewed up in science and technology is similarly the root for radical and desperate questioning. Is the universe cold and void? Is there a chance of putting a stop to homo faber? Is he in process of taking all creative power into his hands? Where is God in the modern cultural world of gene manipulation and space flights? Literature, theater, films—right down to the genre of science fiction and science horror strips—have taken up the theme. Among physicists in modern times there have always been those who have held firm to the notion of a creator (like Albert Einstein, Niels Bohr, and so on). Other Western scientists speak, in the light of Jewish-Christian creation faith, of an anthropic universe, i.e. a universe orientated on human beings and their knowledge and understanding.[6] Yet others reject the existence of any deity: they claim that this cannot be reconciled with the laws of physics. The knowable universe functions without the hypothesis of a divine creation or guidance. "The old covenant is broken; man finally knows that he is alone in the unfeeling expanses of the

---

4. Gelbard, in *Hiob 1943*, 153–54.
5. Gelbard, in *Hiob 1943*, 155.
6. Hawking, *A Brief History of Time*.

universe from which he emerged by chance. Nowhere is either his lot or his duty written down."[7] Here, apparently, all questions about God end.

The Psalms and Us

Of the one hundred and fifty prayers and songs in the Old Testament Psalter, about forty belong to the category of "individual laments." They reflect the personal distress of people whose life is in danger. Serious illness, social scorn, evil circumstances, unexplained misfortunes and anxieties have them in their grasp, heralds of death and the powers of the underworld. The depths, the "maw," reach out for them or seem already to have swallowed them up.

> I sink in deep mire;
>   where there is no foothold.
> I have come into deep water,
>   and the flood sweeps over me.
> I am weary with my crying;
>   my throat is parched.
> My eyes grow dim
>   with waiting for my God.
> (Ps 69:2–4; cf. Ps 88:5–7; 130:1; Jonah 2:3–7).

The distress cannot be explained by chance, blind fate or some mechanical causes. The deity is involved in the threat to life in some still unknown way. The sufferer needs rapid help; his family sends for the healer or man of God (cf. 1 Kgs 14:2–3; 2 Kgs 1:2; 4:22). Only these specialists can make a diagnosis; they know the possibilities for medical and ritual treatment. The prayers in the psalms come from their knowledge; indeed they are liturgical parts of worship which are to bring healing (similar rituals are known from the ancient Near East and many tribal societies), and they give us insight into the symptoms of suffering and their interpretation.

> My heart throbs, my strength fails me;
>   and the light of my eyes—it also has gone from me.
> My friends and companions stand aloof from my plague,
>   and my kinsmen stand far off.
> Those who seek my life lay their snares,
>   those who seek my hurt speak of ruin,
>   and meditate treachery all the day long.
> But I am like a deaf man, I do not hear,

---

7. Monod, *Chance and Necessity*.

> like a dumb man who does not open his mouth.
> Yes, I am like a man who does not hear,
>> and one who has nothing to say. (Ps 38:11–15 [ET 10–14]).

The lament indicates stages in the suffering which to some degree correspond to the attitude of the deity. The physical collapse (v. 11), already vividly described in vv. 4, 6, 8, is the consequence of a divine "curse," an evil reprimand. Other laments identify God's chastisement, blow, punishment, as the direct cause of this suffering. At all events God must be angry, and the reason for his anger can lie with the supplicant himself (vv. 4, 7). However, the punishment—no matter how deserved it may be—must not turn into anger (v. 2), for then compassion could be excluded, and the measure of the punishment be exceeded (cf. Prov 19:18). His closest kinsfolk stand round the sufferer; their solidarity is very important (cf. Pss 35:11–15; 41:6–11). They have become skeptical: perhaps God's anger against the supplicant can no longer be turned away? Has the guardian deity already irrevocably doomed him to corruption? If that is the case, then everyone is exposed to the danger (v. 11). The point is even reached when those closest of all to the sick person give up, in order to save their own skins (Ps 41:10). What is the reaction of those more remote from the supplicant, those with whom he did not formerly get on? They openly and brutally urge the destruction of the one who is doomed to death (v. 12). They quickly come up with the claim that God has clearly rejected this fellow (Pss 22:8–9; 31:14; 55:34; 59:2–5; 69:5; 70:3–4; 71:10–11; 109:2–5; 143:3; etc.). The mass of references to enemies "within," people who live in the same community or share the same faith and yet wish ill to the sufferer, is terrifying. It is a sign of the state of psycho-social tension in which the psalms of lamentation were uttered.[8] Theologically, however, the enemies stand for the turning away of God. It is not fortuitous that a mocking remark is put on their lips: "He committed his cause to Yahweh. Let him rescue him, if he delights in him" (Ps 22:9), along with the decisive, deadly question, "Where is your God?" (Ps 42:4). It casts the one who is threatened into the abyss. The sufferer has already internalized all the objections to him. He has already half given himself over to the ambivalence of hope and despair (vv. 13–14). He no longer has any counterarguments. He believes in his guilt (vv. 17–18); he has noted God's anger and turning away and can only ask against all reason for help (vv. 15–16, 21–22). Despair lowers in the darkest tones, takes up the godforsakenness (Ps 22:2: "My God, my God, why have your forsaken me?") and extends to the sharpest accusations against the one who should really be a protector

---

8. Cf. Keel, *Feinde und Gottesleugner*.

and benefactor (Ps 88:7–19), in extreme cases even cursing the suppliant's own life (Jer 20:14–18; Job 3:2–26).

So the question of God arises in the human environment[9] and on the basis of the personal fortunes of one who has been pursued by unhappiness. It is sparked off by symptoms of sickness, misery and persecution. Those who want to distance themselves from this lapse into death express the issue clearly. Where is the power that keeps you alive? Your God has failed, and now you've lost your chance. This is no metaphysical matter. God is experienced through this-worldly problems. The victims suffer the absence of God to a greater degree than they can say. Job, the great protester—but a literary figure, not a suppliant in a liturgical service—can accuse God of arbitrariness and misconduct (cf. Job 19:6–22). The suppliant keeps silent and hopes.

The starting point for the ancient Israelite suppliant is the wider family which supports him. But that begins to fall victim to the disaster. Following its urge for survival, it withdraws its solidarity from the one who seeks it. One might almost call the godforsaken person in an industrial society fortunate. Such people do not need the social net of the family, and hardly know it from their everyday experience. Left to themselves—as latch-key children, engaged in single combat in school and profession, or as old people living in garrets—such people know what it means to be delivered over to death and marginalization. Indeed, they are there: the cries of the prisoners and the tortured, for mother and children, for wife or husband, brothers and sisters and relatives. But today the question of God seems less affected by the collapse of inter-personal solidarity in the most intimate circle. Rather, it is the triumph of injustice which agonizingly puts God's power in question. Where the family is no longer the sole support, its collapse is no longer experienced as the fundamental shattering of life. By contrast, the collapse of the legal order and of economic existence, chronic illnesses and permanent pain, can still provoke the question of God, even among people who do not regard themselves as being very religious. "How can God do this to me?" "If there is a just God, then he must help me."

At that time, as today, the experience of the remoteness of God oscillated between desperation and hope. There was some prayer and some cursing. And when strength disappears and there is increasingly clearly no way out, apathetic endurance remains as the last resistance against the meaninglessness of suffering and dying. "Hope dies last!"[10] The Psalmists live by the remnants of the primal trust which counts on the solidarity of the

---

9. Cf. Benetti, *Salmos al derecho y al revés*; and Benetti, *Salmos para vivir y morir*.
10. De Melo Neto, *Tod und Leben des Severino*.

guardian deity. This solidarity is part of the family circle, is its invisible head. So it must be taken at its ward and honored, and called on for the help that is owed (cf. Ps 38:21–22: "Do not forsake me, Yahweh my God, be not far from me. Make haste to help me, O God of my salvation"). The petition can be like a hymn praising the qualities of God as protector and savior (cf. Pss 3:4; 13:6; 27:1; 28:1; 71:1–3; etc.). The frequent address to God as "my God," "my fortress," "my deliverer" indicates the close personal tie to the deity. It is indeed shaken by the experience of the remoteness of God, but it is not clone away with by either side. Given their secularized environment, it is far more difficult for modern men and women to activate so close a personal tie to God. Nevertheless, they think, pray and lament in the old patterns.

And what is their hope? Like the psalmists of old, they long for just one thing: a break-through to life. Having escaped once again, we would like a new chance just short of the abyss. In the Psalms that is an occasion for making vows (cf. Pss 35:18; 42:12). The close and familiar deity can be offered something for deliverance (cf. Gen 28:20–21). But the support expected from God does not consist in the bringing in of the eternal kingdom but in the restoration of normal life. Disruptions and hurts must cease. So health and a good outcome are the aim, and often enough the enemies will be punished or destroyed as those who had a share in the cause of the suffering (cf. Pss 31:18–19; 35:26–27; 55:10–16; 109:6–20). Again we come up against the social problem of the absence of God. However much for Christ's sake we may eliminate any thought of vengeance from our prayers uttered in distress, the removal of social evils which cause the suffering of the many is an unconditional presupposition for the rehabilitation of the hungry. Poverty, the "new" poverty, is a scourge of our time. The number of those who have been forced to the margin is growing rapidly, not only in Third World countries, but also in industrial countries, in the midst of the greatest prosperity of all time. The unjust distribution of goods on this rich earth is itself a reason for noting God's impotence—not to mention the mechanisms of exploitation which the followers of the Christian God have invented in the course of history.

The godforsakenness seems to weigh that much more heavily when it affects a community, a people, a nation. The individual may give up after a while, because his strength may no longer be sufficient for the quest. "Deny God and die!" (Job 2:9). Job is an exception. Most of the godforsaken go under, often no longer capable of lamenting. In the Psalms there are collective laments as well as individual laments. They express the desperation in dramatic words. A battle has been lost. God has shown himself incapable of helping his people or unwilling to help them. The accusation sounds very harsh.

> You have made us like sheep for the slaughter,
>   and have scattered us among the nations.
> You have sold your people for a trifle,
>   demanding no high price for them.
> You have made us the taunt of our neighbors,
>   the derision and scorn of those about us.
> You have made us a byword among the nations,
>   a laughingstock among the peoples. (Ps 44:11–14)

The petition is meant to compel God to show solidarity with his people once again. It harasses the absent God:

> Rouse yourself! Why are you asleep, O Lord?
>   Awake! Do not cast us off forever!
> Why do you hide your face?
>   Why do you forget our affliction and oppression?
> For our soul is bowed down to the dust;
>   our body cleaves to the ground.
> Rise up, come to our help!
>   Redeem us for the sake of your steadfast love!
>   (Ps 44:23–26)

The desperation becomes immeasurable when God's dwelling place, the sanctuary, is defiled by enemies (Ps 74; cf. 1 Sam 4–5) or when the holy city, Jerusalem, falls victim to war (Lam 1; 2; 4; 5). Or the dynasty which supports the state falls, is wiped out, and the divine promises publicly given to it are shown to be of no account (Ps. 89). Are not such catastrophes clear evidence that God is impotent or uninterested—or even dead? And the godforsakenness which shows itself in defeats at the hands of enemies bears abundantly within itself the sting of the mockery of enemies (the theme is far less prominent in "natural" calamities like drought and famine, plagues of locusts and earthquakes, cf. Jer 14; Joel 1–2). But the enemies represent another deity, who has become stronger. They love to express their mockery in the cynical question, "Where is your God?" (Pss 79:10; 115:2; also Joel 2:17, cf. the vivid description of the blasphemous talk in 2 Kgs 18:33–35). The taunts and mockery of the vanquished enemy were often ritualized in ancient societies: triumphal marches and victory parades are a survival of such demonstrations of humiliation. Many Old Testament texts speak of the mockery of the enemy and the shame suffered as a result (cf. Pss 14:14–15; 79:12; 80:7; 89:42).[11]

It emerges that even in wider societies conclusions are drawn from the state of the society as to God's absence. The lack of God's support in the

---

11. Klopfenstein, *Scham und Schande*.

face of hostile powers, possibly also in the face of natural threats, raises the question: Where is God? Has he turned away in wrath? Or is he asleep?

In our Western tradition since Constantine the Great the presence of God has been interwoven above all with the rule of the state. Until modern times the princes, kings, and emperors who ruled "by the grace of God" were the basic foundation of the social order. The nation-states of the nineteenth century—including the democratic and later the secularized states—entered into this heritage. So it is that down to the present day the question of God plays an essential role at the national level that is not always clearly recognized. How does a people feel in times of national depression? Why do self-reproach, inferiority complexes, the feeling of forsakenness and victimization so easily turn into fanatical, nationalistic aggression? Are not mechanisms at work here which can only be explained by the desperate and continually frustrated search for the Absolute, for God? What happens in populations the majority of which belong to what Frantz Fanon called "the wretched of the earth"? For decades they have experienced a steady deterioration in the economic situation and an ongoing lack of even the most basic human rights. How often in the past have people groaned in the endless slum settlements of the Third World (and sometimes even in the rich industrial world!) that starvation wages are no longer enough to live on! There have been short-term improvements and a long-term decline into an increasingly deep and unspeakably humiliating poverty. Can trust in God survive in such circumstances? It is a miracle that there are still communities of believers in the shanty-towns of Latin America. But for how long will the absence of God be tolerated? Atahualpa Yupanqui (cf. above) thinks less than a generation.

The various conflicts of groups, classes, and nations explode into bloody battles. Where is God in human wars? Apparently every armed struggle needs the support of God. Inhibitions about killing must be suppressed.[12] The name of the God who is the patron of the war does not matter. It must simply be seen as the supreme goal. All wars take place in the name of a God. Perhaps the situation of war in modern times is the last place where there is no problem in rapidly setting rationality aside, and the God who has long been said to be dead is again enthroned overnight.

But must we not distinguish between just wars and unjust wars, between exploitation by force and militant love? Indeed the distinction is necessary: the sober passion for justice and human dignity in many liberation movements is something fundamentally different from the blood-lust of monstrous bands of killers. With whom could God really be? May we make this question a test-case for the existence of God in our world?

---

12. Girard, *Violence and the Sacred*.

The question of God which is derived from experience but is worked through intellectually is not alien to the Old Testament. It may have the upper hand in our time, and in the prosperous levels of society where people need not be concerned for their very existence. Science, technology and dissociation from "primitive" pictures of the world guarantee it a high status. But antiquity knows similar reflections, and they are also expressed in the Psalms. The supplicant himself concedes that he has been drawn into intellectual doubt, like Job and Koheleth:

> But as for me, my feet had almost stumbled,
>   my steps had nearly slipped.
> For I was envious of the arrogant,
>   when I saw the prosperity of the wicked. (Ps 73:2–3)

However, the Psalms often depict the type of the man of violence who has forgotten God, who stands over against God. They clearly indicate what a great impression these godless people make. The scornful confession "There is no God" or—in complete indifference—"I'm not bothered" causes serious inner conflicts among believers. This goes uncontradicted in practice. The supplicants in the Psalms suffer directly from the cynical claims of their tormentors. At the same time they are fascinated with the autonomy of these people, who have apparently cut out God's power.

> In the pride of his countenance the wicked does not seek God;
>   all his thoughts are, "There is no God."
> His ways prosper at all times;
>   your judgments are a matter of indifference to him.
>   As for all his foes, he puffs at them.
> He thinks in his heart, "I shall not be moved;
>   throughout all generations I shall not meet adversity."
> His mouth is filled with cursing and deceit and oppression;
>   under his tongue are mischief and iniquity.
> He sits in ambush in the villages;
>   in hiding places he murders the innocent.
> His eyes stealthily watch for the hapless,
>   he lurks in secret like a lion in his covert;
>   he lurks that he may seize the poor;
>   he seizes the poor when he draws him into his net.
> The hapless is crushed down,
>   sinks down and falls by his might.
> He thinks in his heart, "God has forgotten,
>   he has hidden his face, he will never see it."
>   (Ps 10:4–11; my trans.)

The attitude in the double Psalm 14/53 is quite similar. However, here the Psalmist reflects more on the enemies from outside who put on godless airs. Still, the problem is the same: God is no longer there, and the others claim at least with the semblance of justice and truth that for practical purposes he can be excluded. The suppliant himself becomes doubtful when confronted with this assertive atheism.

Where Is Our God Now?

Today, are we more "godforsaken" than earlier epochs? Hardly. However, the absence, inactivity and silence of God do of course oppress us, in the structures of society and thought which now prevail, as they did not in the biblical period or in the Middle Ages. The industrial revolution, the Enlightenment or post-modernity have come upon us like an avalanche, and they bear within themselves the deposits of earlier periods. Our age is surely characterized by the boundless individualism which is proclaimed on all sides, and the gnawing doubt that can rob the atomized masses of the right seedbed for a fulfilled life. Autonomous man easily freezes in his solitude. He is prone to being manipulated. To a terrifying degree he falls beneath the wheels of a society orientated on success. The phenomena of disintegration are multiplying in the economic gap between North and South. Majorities are excluded from an existence which is worth living. Minorities rule, exploit and appeal to divine right.

The call for the absent God who wills to be there for every creature can still be heard clearly. It is also taken up here and there and translated into saving reality. Wherever "one of the least of these" (see Matt 25:40) experiences the solidarity of others, God shows his presence. But we should not give way to any illusions. Even if quantifying thought is hardly in place in any "proof of God," many, very many, of "the least of these brothers" are dying "in the fields, without prayer or confession" (see above). It is not a matter of their number; anyone who perishes in this way is a proof against God. Anyone who is forsaken is an accusation; any of them indicates that those around him or her who talk of God do not want to do anything for the survival of God in this world. For God does not die from intellectual erosion but from the twisting of righteousness and love.

The same can be said of the manifold human societies. Every conceivable formation, from the perspectives of class, race, gender, faith, language, culture, nationality or race, is an artificial construction, as it were a corset for life. Wherever these groups pursue their interests in a self-centered way by exercising power—and unfortunately that is the rule—and claim religious privileges in doing so, other groups are forced to the margin, disadvantaged, deprived of their rights and no longer have any possibilities in life. Blacks, foreigners, handicapped, women, old people, children, in prosperous societies are discriminated against by the ruling groups. According to the biblical understanding, such devaluation of the socially weaker is directed against the God who takes the side of the least ones. Discrimination kills God. That can be demonstrated from the biblical tradition. If only one God is the creator and sustainer of all human beings, then every creature is his child. But according to our ethical standards there cannot be any legal distinctions between the children of a couple. Anyone who in the name of his God encourages the power-struggle among groups on this earth betrays the one God who wills to be mother and father of all.

Last of all we must also reflect theologically in the narrower sense on the crying of the sufferers and the demands for the social equality of all people. Where do we find the God who can be so present in our contemporary situation that the desperate cries of humankind are answered and the spreading apathy is transformed into life? Where is the God of Jesus Christ, who heals individuals and groups by his love? He does not sit on thrones nor does he dwell in cathedrals. He is also among injured men and women and in his maltreated creation. He is the victim of blasphemous power.

> This swollen face, dirty and covered in sweat,
> marked by falls or blows,
> is the face
> of a drinker, a beggar,
> or are we even standing on the mount of Calvary
> and looking into the holy countenance of the Son of God?[13]

---

13. Câmara, *A Thousand Reasons for Living*.

3

Complaint and Confession

Psalm 69

WORKING TOWARDS A COMMENTARY on the book of Psalms,[1] I thought that as I offer my contribution to a Festschrift I would also ask my honored friend to partake in my labor. Fredrick Holmgren, respected colleague and dear visitor at Marburg University, will appreciate the general topic and will offer his judicious critique of my exegesis, thus helping me in my interpretive efforts.

The Psalm

Psalm 69 has always received much attention from Bible readers and interpreters. There are connections to the New Testament passion narratives, as well as to other writings within and without the New Testament and the early Jewish communities. It is possible that the Jeremianic tradition was linked to our psalm, and the history of exegesis through the Christian era has given it special recognition as a powerful song of suffering and salvation.[2] Form-critical exegesis has unanimously labeled the psalm a clear example of "individual complaint," with its main elements of complaint, petition, imprecation, and vow.[3]

---

1. [Ed.] Gerstenberger wrote this before the second volume of his Psalms commentary had been completed; see now Gerstenberger, *Psalms, Part 2*.

2. To my knowledge, there has not yet been written an extensive, book-length study about this psalm, but treatment in commentaries and articles has been intensive; also, in past centuries, see Augustine, *Enarrationes in Psalmos*, 930–39; and Luther, *Psalmenauslegung*, vol. 2, 349–61.

3. For a brief discussion of this genre, cf. Gerstenberger, *Psalms, Part 1*, 11–14.

Besides the force of language and imagery, daring metaphors, and theological depth, modern observers will note the unusual length of this prayer. Individual complaints are the most frequent genre within the Psalter, comprising about thirty to forty texts.[4] Psalm 69 is one of the largest of its kind, extending over forty-four poetic lines, in comparison to an average length of between ten and twenty lines for the bulk of the Psalter's individual complaints.[5] If we consider the original *Sitz im Leben* of such complaint psalms, the normal size of the text becomes quite plausible. Individual complaints were part and parcel of prayer services for sufferers. They used to be recited by the "patient" under professional supervision of a "man of God" (or perhaps a prophet, Levite, singer, healer, etc.), as Akkadian ritual texts of Mesopotamia indicate.[6]

These prayers, preserved in healing liturgies of Israel's older neighbors, are quite similar in content, form, and size to the Old Testament ones.[7] Because these prayers are similar in purpose, one may conclude that the patient was obliged to recite a limited text only, never approaching the extent of our Psalm 69. Moreover, no matter how far the Old Testament prayers for suffering persons were removed from the familial service or ritual, they preserved, as a rule, the old structure and size. Why, then, did Psalm 69 outgrow this traditional mold and attain this double size?

The Elements

Closing Lines

Form-critical analysis of the Psalms starts out from the presupposition that complaint psalms consist of specific form-elements that correspond to certain liturgical necessities. There should be an invocation, because no suppliant may approach his or her God without preparing for the appearance before the deity by such a preliminary appeal. There should be a statement of the sufferer's case—be it complaint, lament, or protestation—as well as a formal petition. There should also be some kind of response to divine exigencies in terms of loyalty and faith. All these expectations are fully met in

---

4. Cf. Gunkel and Begrich, *Einleitung in die Psalmen*, chap. 6, 172-265 (ET *Introduction to the Psalms*, 121-98); Mowinckel, *The Psalms in Israel's Worship*, 2:1-25.

5. Statistics about size of individual complaints can be found in Gerstenberger, *Der bittende Mensch*, 123-27.

6. Text editions of these rituals containing outright prescriptions of cultic procedure, prayers, and incantations include Caplice, *The Akkadian Namburbi Texts*; Ebeling, *Die akkadische Gebetsserie "Handerhebung"*; Pritchard, ed., *Ancient Near Eastern Texts*.

7. Gerstenberger, *Der bittende Mensch*, 64-72.

Psalm 69. We find also some identification of evildoers and enemies, as well as imprecations against them (this element corresponds negatively to the petition for one's own cause). The opening part being typical, what immediately calls our attention are the closing lines (vv. 33–37 [ET 32–36]). Extending well-wishes to the poor, more specifically to "distressed, miserable, and captives" (vv. 33–34 [ET 32–33]), and summoning to praise—a hymnic element[8]—a whole universe and a whole people (vv. 35–37 [ET 34–36]) seems to exceed by far the concerns for an individual sufferer within his primary group. These observations lead us to suspect that the individual complaint has been reworked in a wider, communal setting. Such a reworking of older psalms becomes obvious to the scrutinizing eye of interpreters, as for example in Psalms 12, 31, and 102.[9]

Complaints

If we next look at the structure of Psalm 69 to determine the liturgical nature of each element, we soon find out that there indeed has been a thorough reworking of the text. We see that a quite different psalm of individual complaint has been brought into an older text.

The first compact element of our psalm is found in vv. 2–5 (ET 1–4). Invocation is, as in some parallel texts (cf. Pss 7:2 [ET 1]; 54:3 [ET 1]; 86:2 [ET 1], combined with an urgent cry for help. This sense of emergency alone justifies such a modification in word order and etiquette: "Help me, God" (v. 2a [ET 1a]). Perhaps we may assume that preparatory liturgical elements, when recited before the complaint proper, furnished a more adequate appellation of God and a proper initial plea to be heard (cf. Pss 4:2 [ET 1]; 5:2–3 [ET 1–2]). In our text, anyway, the complaint element begins right away with strong expressions of despair in tight, extremely short phrases of three and two stressed syllables, which occasionally dwindle to breathless two and two accented shouts (vv. 4–5 [ET 3–4]). The imagery is rich and shifts rapidly: the chaos-waters are rising, and the mire of the netherworld is ensnaring the feet of the supplicant. Dangers of this mythical dimension were ordinarily seen in all kinds of threats to life and well-being (cf. the Psalm of Jonah in Jonah 2; but also Psalms 6 and 88, and the general picture of the netherworld in Isa 14:4–21).[10]

---

8. Typical for one type of hymn is a call to praise issued by the leader of the assembly; cf. Pss 105:1–6; 136:1–26; Crüsemann, *Studien zur Formgeschichte von Hymnus und Danklied in Israel*; Gerstenberger, *Psalms, Part 1*, 16–19.

9. Cf. Becker, *Israel deutet seine Psalmen*; Zenger and Hossfeld, *Die Psalmen*, vol. 1.

10. Cf. Barth, *Die Errettung vom Tode*.

A sordid description of crying and pleading to God follows the initial outburst of anguish. It is a standard motif of complaint-psalms (cf. Pss 17:1; 28:2; 38:9 [ET 8]; 61:3 [ET 2]; 88:2, 10 [ET 1, 9]; 130:1; 142:2-3 [ET 1-2]) intended, liturgically, to move the heart of the deity. What a demonstration of tearful and helpless suffering! The three concluding lines of the complaint (v. 5 [ET 4]) are reserved for an intense complaint against the enemies. Naturally, as ancient Hebrews took it, suffering and the danger of losing one's life had to be attributed to some malevolent entity, whether it be human, demonic, or divine. Certain identification in naming those evil-mongers possibly could be won in those days by ordeal or oracle. Several times we read in the Hebrew Scriptures that people in distress would consult God, trying to clarify the root and the outcome of a personal crisis (cf. 1 Kgs 14:1-3; 2 Kgs 1:1-2; 4:21-25). Asking God for guidance had a long tradition in the ancient Near East; there were many professionals involved in these inquiries. Israel took part in general divination practices, even if the Deuteronomic movement tried to interdict popular inquiries (Deut 18:9-13). In our case, some enemies who slanderously mise accusations against the supplicant have been identified as the sources of his bad state. The (false) charge is a criminal one, as reflected in civil laws and customs (cf. Exod 21:37—22:8; Lev 19:13; Prov 22:22). The Psalms treat this type of false suing for criminal offenses in various places: Ps 7:4-6 (Eng. 3-5) is a protestation of innocence and a conditional curse in this kind of situation. In Ps 26:6, 11, an accused refutes the charges against him in a more general way and does not hesitate to denounce his opponents as totally corrupt (Ps 26:9-10).[11] It is important to realize that these charges are leveled against the sufferer on the basis of alleged criminal conduct. This very horizon changes drastically in the next liturgical section (vv. 6-14a [ET 5-13a]). Now a definite moment of loyalty to Yahweh alone and to his congregation enters the scene. Religious faith becomes the central problem now, not criminal offense. Formally as well as in regard to contents and theological motivation, vv. 6-7 (ET 5-6) are different from the introductory complaint. The poetic lines are fuller; v. 6 (ET 5) seems even overcrowded with words (4 + 3 stresses). There is also a new invocation, and its wording, "God, you know my stupidity" (*'iwwelet*) and its derivates are typical wisdom jargon), derives from prophetic or sapiential dialogue rather than from formal, cultic prayer language.[12] Or,

---

11. Hans Schmidt designated a subgroup of individual complaints as "Psalms of falsely accused persons." Schmidt, *Das Gebet des Angeklagten*.

12. "You know," as an affirmation made about God himself, occurs with some frequency in the book of Jeremiah (cf. Jer 12:3; 15:15; 17:16; 18:23) and rarely elsewhere: for example, 2 Sam 7:20; 1 Kgs 8:39; Ezek 37:3; Pss 31:8 (ET 7); 40:10 (ET 9); 139:2, 4; 142:4 (ET 3); 144:3; Neh 9:10; 1 Chr 17:18; 2 Chr 6:30 (all passages cited). The formula

to put it differently, the old rituals of worship apparently did not use the expression very much, although it was used more frequently in later times. The first stichos (v. 6a [ET 5a]) already admits, in sapiential terminology, faulty existence, but the formal confession of guilt is articulated in v. 6b (ET 5b). Terms related to *ašam*, "guilt," however, are very rare in the Psalter (only in Pss 68:22 [ET 21] and 69:6b [ET 5b] they strictly belong to Priestly layers of the Hebrew Scriptures, cf. Lev 5, etc.). The whole line, therefore, comes close to becoming a rather exquisite confession of sin. (For contrasts in the line of old complaint songs, cf. Pss 38:5 [ET 4]; 51:5-8 [ET 3-6].) These last mentioned passages straightforwardly employ the regular words for "sin," "error," and "guilt," placing the supplicant directly before his God.[13] "I have erred" is a recognized confessional formula (Ps 51:6a [ET 5a]; cf. Josh 7:20; 1 Sam 15:24, 30; 2 Sam 12:13; 19:21; 24:10, 17; etc.).

Just as the beginning line of the actual section does not fit well into the linguistic and theological patterns of the old complaints, the other two lines (v. 7 [ET 6]) have their own peculiarities, which make them look a little strange in the context of the initial complaint. The phrases are formulated as negative wishes, and each of them ends up with a weighty invocation first, "Yahweh Sebaoth," and second, "God of Israel." While the double negative (an almost apotropaic imploration with concomitant appellation of God) does have some parallels in other prayers (cf. Pss 6:2 [ET 1]; 27:9; 35:22, 25; 38:22 [ET 21]; 83:2 [ET 1]), the specific affirmations of our two lines are unique in the Psalter. Instead of asking God to keep the supplicant from shame, that is, the impending disgrace of being sentenced and ostracized by society, and instead of trying to put the full blame on the "enemies" (cf. Pss 31:2b, 18 [ET 1b, 17]; 35:26), our text pleads that those who "hope for you" and "seek you" "will not be put to shame on my account." The "I" of the supplicant suddenly takes on a different quality or character. He becomes the intermediary—the messenger, or servant, of the Lord—whose existence is bound up with the message to the faithful. "Shame" now does not simply mean the destruction of human existence under the onslaught of false or right condemnation. Shame is a consequence not of unethical actions committed but of attitudes taken over against a person of Yahweh's confidence (or at least a person who thinks him- or herself in line with the ordinances of God). Theoretically, this can be only persons of very special standing in the community, figures like Moses, Jeremiah, or Ezra, who are portrayed in the Scriptures as special representatives of their God. Still, it is needless to

---

in most cases conveys a feeling of deep personal piety.

13. The very traditional triad of terms (*pešaʻ, haṭṭaʼt, ʻawon*) has been studied by Rolf Knierim, *Die Hauptbegriffe für Sünde*; cf. also the relevant articles in the *TDOT*.

say that all successors of crucial leaders tend to step into the footprints of their masters and think of themselves as equally important.

The remaining lines of the section under discussion, vv. 8–14a [ET 7–13a], spell out in greater detail that peculiar relationship between the supplicant and God which makes the main difference over against the older complaint pattern. Because of God, the sufferer is being despised (v. 8 [ET 7]); or, more precisely, he fell into disgrace with (some of?) his brothers because of his zeal for the "house of God," that is, the temple (v. 10 [ET 9]). Alienation from his compatriots is the result (v. 9 [ET 8]). This latter motif, alienation from kinfolk and neighbors, is a standard theme in complaint (cf. Ps 88; Job 19:13–22). However, the reasons recognizable in the common model are either suspicion of criminal record or "evidence" of divine castigation because of some grave aberration (cf. Job). In our case, the alienation is caused by religious zeal in favor of God Yahweh and in support of the sanctity and integrity of his temple. The only way to make sense of these statements is to visualize a religious rift in the community which makes for vicious animosity among its members. What for some may be considered zealous endeavor for the God of Israel and his holy dwelling place, for others is unnecessary or even detrimental fanaticism.

We note the difference between the two complaint sections. The first one (vv. 1–7 [ET 1–6]) deals with serious dangers threatening from slander and false accusation within a political and social community. The second complaint (vv. 8–14a [ET 7–13a]) tells us about religious hatred within a religious congregation. The passage uses traditional imagery and metaphors to voice the lament. For instance, going in sack and ashes in order to demonstrate solidarity with mourners or people practicing penitence (vv. 11–12 [ET 10–11]) is well attested also in Ps 35:13–14 or in Job 1–2. Likewise, being scorned by those sitting in the gate (v. 13 [ET 12]), that is, by people in a public place, has its counterpart in other texts (Job 30:9; Lam 3:14; Isa 28:7–10). In our second complaint section, however, the traditional motifs and expressions of dissonance are all subjugated to the general claim: "For your sake am I being disdained." The supplicant is suffering because of his loyalty to Yahweh. Wearing clothes of mourning, then, would also have some religious or confessional connotations that escape our knowledge. A concluding line wants to ascertain the prayer of frustrated zeal for the Lord (v. 14a [ET 13a]). Reference to one's own prayer more likely than not is a matter of introductory or concluding words (cf. Pss 4:2 [ET 1]; 6:10 [ET 9]; 17:1; 39:13 [ET 12]; 88:3, 14 [ET 2, 13]; 109:4; 141:2, 5; etc.

Petitions and Imprecations

The petitionary section of vv. 14b–19 (ET 13b–18) apparently has two distinct parts. The first unit, vv. 14b–16 (ET 13b–15), is intimately linked to the opening complaints of vv. 2–5 (ET 1–4) in its vocabulary and style. After renewed invocation ("God . . . hear me," v. 14b [ET 13b]), the supplication is precisely for rescue from the waters and the mire in which the sufferer is drowning. Thus there can be no doubt about the original linkage between the passages.[14] On the other hand, vv. 17–19 (ET 16–18) turn to Yahweh only in the most general way, pleading for recognition and acceptance of the supplicant for the sake of God's graciousness and mercy. The words used for God's hoped-for closeness and deliverance are partly traditional (for example, in vv. 17–18 [ET 16–17]), partly unusual and rare; "Be close to me and redeem me" (v. 19a [ET 18a]) does not have an exact counterpart in the Hebrew Scriptures. Therefore, neither vocabulary nor style will easily reveal anything about the literary affiliation of the lines in question. Perhaps, however, the lone self-designation "your servant" in v. 18a (ET 17a) has some significance. It does not occur verbatim in vv. 6–14a (ET 5–13a), but the concept of God's mediator and servant, as pointed out, is there. Also, the pointed use of "Yahweh" in v. 17 over against "Elohim" in v. 14b would support the literary analysis linking the first segment of petition to the old complaint, and the second one (vv. 17–19 [ET 16–18]) to the "confessional lament" of vv. 6–14a (ET 5–13a).

Looking for cross-connections of this type, we have to ask, however, what about the "enemies" and "persecutors," which are so important in both complaint sections already discussed. This may be a test case for our analysis. The petition, so far, is hardly concerned about these dangerous adversaries. Our present petitionary passage, vv. 14b–19 (ET 13b–18), briefly touches the opponents in vv. 15 and 19 (ET 14, 18). The first reference is in the middle of demands for help and deliverance from deadly mire and wild waters; "from my haters" seems misplaced in this context, and some exegetes suggest a textual emendation. The second reference to "my enemies" (v. 19 [ET 18]) moves the supplicant to ask God for nearness and intervention. In other words, the formulation "because of my enemies"—please help me— does possibly suggest a special relationship of the supplicant to Yahweh, and a special situation with regard to Israel and her neighbors.[15]

---

14. Cf. Allen, "The Value of Rhetorical Criticism in Psalm 69."

15. "Because of" (*lemaʿan*) in this context means "in order to refute the adversaries, to silence them and put them to shame." Exilic and post-exilic preaching characteristically has dwelled on this motif for asking divine help (cf. Ps 83; Exod 32:12; Lev 18:24–25; Deut 7:17–26; etc.), but there also may have been an older variant in

Our psalm does not end, as we might expect, with petition and possibly a vow, but starts another round of complaint, this time joined to extended imprecations of enemies (vv. 20–29 [ET 19–28]). Are we able to continue the work of partitioning the prayer to find two distinct layers of tradition in it? The section again begins with that ominous formula, "You [God] know" what trouble I have seen, namely, three kinds of shame (in Hebrew: *herpah, boset, kelimma*).[16] The formula itself, as well as the suspicious accumulation of shame words, suggests that this line had some connection with the confessional version of complaint.[17] The next line (v. 21 [ET 20]) also talks about *herpa*, "shame," but lacks the usual reinforcement with synonyms. It also paints a rather typical kind of alienation between supplicant and villagers. The supplicant is counting on neighborly solidarity, but does not receive it, just as in Psalms 35 and 41. Neighbors and friends have turned hostile for practical reasons; you have to steer clear of a person punished by God so as not to be caught in the same castigation. The expression "give vinegar for water" probably is proverbial for "to recompense evil for good" (cf. Pss 35:12; 41:10 [ET 9]). The metaphor at this point does not have a cultic meaning, but comes from everyday experience. Most probably, then, the renewed complaint fits the pattern of traditional articulations. No specific reference is made, either, to the precarious existence of a messenger of God, nor is there any hint as to actual persecution for the sake of Yahweh or any conflict or rift between factions of the Jewish community.

Instead of positive petitions for one's own cause, this new round of liturgy presents a series of imprecations. Form-critical study long has recognized that petition and imprecations in ritual practice are but two sides of the same coin. Both actively deal with overcoming evil, imprecation choosing direct action (via the deity appealed to) against the evil-mongers and sources of all suffering. Thus, imprecations belong to the basic structure of those complaint-psalms that deal with personalized enemies.[18] Destructive prayer-wishes, to be executed by God himself, are flung against those who cause mischief (vv. 23–26 [ET 22–25]; cf. Ps 109).

The evil-mongers are to be hit in their religious practice; their very sacrifice is to be perverted, producing nothing but bad luck (v. 23 [ET 22]). Their physical health is to be impaired and their homes destroyed (vv. 24, 26 [ET 23, 25]). All these bad effects on the evildoers are to flow out of

---

liturgical practice: Pss 5:9–11 (Eng. 8–10); 143:11–12.

16. The words really are synonymous; cf. Klopfenstein, *Scham und Schande*.

17. Cf. Olyan, "Honor, Shame, and Covenant Relations."

18. There are many special studies about the problem; cf. Keel, *Feinde und Gottesleugner*; Gerstenberger, "Enemies and Evildoers."

God's wrath (v. 25 [ET 24]). Up to this point, there is no sign of any specific condemnation of internal opponents based on true or false worship of Yahweh. The motive clause in v. 27 (ET 26), the only line legitimating the brutal punishment of the wicked, sums up, in a way, the whole scenario: "persecute" the sufferer who has been castigated by God. Now, is the concept of "persecution" to be understood in a religious or confessional way? Hardly so. Many individual complaints use the term for "regular" harassment of suspects who are considered punished by God and therefore are being treated as outcasts (cf. Pss 7:2, 6 [ET 1, 5]; 31:16 [ET 15]; 35:3; 109:16). The tenor of the two cola (which again seem "overstretched," with altogether nine lexemes, but regular three and three accented syllables) goes in the same direction. God himself has hit the sufferer, and he is not—like Jeremiah—a messenger zealously engaged in the work of the Lord.

In fact, v. 27 (ET 26) closes the liturgical set-up. The motive clause gives the reason for the preceding imprecations. The two lines that follow (vv. 28–29 [ET 27–28] are imprecative in the same style (imperatives and jussives directed to God), but they do employ different vocabulary and betray a very distinct purpose. No longer does the supplicant demand the destruction of physical conditions and the frustration of religious endeavors of his adversaries. Instead, he clearly moves within the community of the "just" and is trying to expel the others from the ranks of the *ṣaddiqim*. The "book of the living" is a late concept used to symbolize the loyalty and homogeneity of the true faith community.[19] The request to blot out enemies from this book can only refer to acts of purification within this community. For all these reasons, vv. 28–29 (ET 27–28) are to be considered a new layer of imprecation corresponding to a different life-setting.

Vow and the Rest

Having studied the complaint and petition blocks of Psalm 69, we once more must look briefly at the closing units of this prayer. Form-critical research from the beginning has held petition to be the most essential and climactic element of complaint-songs. Theoretically and liturgically, a prayer may end at this high point (cf. Pss 36:11–13 [ET 10–12]; 44:27 [ET 26]). As a rule, however, complaint-songs close with some praising affirmation or a vow to offer thanks to the helpful deity. This liturgical feature is quite natural and

---

19. All occurrences of the term seem to be late, even the one in Exod 32:32–33. Being a list of the recognized "righteous" in Israel (Isa 4:3; Jer 17:13; Ezek 13:9; Mal 3:16; Dan 7:10; 10:21; 12:1; Pss 87:6; 139:16), it must come out of those periods in which the confessional state became decisive in evaluating membership in Israel.

in line with general human behavior.[20] The benevolent God who will rescue the sufferer is to receive laudations and even a certain recompense.

The vow of praise appears at the close of Psalm 69. The distribution of the closing elements is problematic due to the two layers of psalmic tradition. Verses 30–32 (ET 29–31) sound like old affirmations of humility and anxiety (v. 30a, cf. formulaic expressions of this type in Pss 40:18 [ET 17]; 70:6 [ET 5]; 86:1; 109:22), a final plea for help (v. 30b [ET 29b]), and a vow to sing praises if God's help will materialize (v. 31 [ET 30]). In both lines *elohim* is either addressed directly or mentioned in the third person. The next line (v. 32), however, appeals to Yahweh and seems to add a second thought on the value of thanksgiving songs in contrast to thanksgiving sacrifice. The term *todah*, "thanksgiving offer," at the end of v. 31 thus is being reinterpreted in the light of non-temple worship (cf. Pss 40:7 [ET 6]; 50:8–13; 51:18–21 [ET 16–19]). Therefore, the verse may not be an original part of the first closing passage, but neither is it to be linked with the confessional psalm, in which the temple plays such a central role.

All the rest of this long prayer (vv. 33–37 [ET 32–36]), as stated in the beginning, goes beyond the boundaries of special worship for some patient seeking help because of sickness or social ostracism. Well wishes for "oppressed ones" and frequent references to Zion, the Zion community, the cities of Judah, and the cosmic universe[21] are significant indicators of the place of origin of this final part of Psalm 69. Delimitation of the congregation of the faithful implicitly wards off those traitors who persecute people for their zeal in regard to Yahweh and his holy abode.

Life Situations

At various points we have hinted at the *Sitz im Leben* of the two layers of our rich and lengthy text. This diachronic view has to be systematized briefly, so that we may draw some theological conclusions afterwards.

We identified a first and traditional individual complaint that possibly comprises vv. 2–5, 14b–16, 21–27, and 30–32 (ET 1–4, 13b–15, 20–26, 29–31). Speaking in general terms and not insisting on locating every single word, we estimate that about twenty-three of the forty-four lines may have

---

20. Anthropological, cultural, historical research has long discovered a subtle system of exchanging gifts as a kind of fundamental constant; cf. Mauss, *The Gift*.

21. Self-descriptive terms are used abundantly in vv. 33–34 (ET 32–33); and Zion, the cities of Judah, and the congregation of faithful ("descendants of his servants," "those who love his name") are repeatedly referred to in vv. 36–37 (Eng. 35–36). The line in the middle between these two subunits bursts out in universal praise (v. 35 [ET 34]).

constituted the basic layer an independent complaint song the individual sufferer. The essential form elements are present in a liturgical sequence: invocation and complaint, petition, complaint, imprecation, final plea, and vow. This original complaint is concerned with the individual in his or her primary group. Life is in great danger, threatened by abysmal forces of destruction and personal enemies raising false accusations. The only possible salvation is with the personal God who is able to help against powers of death and deadly calumny. Significantly, most parts of the traditional prayer are oriented towards *elohim*, "God," and not to Yahweh. Thus *elohim* appears in vv. 2, 14b, 30, and 31 (ET 1, 13b, 29, and 30), that is, out of seven times within the traditional prayer. The only use of YHWH (out of five occurrences) within this older text is in v. 32 (ET 31). But, as discussed above, the line in question may be a later addition to the text. If our analysis is correct, the traditional prayer, coming out of the older family religion in Israel,[22] was oriented towards *elohim*, most likely the deity of family or clan. The widespread belief that a so-called "Elohistic Psalter" (Pss 42–83) originally was composed of Yahweh psalms that at some indefinite point suffered an "elohistic redaction" is hardly tenable.[23] Especially in the case of Ps 69, it proves absurd. Five uses of YHWH compare to seven occurrences of *elohim* in this prayer.

To test our identification of a later "confessional" layer, extending over vv. 6–14a, 17–20, 28–29, and 33–37 (ET 5–13a, 16–19, 27–28, and 32–36), at this point we observe that the later part of Ps 69 does use YHWH in a demonstrative way throughout. Verse 7b (ET 6b) has the first emphatic appearance, after v. 6 (ET 5) named the deity (by mistake? scribal error?) *elohim* in its invocation. Verse 7d continues with *elohim yisra'ely* "God of Israel," which is, of course, equivalent to YHWH. Next, vv. 14a and 17a (ET 13a and 16a) are prominent lines, closing and opening a liturgical section. Both carry the name YHWH and no other designation of divinity. Lastly, v. 34 (ET 33) has YHWH in a prominent place, the difficulty being that twice in this last section *elohim* appears in contexts where one would expect YHWH. The verb drs, "seek"(v. 33 [ET 32]), can be linked to *elohim* (cf. Ps 14:2) the psalm in general does not discriminate between the two designations) or to YHWH (cf. Ps 22:27 [ET 26]; 34:5, 11 [ET 4, 10]; 105:4; the latter has no *elohim* as an independent name but three times uncontested

---

22. Family religion should be recognized as a distinct reality in Israel, in the ancient Near East, even in modem societies; Vorländer, *Mein Gott*; Gerstenberger, *Der bittende Mensch*; Gerstenberger, *Jahwe—ein patriarchaler Gott* (ET *Yahweh the Patriarch*); Rainer Albertz, *A History of Israelite Religion*.

23. I raised that suspicion already in my commentary (cf. Gerstenberger, *Psalms, Part 1*, 37); it has been getting stronger ever since.

YHWH). Even worse, *elohim* is attested even in connection with Zion in v. 36 (ET 35). This means that the evidence is not as clear as one would wish; therefore, the only plausible answer would be that the later prayer uses YHWH pointedly in some parts, but obviously does not attribute much weight to it in the closing section.

We should still examine the "confessional" prayer in Ps 69 to answer the question whether or not it may have been an autonomous liturgical text at one time. We tried to understand the opening element in vv. 6–7 (ET 5–6) as a plaintive petition with a peculiar, Jeremianic twist to it. In the Psalter there is no comparable introductory statement. The four parallels from Jeremiah do not lend much force to the hypothesis that "God, you know my stupidity" could have been used as a first line of a prayer. (Jeremiah 12:3; 17:16; and 18:23 place the formula "you know" into a larger context; only in Jer 15:15 does it open a new section.) The complaint of vv. 8–13 (ET 7–12), ending with a petition in v. 14a (ET 13a), is a full-fledged liturgical element. Similarly, the petition in vv. 17–19 (ET 16–18) qualifies as an autonomous part of a complaint-song. Verses 20 and 28–29 (ET 19, 27–28), however, are most likely redactional accretions that interpret the older text at hand. The final section, vv. 33–37 (ET 32–36), then, places the whole prayer into the context of a congregation of poor and righteous believers, the so-called "community of the oppressed"[24] (extant in some psalms, for example, Pss 9/10, 37, 49, and 73), without mentioning explicitly the internal split between warring factions.[25] In that the closing section by itself transcends the border of complaint service for individuals, it cannot be a trustworthy witness to our question. To summarize, the younger layer, identified as confessional in nature, most probably never existed as an independent, liturgical text, but most likely does consist of redactional additions to the standard complaint song pointed out earlier.

Therefore, Psalm 69 derives from earlier family traditions where prayer rituals in support of ailing members of the intimate group were performed, usually under the auspices of expert healers and liturgists. The treasure of this old family religion was handed down to the exilic and postexilic communities of Yahweh-believers. They expanded the old texts. In the case of Psalm 69, emphasis shifted from the individual sufferer towards a whole community of persons struggling to survive in a foreign-dominated world. The early Jewish congregations in Palestine as well as in Babylonia, Persia, Egypt, and Syria had to rally around their traditional faith. In doing

---

24. Cf. Lohfink, *Option for the Poor*; Lohfink, *Lobgesänge der Armen*. Also Zenger, *Die Psalmen*, and Latin-American liberation theologians highlight the presence of autonomous congregations of poor people.

25. This aspect has been little treated so far; cf. Smith, *Palestinian Parties and Politics*.

so, it was natural that schisms arose on confessional and social grounds. Quite early, some groups were more zealous than others in defending the traditional values. The community of the "poor" and "oppressed" seems to have developed not only a strong conscience of justice and equity for Israelites, but also a keen sense of temple orientation. The heated discussion in Haggai 1 about reconstructing the temple could be an example of two opposing positions on this issue. As a consequence of that particular zeal for Yahweh, those who would not join the active confessors were viewed with suspicion and sometimes banished from the community. Or, perhaps more frequently, the internal distribution of power worked the other way around. As we have seen, the poor and oppressed complain very succinctly in the Psalter (cf. Psalms 9/10, 37, 49, and 73). In any case, the redactional or "confessional" layer in Psalm 69 poses the problem of survival for each member of the Jewish community in the sixth and fifth centuries. Apparently, the details and degrees of allegiance to Yahweh were at stake at the time, as happened again and again in succeeding centuries.

Incentives

Considering diachronic developments of biblical texts which are clearly distinguishable through critical analysis, I cannot see a theological justification to evaluate only the very last or canonical stage of Scripture when asking for theological significance.[26] This means with regard to Ps 69 that we have to acknowledge at least two different levels of interpretation in this composite complaint song. The first level is that of primary group relationships, and in particular the way of dealing with extreme situations of threats to life and social ostracism. No matter how grave the deviation, guilt, or abnormality of a person, we may judge, in the light of Old Testament concern for the marginalized and powerless, that the "outcast" always had to get a chance for rehabilitation.[27] The traditional complaint-prayers and their concomi-

---

26. The discussion about "canonical interpretation" has been held for some time already; cf. Childs, *Old Testament Theology in a Canonical Context*. To "canonize" the final text is in itself an illusion, because there never has been one definite, final text, as the Greek tradition proves beyond any doubts. Furthermore, the freezing of one particular text, trying to make it normative, absolutizes one particular historical and social structure, which in itself is an affront against the living ever-concrete word of God. Cf. Gerstenberger, "Canon Criticism and the Meaning of 'Sitz im Leben'"; Seybold and Zenger, eds., *Neue Wege der Psalmenforschung*.

27. Of course, Hebrew Scriptures also let us know about circumstances of official banishment of culprits or sick kin, perhaps the worst example being the exclusion from social solidarity of persons stigmatized by a certain skin disease (Lev 13:45-46; 2 Kgs 7:3-10; Matt 8:1-4). Cf. Gerstenberger, *Leviticus* (in both German and English). But

tant worship services are witnesses to this effect. Even in cases when family solidarity already had broken down, there still existed the possibility of performing rehabilitation rituals (cf. Pss 41; 88).

Another point needs clarification. In antiquity the family or clan was the last resort for persons suffering from any deficits, losses, disorientations. If these primary groups failed to provide help, chances were slight of finding outside sponsors, counselors, ritual experts, priests who would venture salvatory action. When all these options were exhausted, the afflicted person was left alone and lost in the wilderness like those "embittered" and "distressed" men whom David collected (1 Sam 22:2). In our own industrial and urban societies, primary and natural groups long have lost their financial and emotional capacities to take care of their marginalized members. The worst cases in question are children and elderly persons.[28] To whom are we addressing ourselves if we try to preach the gospel of the complaint genres in the Old Testament? Certainly we need to address the church community, which already in ancient times took over some of the social responsibilities, as the second layer of Psalm 69 attests (cf. also Pss 12; 37; 102; 146; etc.). But unfortunately, churches cannot possibly heal all the ills of any given society. Millions and millions of poor people nowadays are not able to benefit from church aid and engagement. Therefore, we have to sensitize our political and economic entities to the discrepancies of our own society. Human fallout in social terms is alarmingly high and increasing rapidly, and there "should not be any poor in your midst" (Deut 15:4).[29] Eventually our Christian or Jewish communities must reflect about the social, political, and economic structures that produce all the typical miseries of this world.

But what kind of rehabilitation do the needy of our time want? And what kind of assistance should be supplied according to the will of God today? Needless to say, protection from evil spirits does not rank high in our day, nor does it help against calumny or the evil eye. But the basic demands are very elementary. The needy have to be freed from the worldwide slander that they cause all the evils on this planet by multiplying too fast, by being

---

the overwhelming impression from Old Testament texts is this: Our spiritual forebears went to the limit of their knowledge and capabilities to incorporate those at the margins, and Jesus, under different cultural conditions, did the best in his time to overcome exclusivistic barriers.

28. We hear about substandard living conditions of large numbers of young and elderly persons all over the world; cf. key words in the news: "abused children," "abandoned children or older persons," "child prostitution," "child gangs," etc.

29. Read and discuss the latest UN report on world social conditions. Also, national statistics on economic growth and incomes, unemployment and web fare, the situation of children and school opportunities, single mothers and old-age poverty, and many more areas should inform us.

idle and living on the income of innocent working people, by not adapting to the rules of honest labor. Next, the millions of marginalized are in desperate need of food, clothing, housing, health care, education, and (most of all) real job opportunities. Millions of abandoned children, millions of hopelessly overburdened women, and again millions of persons discriminated against on account of their color, ethnic identity, minority position, or quantity and special situation probably are the groups most exploited and abused on this earth.

Of course, there is a whole category of poor and despised who are suffering on a different level. They do not lack so much the physical means to lead decent lives, but they are deficient in psychic stability, moral orientation, and personal posture. They too are clamoring for attention and rehabilitation in our days. Again, congregations and churches cannot possibly provide all the psychological and spiritual assistance necessary. We should do what is possible, and alert others to the necessity of integrating efforts and social structures. God wants those who believe in him or her to be open to the supplicants of our times and their specific complaint-songs. In front of the cathedral of the city of Cologne there has been, these past decades, a "wailing wall." Everyone is allowed to publicize his or her lament on a poster right there. Many church officials are working to clear the place of what they think is a nuisance and an insult to the harmonious world of the well-to-do Christians. They may prevail in the courts—a bad omen for Christian witness, which should proclaim the gospel to the poor.

On the second plane of our psalm, the problem of the needy shifts from basic needs for a decent human life towards the survival of the individual and the community in the face of external oppression and injustice on the one hand and internal rifts and parties on the other, just as happened in early Jewish antiquity, our Christian existence today is overshadowed by innumerable conflicts among believers, brought about by exaggerated confessionalism and self-centered fundamentalism. Christianity (and for that matter also Judaism, but in this regard I am not able to evaluate the situation), in spite of all efforts to come together and live in brother- and sisterhood according to John 17:21 and the love of Christ, still represents a torn body of believers in the one and undivided Savior. This is an extremely sad picture that constantly defies the preaching of the proper gospel.

What are we to make out of this dreary reality? How could we demonstrate that believed and confessed unity in Christ? What are possible ways to assist those who are feeling maltreated for their zeal in regard to God and the correct faith? Again, we are living in different times and circumstances from those psalmists who complained about wicked persecutors among their own people. For most of us there is no place to defend that could be declared the "holiest of holy," no particular church to protect that considers itself exclusively correct and absolutely unique in this world. We have to rethink the essence of zeal and zealousness in matters of faith and religious community.

Some critical observers of Western culture have noted that in our days Christian faith has lost most of its ground, but Christian zeal is surviving in secularized forms. In fact, nowadays we are witnessing many active Christian militants who have few scruples as to the means available to achieve their ultimate ends. They are rivaled only by some Muslim, Hindu, or other religious fundamentalists. Such zealousness for the cause of others (preferably helpless persons or the altogether defenseless nature) may be entirely justified. Zeal means identification with a lost cause and sacrifice of one's own self for others. In this sense, Jesus may be considered a zealous preacher, and some interpreters of his life actually link the narrative about his cleansing the temple with Ps 69:10 (ET 9). John 2:17 reports that his disciples remembered that passage of our psalm. So there is, from the beginning, a legitimate holy wrath in our tradition, which even implies a degree of violence (cf. Exod 32:19; Judg 14:6; 1 Sam 11:6–7; etc.). Still, no zeal should become in any way arbitrary and authoritarian; it must be controlled by justice and love. We constantly need to discuss the goals and methods of full engagement for "holy" causes in our own time. To go to war and slaughter innocents in order to achieve supremacy of one's own ethnic or religious group does not qualify as legitimate zeal, in my opinion. On the other hand, to join a liberation movement of oppressed, dehumanized classes or minority groups and fight for their rights might be a direct consequence of preaching the gospel of love. The ends of zeal and the methods of actualizing zealousness are decisive in evaluating its legitimacy before God and Christ.

The existence of assemblies of poor and oppressed that also claim to represent true faith in God is another challenge to Christian convictions. During centuries of ecclesiastic tradition, the well-to-do churches, often intimately aligned with political powers, have become the dominant force in the Western world. Poor congregations or movements, exercising full solidarity with the exploited, mostly survived (if at all) in niches and undercurrents of official religion. Today, so-called underdeveloped countries and some ghettos or slums of our big cities shelter authentic congregations of disenfranchised people, while a few groups within the academic world and the mainstream of middle-class religion try to maintain sympathetic connections with the outcasts of our system. In the light of heavy biblical evidence that God and Christ side with the poor, we should be aware of the consequences of our social standing. After all, truth and the practice of truth have something to do with plain property rights, as Jesus pointed out succinctly: "How hard for those who have riches to enter the kingdom of God" (Luke 18:24).

To sum up, by using the diachronic method to study the Bible and the Psalter as a highly important part in it, we discover layers of communal life, each with their different articulations of theological problems and answers. Although our world has changed greatly over the centuries, basic insights of our spiritual ancestors remain active and challenging for us because human beings do not change much in their different environments. The parameters of our times have to be brought into account, however, to get down to that theological orientation for which we are legitimated by Christ to be zealous.

4

Form Criticism in Action

Psalm 22

Origins

RECURRING PATTERNS OF LIFE, cycles of rise and decline, a revolving earth and endlessly repetitive seasonal sequences may suggest to the human mind that there is "nothing new under the sun." "Is there a thing of which it is said: 'See, this is new'? It has already been, in the ages before us." (Eccl 1:9–10). For millenniums thinkers were preoccupied with the ongoing, but known and enduring qualities of history. Medieval painting presented all events—and, as a rule, each one belonged to the sacred category—before the golden background of eternity. This attitude changed dramatically only with the advent of renaissance[1] and enlightenment. Gradually, people became aware (and actively construed their world-view in this vain) that history consisted of a never ending chain of new developments, every one unheard of in the past, none comparable to its antecessors. The past lost its formative power, future stepped in and took charge as the decisive molding force of present destinies.[2] One driving impetus behind such a fundamental change of world-views probably was the discovery of human potentialities to understand, explain, and manipulate nature. People governing the new age of science and technology considered themselves co-creators of the world, and they dreamed of human autonomy and glorification. This scenery is the remote background also of form-critical designs,[3] but before the new

1. Cf. Burckhardt, *The Civilization of the Renaissance in Italy*.
2. Cf. Howard, *Religion and the Rise of Historicism*.
3. Martin Buss in his voluminous work on biblical form criticism traces its roots

method of Biblical exegesis really could come to life the concepts of "history" and "literature" had to undergo considerable changes, if not outright metamorphoses.

The advent of a historical-critical perspective for a long time led thinkers to believe that history, as a man-made enactment in contradistinction to divinely cast destinies, was the product solely of leading figures, monarchs, generals, merchants, poets and the like. Literature, according to this line of thinking, reflected that heroic interpretation of reality. Any literary work could be acknowledged only if some individual hero, a spiritual or literary genius, was accredited with its authorship. In this fashion, all Biblical books had to be vested with the names of extraordinary writers, like Moses, David, the "literary" prophets, etc.[4] During the reign of this type of historical-critical investigation of the Hebrew Scripture form criticism did not yet have a chance to be invented. But literary analysis in the long run came up with the insight, that authorship of biblical books quite often was uncertain, to say the least. Gradually suspicions arose that nobodies might have a hand in the making of Hebrew Scriptures. Consequently, the aura of outstanding literary quality waned and a good number of exegetes would not hesitate to disqualify Biblical passages of lesser standing.[5] Personal authorship of superior literary quality continued to be an essential feature to be looked for in the Biblical tradition.

The religious-historical school of thinking, starting at the University of Göttingen near the end of the nineteenth century broke away from older patterns of doing historical-critical research. To be sure, there have been earlier movements in European philosophical and theological tradition[6] which partly anticipated attitudes and evaluations taken by the group of young scholars leaning on some older professors like Albrecht Ritschl (1822–1889) and Karl Albert Eichhorn (1856–1926). The young and rebellious troop of theologians included Johannes Weiß, Hermann Gunkel, Wilhelm Bousset,

---

to Greco-Roman philosophy (*Biblical Form Criticism*, 31–47). I prefer to begin at the dawn of critical analysis of history and literature.

4. Progressive scholars like Wilhelm M. L. de Wette (1780–1849) or Julius Wellhausen (1844–1918) and many others, after declaring Old Testament sources to be of unknown authorship continued to treat such "anonymous" writers reverently as individual scholars without analyzing their modes of articulation in generic terms.

5. Cf., e.g., Bernhard L. Duhm (1847–1928) in his famous study on the prophets: *Israels Propheten*, 3–12, etc.

6. As already stated, Martin Buss goes a long way to point out anteceding movements; I would place special emphasis on the literary and philosophical romanticists of the period around 1800, like Johann Gottfried Herder (1744–1803); cf. Herms, "Herder, Johann Gottfried"; he is mentioned in passing by Buss, *Biblical Form Criticism*, 143–44, 147, etc.

Ernst Troeltsch, Wilhelm Wrede and others, promptly to be followed by a new generation of "disciples" who continued into the same direction. It is the merit of the initial set to have generated a new way of reading and interpreting the Bible. Hermann Gunkel was the leading Old Testament expert in this group; he soon had brought up a good number of form-critical disciples, e.g., Hugo Gressmann, Sigmund Mowinckel, Hans Schmidt, Joachim Begrich, Hedwig Jahnow, and Walter Baumgartner. In the New Testament camp Johannes Weiß, Wilhelm Bousset, Wilhelm Wrede were leading the field, before long to be supported and overtaken by Martin Dibelius, Rudolf Bultmann, and others. Form-critical work in the narrower sense, as it is commonly used in Old Testament studies, thus can be linked in its origin with a definite group of people, a concrete starting point at Göttingen University, a special climate of intellectual and spiritual curiosity and learning, a limited span of time, about 1890 to 1920. It is in this environment that form and genre criticism came into being as a feasible way to reconstruct the early unfolding of old Israelite literature. And we should not forget to remember the strong religious-historical interests of the whole group. Form-critical analysis, from the beginning, was not restricted to biblical texts.

Forms and Genres

The religious historical school realized that human intellectual and religious development has been going on since times immemorial in a coherent stream of changing patterns of thought and experience. Since, however, the oldest periods of history have not been documented in writing, let alone in modern critical reports on factual events, extant texts of those times have to be analyzed in an adequate "pre-literary" fashion. There are no authenticated authors e.g., in Old Testament traditions nor in much other antique literature, for that matter. Consequently, the emergence of the oral and written sacred heritage must be due to other formative powers besides individual geniality. The century-old romanticist tendency to pay heightened attention to folk-literature like fairy-tales, legends, sagas, poetry in literary and religious anthropological studies proved to be an additional motivation to design a new exegetical method opportune for the analysis of biblical materials. A third thrust was, of course, the development of religion! Religion, used in the singular, bespeaks that universal spiritual power permeating all mankind and history, and manifesting itself on all levels of human development.

Thus grammatical, stylistic, rhetoric, and structural observations became the logical starting point for a closer evaluation of any ancient text. This certainly does not mean to say that the "outward form" of literary tradition was studied by form critics as an end in itself. Aesthetic appreciation from the outset has to serve recognition of oral and literary genres, and they in their turn are only indications of their "life-settings," those "recurring opportunities in real life, which give rise to any stereotyped linguistic expression."[7] But since life situations can only be deduced secondarily from the appearances of written traditions and a tentative genre description, the investigation *de facto* has to start with an analysis of formal elements of a given textual unit[8] without losing sight of the fertile soil it has been rooted in. A corresponding procedure is followed by most handbooks on form criticism[9] as well as by guides or work-manuals for pre-seminars.[10] To make the system of correlating speech forms and particular communicative actions more plausible to modern readers all form critics do point out present-day examples of standardized speech or writing, like e.g., the relatively fixed patterns of death-announcements, love songs, bills or greeting formulas. Usually, we are unaware of the formative moldings of verbal articulations but nevertheless readily comply within our own culture and environment to the customarily fixed rules. If we would ignore speech conventions we would probably get into serious trouble for not understanding partners in dialogue and/or irritating them. Standardized, sometimes formulaic language for all kinds of human communications, therefore, is by no means an archaic or low-class phenomenon but a social must, even more so in modern societies. Theoreticians and practitioners in the fields of literature, communication-sciences, marketing, public relations, etc. are fully aware of this fact.[11] We may conclude: Much more at present times than at the

---

7. This is about the gist of Hermann Gunkel's definitions of *Sitz im Leben*; cf., e.g., Gunkel and Begrich, *Einleitung in die Psalmen*, chap. 1 §§4–5 and passim (ET *Introduction to the Psalms*, 7–10 and throughout).

8. To single out literary units, consequently could be called the very first step of formal analysis; this is evident. The task calls for employment of literary techniques, and this is exactly the reason, why form critics usually have engaged quite a bit in literary criticism. We also should keep in mind that Gunkel himself in all his work was aiming at a comprehensive "literary history" of Old Testament writings; cf. Gunkel, "Ziele und Methoden der alttestamentlichen Exegese"; Gunkel, "Die israelitische Literatur" (ET "The Literature of Ancient Israel"). Furthermore, cf. Gunkel, *Das Märchen im Alten Testament* (ET *The Folktale in the Old Testament*).

9. To give but one example: Koch, *Was ist Formgeschichte?* (ET *The Growth of the Biblical Tradition*), deals with formulaic language, genres, and *Sitz im Leben* in his first three paragraphs (3–44).

10. One item may be sufficient, too, for the moment: Steck, *Exegese des Alten Testaments* (ET *Old Testament Exegesis*).

11. A few examples: Gunn, *Modern Occult Rhetoric*; Furht, ed., *Encyclopedia of Multimedia*; Placencia and Garcia, eds., *Research on Politeness in the Spanish-Speaking World*; Williams et al., eds., *Diversity in Advertising*; Longmire and Merrill, eds.,

beginning of form-critical research the issue of patterned speech has to be taken into account, always, to be sure, in relation to real life situations.[12] Of course, perspectives and interests have changed along the time. While biblical researchers at the beginning tried to verify the functions of words within their communication systems of old, modern word-strategists try to invent new, potent words, formulas, texts in order to stimulate people and markets. Still, the decisive importance of moulded speech is operative in both contexts.

What have been, in broad terms, the main aspects of form-critical endeavors in Old Testament literary tradition? Finding adequate categories in the analyses of past literary phenomena and define properly forms and genres is not an easy task because our own, twenty-first-century Western ways of distinguishing extant materials unwittingly enters the scene. For this reason, all our efforts remain tentative. A basic separation of prose and poetic language[13] and concomitant sub-divisions, for example, is of little help: Actual performances of ritual in most environments may include both literary styles, as social anthropologists commenting on life-ceremonies confirm. There is no way, consequently, to ignore real life situations already at this stage of analyzing and determining speech-forms (see below). Hermann Gunkel and Sigmund Mowinckel, parents of form-critical methodology, did acknowledge this fact,[14] while many of their successors blithely passed over it. The generally accepted division of speech-forms in Old Testament scholarship—narrative, prescriptive, poetic, etc. discourse, particular attention going to Israelite "prophetic" speech—needs to be handled carefully.[15] Taking it as a provisional guideline we certainly are able to point out a whole range of valuable "discoveries" in the field of forms and genres over some eight or nine decades, even admitting a good number of errors,

---

Untying the Tongue.

12. There has been a notion of this fact in Old Testament scholarship; cf., e.g., the work of Hardmeier, *Texttheorie und biblische Exegese*; Hardmeier, *Erzähldiskurs und Redepragmatik im Alten Testament*; Hayes and C. Holladay, *Biblical Exegesis*.

13. Cf. Gunkel, "Literature of Ancient Israel," 29. Under the influence of form criticism, standard textbooks on introduction to the Old Testament adopted this major division of (pre-literary) Hebrew tradition; cf. Eissfeldt, *Einleitung in das Alte Testament*, §3–16 (ET *The Old Testament: An Introduction*); Fohrer, *Einleitung in das Alte Testament*, §4–13 (ET *Introduction to the Old Testament*).

14. Gunkel and Begrich, *Einleitung in die Psalmen*, 10; 22–23 ($1/4, 8) (ET *Introduction to the Psalms*, 7–8, 15–21).

15. Most recent publications still follow this path, cf., e.g., Sweeney and Ben Zvi, eds., *The Changing Face of Form Criticism* (limitation to "narrative" and "prophetic" speech); Utzschneider, ed., *Lesarten der Bibel*, 97–182 ("narrative," "prescriptive," "psalmic," "prophetic" literature).

and uncertainties in the course of form-critical research. Shifting presuppositions, altered theological outlooks and exegetical aims did prompt a rich variety of analyses and genre definitions.[16]

Biblical *narratives* always have attracted very much the attention of form critics.[17] Small wonder, since communication of plots and events is an essential preoccupation of humans. Suggested life-settings for the biblical world range from folktales recounted at campfires or on doorsteps for a pastime, aetiological and educative stories for young people, reports of historical and/or heroic events, sacred and prophetic depictions of religious import, etc. Over time not the biblical stories changed, but modern interpreters acquired new vantage points and literary theories, going far beyond the plain folk tale rubrics of the Brothers Grimm[18] and the psychological and religious-historical constructions of W. Robertson Smith, Wilhelm Wundt, or Johannes Pedersen.[19] More recent (i.e. in our modern and postmodern age) developments in "narratology" clearly demonstrate a host of new angles under which story-telling can be viewed, mostly derived from formalist, structuralist, and psychic concerns about spoken and written texts and their readers or listeners, respectively.[20] All these new ventures help immensely to evaluate the kinds and ways of telling stories, to understand their surface, and even depth-structures including reader-response-relationships. In this function literary scholarship in its fascinating ramifications also is a big aid to form-critical studies, in that it may illuminate also the nascence of texts in real life. As long as the fundamental concern of form criticism is heeded, namely to take account of the *Sitz im Leben* of determined genres, any analytical tool for literary exposition is welcome.

---

16. Exact delimitations of literary "forms" (motifs) and "genres" (kinds/units of literature) need not to be discussed at this point. Suffice it to work with the general concept of several formal elements constituting a "genre" or "species" of literature. This latter, larger connotation, for its part, may be widened to include conglomerates of genres like in a biblical book or even the whole canon. Genre, consequently, is any piece of literature serving as a coherent text in some communicative act.

17. The literature on the investigation and classification of narratives alone is immense, cf., e.g., Gunkel, *Genesis* (ET *Genesis*); Gunkel, *Das Märchen im Alten Testament* (ET *The Folktale in the Old Testament*); Coats, *Genesis*; Coats, *Saga, Legend, Tale, Novella, Fable*.

18. Jacob and Wilhelm Grimm in the first half of the nineteenth century were the pioneers in collecting and appreciating "pure," "unspoiled" popular traditions.

19. The influence of all three of them on form criticism is considerable, proof of an astonishing openness of this method to new insights.

20. Cf., e.g., Herman, ed., *The Cambridge Companion to Narrative*; Ryan, *Narrative as Virtual Reality*.

Prescriptive genres[21] are widely used in Hebrew Scriptures; there are even those scholars who claim ordinance character for most of the biblical narratives, too.[22] Excluding the latter from our purview at this moment we still find a large diversity of norms and orientations, visibly taking up the needs of different groups of people. Old Testament prescriptions extend through all parts of the canon, and within the Pentateuch alone distinctive lists of commandments are found, ranging from sexual taboos (Lev 18), purification laws (Lev 11–15), pedagogic principles (Exod 20:12–17), civil laws (Exod 21–22), juridic procedures (Exod 23:1–8), community provisions (Deut 17–19), festive calendars (Lev 23), curses and maledictions (Lev 26; Deut 27–28) and others. A large number of form-critical studies have been dedicated to this area of Hebrew literature. Albrecht Alt really started a flood of scrutinies when he published his "Die Ursprünge des israelitischen Rechts" in 1934.[23] Studies included those on specific formulations like "case-law," "admonitions," "curses," "oath," "treaty- or covenant stipulations," "sacrificial rules," "purity precepts," and the like, but also extended to multi-layered collections like the Covenant Code and the Holiness Code and parts of Deuteronomy. In some instances whole books and compositions of sources were investigated form-critically. Instead of trying to give an exhaustive report on everything designed and published in this particular area I would like to point out only a few pertinent studies: Hans Jochen Boecker carefully analyzed juridical speech forms (mostly in secondary, e.g., prophetic usage!) leading to and being employed at hearings and trials by the court of elders in ancient Israel.[24] Klaus Koch looked closely at a segment of the Priestly source discovering an array of remarkably consistent forms.[25] Rolf Rendtorff, just like Gerhard von Rad, tried to explain form-critically and along tradition historical lines (which are nothing other than literary forms in culturally changing situations) the emergence and functioning of the whole Pentateuch, even the Hexateuch.[26] Sigmund Mowinckel, besides

21. Most of all, cf. Schwienhorst-Schönberger, "Präskriptive Texte"; but also Clark, "Law."

22. Cf. Daube, *Studies in Biblical Law*; Carmichael, *Law and Narrative in the Bible*, Ithaca: Cornell University Press 1985; Carmichael, *Illuminating Leviticus*.

23. English translation, Alt, "The Origin of Israelite Law." It may be opportune to mention my Bonn dissertation, accepted by Martin Noth, challenging Alt's evaluation of the "uniquely Israelite" "apodictic" law; cf. Gerstenberger, *Wesen und Herkunft des 'apodiktischen' Rechts*.

24. Boecker, *Redeformen des Rechtslebens im Alten Testament*.

25. Koch, *Die Priesterschrift von Ex 25 bis Lev 16*.

26. Rendtorff, *Das überlieferungsgeschichtliche Problem des Pentateuch*; von Rad, *Das formgeschichtliche Problem des Hexateuch* (ET *The Form-critical Problem of the Hexateuch*, 1–90).

putting an immense amount of work into his studies of the psalms, messianic prophecies, and late narrative sections of the Old Testament also followed up thoroughly the genesis of the Decalogue.[27] George E. Mendenhall and other scholars looked to ancient Near Eastern treaty-covenant patterns in order to understand biblical law and ensuing "covenant trials" (the so-called *rîb*-pattern).[28] Since sapiential traditions contain a great deal of prescriptive materials there also have been numerous works on admonitions, teachings, etc., quite often in comparison with Egyptian and Mesopotamian parallels.[29] The book of Job poses specific problems, so it came to be scrutinized more than once from a form-critical angle.[30] Influences of sapiential forms on the prophets were investigated[31] just like parenetical, prohibitive, and comforting words of the prophets themselves.[32] The field of literature on prescriptive genres is vast all by itself. Form critics have been working on them often trying to penetrate towards an appropriate life-situation. Sometimes they definitely erred in their proposed localization of genres. Nevertheless, the efforts have been fruitful; we know much more about Old Testament ceremonies, juridic activities, etc. today than before the times of form-critical research.

Poetic and prophetic literatures constitute a large part of Hebrew Scriptures. The former, clear enough, are present in the whole book of Psalms (see below Chap. 5), but they extend far beyond sacred songs and prayers. Working songs, love poetry, voluminous parts of wisdom literature, even prophetic discourse, all partake in poetic forms. Also in this area, we have to count on a great variety of specific modifications of genres serving a good number of communicative actions. Prophetic speech, on the other hand, already referred to above,[33] drew much attention by protestant scholars,

27. Mowinckel, *Le Décalogue*.

28. Mendenhall, "Ancient and Biblical Law"; Mendenhall, *Law and Covenant in Israel and the Ancient Near East*; Huffmon, "The Covenant Lawsuit in the Prophets"; McCarthy, *Treaty and Covenant*; Gerstenberger, "Covenant and Commandment."

29. Cf. Lang, *Die weisheitliche Lehrrede*; von Rad, *Weisheit in Israel* (ET *Wisdom in Israel*); Murphy, *Wisdom Literature*; Gerstenberger, "Proverbia."

30. Westermann, *Der Aufbau des Buches Hiob* (ET *The Structure of the Book of Job*); Albertz, "Der sozialgeschichtliche Hintergrund des Hiobbuches und der 'Babylonischen Theodizee.'"

31. Cf. Whedbee, *Isaiah and Wisdom*.

32. Cf., e.g., Westermann, *Grundformen prophetischer Rede* (ET *Basic Forms of Prophetic Speech*). To indicate one particular example of form-critical work on the prophets: Isa 40–55 came into focus ever since Joachim Begrich singled out the oracular formula "Do not fear . . ."; see Begrich, "Das priesterliche Heilsorakel."

33. Besides Westermann's standard analysis of speech forms (cf. above, n32) cf. e.g., the work of Hans Walter Wolff, Klaus Koch, Siegfried Herrmann et al. on prophetic

because it is in the second part of the Hebrew canon more than anywhere else that reformation theologies find their ultimate *raison d'être*.[34] After Bernhard Duhm, the staunch literary critique, had concluded his standard work on the prophets,[35] the field increasingly was swept by form-critical, tradition-historical, psychological, anthropological, and religio-historical interests.[36] As far as prophetic speech forms are concerned emphasis was placed on legitimation formulas (messenger- and revelatory rubrics),[37] judgment and punishment announcements, invectives and reprobations as well as oratory of hope and salvation presumably articulated by some species of cultic functionary.[38] All in all, prophetic articulations have been thoroughly explored, but, as it seems in our days, based on traditional concepts of biblical prophecy which presuppose certain reconstructions of prophetic office. If it proves to be true, that we are facing a "paradigm switch" in prophetic research,[39] also implying new life-settings for divine messenger proclamations, form-critical work has to be taken up from scratch once again.

The quick survey of form-critical work given above leads us to some conclusions. We realize the complexity of the method introduced some one hundred years ago. Outwardly, formal and generic analyses of texts may be undertaken from different theoretical platforms with varying goals and intentions. The merely descriptive task of identifying formulas, literary motifs, textual units (genres), conglomerations or compositions of entities, biblical books and canonic assemblages remains volatile, because it is intimately, but very often unadmittedly tied to alternating assumptions. The resulting imprecision of form criticism has often been accused by confessed

---

books and speech-forms; also n38 below.

34. A comprehensive evaluation of prophetic research has been given by Blenkinsopp, *A History of Prophecy in Israel* (cf. also the translation into German by Gerstenberger, *Geschichte der Prophetie in Israel*, with a chapter "Ausblick" by the translator, 266–90).

35. Duhm, *Israels Propheten*.

36. The literature produced is unfathomable; see Koch, "Propheten/Prophetie II. In Israel und seiner Umwelt"; Ben Zvi and Floyd, eds., *Writings and Speech in Israelite and Ancient Near Eastern Prophecy*; Köckert and Nissinen, *Propheten in Mari, Assyrien und Israel*; Schipper, ed., *Apokalyptik und kein Ende?*

37. Cf. the recent monograph by Wagner, *Prophetie als Theologie*, referring also to previous studies.

38. Sample publications: Wilson, *Prophecy and Society*; Herrmann, *Die prophetischen Heilserwartungen im Alten Testament*; Reventlow, *Liturgie und prophetisches Ich bei Jeremia*; Janzen, *Mourning Cry and Woe Oracle*; Tucker, "Prophetic Speech"; Tucker, "Prophecy and Prophetic Literature"; Sweeney, "Formation and Form in Prophetic Literature." See also the volumes on prophetic books in FOTL.

39. Cf. Deist, "The Prophets: Are We Heading for a Paradigm Switch?"

"non-" or "trans"-form critics as a weak point of the method. In my opinion it may well be the strong point of formal analysis, since it does do justice to the only material at hand, the written tradition of ancient Israel and the emerging Jewish community of old. Old Testament scholars cannot possibly start out their work from known biographies or psychic portraits of biblical authors, nor from dogmatic presuppositions fixing the contents of the Divine Word, nor, for that matter, from everlasting models of given speech forms and genres. Rather, we have to recognize the ever changing face of literary forms over the centuries, according to a) the occurring shifts in social life, religious ceremony, political institutions during antiquity and b) our own mutating conceptualizations of what is real, worthwhile, desirable for us to know. These two variables are causing constant changes in our biblical evaluations, correctly and necessarily so. We shall briefly discuss the impact of both tendencies before going ahead with the form criticism of the Psalms.

Life Situations (*Sitz im Leben*) and Interpreters' Standpoints

The fathers and mothers[40] of form criticism took particular care in trying to link forms and genres with their appropriate (even changing) life-settings. Hermann Gunkel, as already indicated, rated the search for a plausible *Sitz im Leben* as the very first task of a form critique.[41] Sigmund Mowinckel in practically all his studies is looking for the real life situations, e.g., of the Psalms.[42] Taking this perspective seriously we may postulate: Form criticism does attain its full value only if linked with a search for the life matrices of communication that gave birth to given forms and genres of speech. The argument is widely spread in linguistics and literary scholarship. Any word articulated by humans becomes meaningful only within a proper context. It turns important for subsequent listeners or partners in dialogue only when repeated in determined (ritualized) actions. The fact that written texts become potentially separated from their original *Sitze im Leben* is an artificial, technical chance development.

It does not really sever the ties of texts to real life, because a written piece in itself is dormant and totally insignificant until brought to life in a real life situation, being recited, heard, read, acclaimed, disdained,

---

40. One of the earliest pupils of Hermann Gunkel was Hedwig Jahnow (1879–1944, died in the Nazi concentration camp Theresienstadt); she wrote a careful study on *Das hebräische Leichenlied im Rahmen der Völkerdichtung*, still quoted today.

41. Gunkel and Begrich, *Einleitung in die Psalmen*, 10; 22–23 (ET *Introduction to the Psalms*, 7–13).

42. Cf. Mowinckel, *The Psalms in Israel's Worship*, passim, starting with pp. 3–4.

modified, or annulled. Solely real life gives concrete meaning to any text. Written words in the context of which has been lost are prone to severe misinterpretations, like the word "Cargo" on some wooden planks found by Pacific Islanders during the Second World War (and earlier). Words, it seems, are much like plants: They need to be treated together with the soil in which they are growing in order to be understood correctly.[43]

If this assumption is halfway acceptable, the big question arises: How do we learn about or reconstruct those ancient life settings pertinent to the forms and genres of ancient literature? What we need would be a whole road-atlas of old Israelite social stratifications and institutions,[44] ceremonies and rituals, feasts and customs together with their changing agendas, in order to classify speech patterns and genres extant in the Old Testament. Of course, we are far from possessing all the information necessary to achieve a complete picture in this area. But there are hosts of additional data won by archaeology and through the study of ancient Near Eastern cultures in general. Also, comparable cultures through the ages may be consulted; they also are able to complement our knowledge thus facilitating a better reconstruction of life-situations.[45] Accepting such outside help we could discover a good many speech forms originally tied in with family-, clan-, and village life and its social configurations, like proverbs, ethical norms, love and marriage songs, individual laments, ancestral tales, etc. Tribal and later on state structures did produce quite a different kind of oral and written literature, in correspondence with social and religious functions and actually performed rituals like warfare, coronation of kings, etc. We have examples in the Old Testament of victory songs, enthronement rites, heroic tales, royal genealogies, annals of the court and other activities of ruling classes. What weighs more, however, in all the literature which has come down to us of ancient Israelite provenance is visible in the formation of the Jewish community of faith in exilic/post-exilic times. The particular conditions of the remnants of the Judean populace, partly deported to Babylonia, partly fugitive in Egypt and other Near Eastern countries, forming a religious Yahweh-community are recorded only precariously in a direct way by Old Testament witnesses, because scribes and community leaders focused on the ancient history and their divine revelations when compiling Torah. Still, the emerging institutions of Judaism were most important for the generation of Old Testament

---

43. More about the subject in Gerstenberger, *Psalms, Part 1* and *Part 2*; Gerstenberger and Schoenborn, eds., *Hermeneutik—sozialgeschichtlich*.

44. Cf. Gerstenberger, "The Religion and Institutions of Ancient Israel"; Gerstenberger, *Theologies*.

45. In my book *Theologies*, I try to recover five levels of social organization in ancient Israel and to reconstruct their specific theological concepts.

forms and genres. The reason for this judgment simply is this: Very probably, torah, prophets and writings in their overwhelming majority came into being or were modified during this formative, exilic/post-exilic period of Israel's history.[46] Therefore, we should expect a massive imprint of respective community structures and ceremonies on all the literature composed in this same period. Older forms and genres at that point had to be adapted to the new institutions and rituals of emerging Yahweh-faith-congregations. That we have to use the plural and take into account diverging tradition within early Judaism already, can easily be proven by putting religious practices of Jews from Jerusalem, Samaria, Babylonia, and Elephantine in Egypt side by side. Still, community organization and basic belief in Yahweh and his *torah* has been the common ground for all the Jews in the Persian, Hellenistic, and Roman periods. Prominent speech forms in this time of nascent Judaism where the teaching, preaching, exhorting genres so abundantly used in the Old Testament but also cultic poetry. They for the most part reflect "parochial" activities later on turning into synagogue liturgies and rites; Neh 8 exhibits the central communal act of torah-reading with some corollaries.

As to the second observation: Biblical research, as any other kind of scholarly endeavor, always is conditioned by the *Sitz im Leben* of the persons performing their work in the midst of determined social, cultural, and religious parameters of their own environments.[47] Lamenting over missing unanimity in the field is oblivious of this basic fact of all human learning and knowledge. There cannot possibly be unanimity in interpretation as long as the diversity of contextual situations on the side of the interpreters will last.[48] The crucial question will be: to what extent the perception of reality and the virtual reconstruction of ancient parameters will enter our consciousness and from there into the hermeneutics of understanding? The underlying issue is again the interpreter's relation to surrounding reality, this time the contemporary variety of reality. Do we maintain an idealistic stance, working exclusively in the realm of a spiritual world, or do we admit an insoluble relationship of word, meaning, and social reality?

Form-critical analysis, starting from specific texts but looking for patterned language that is intimately linked to communicative action, is best prepared to do justice to ongoing and changing life situations. They, in turn, continuously give birth to texts and text interpretations, and even the most original text may be considered an interpretation already.

46. Cf. Gerstenberger, *Israel in der Perserzeit* (ET *Israel in the Persian Period*).

47. Twenty-two recent self-portrayals of German Old Testament scholars beautifully illustrate this common truth: Sebastian Grätz and Schipper, eds., *Alttestamentliche Wissenschaft in Selbstdarstellungen*.

48. Cf. Gerstenberger and Schoenborn, eds., *Hermeneutik—sozialgeschichtlich*.

The Psalms

In line with what has been stated above it seems most appropriate to ask for germinal life-settings in the first place that gave rise to specific genres of psalms. Ancient Near Eastern parallels as well as occasional modern anthropological data may help to define such "repeated occasions of communication" on different levels of society. "Patterned language" does suggest a certain amount of formalized speech, but by no means total schematization. Form criticism recognizes a good amount of variation in individual texts.[49] But the existence of formal stereotypes and generic molds should not be denied. Especially in cultic contexts, it seems to me, we have to expect a fairly high level of generality. The Old Testament itself gives us sufficient indications about several main social organizations in Israel that produced distinct genres of psalms, and the diachronic perspective sometimes becomes visible, too.[50]

Psalms for Individuals and Their Families

The most basic and archaic type of human socialization is that in small family (lineage) groups, which for millennia had been—until the advent of industrialization in the Western Hemisphere—firmly knit units of a limited number of persons mastering life together. Not only joint labor was called for to guarantee survival, but also a household cult. There are clear traces of domestic religion in the ancient Near East,[51] as well as in biblical tradition[52] testifying to the veneration of "personal" deities, which, of course, were tied to the family, like Jacob's "God of my father" (e.g., Gen 31:5, 42). Proof of domestic cult-rites comes from passages like Exod 21:6, and other references to small idols (*teraphim*) which have been unearthed also in private homes of ancient Israelite towns besides other implements of small cult practice.[53] Our interest is: How were psalms used in a domestic

---

49. Rhetorical criticism—as represented, e.g., by James Muilenburg and Phyllis Trible—has vehemently denounced lacking regard for individualism in form-critical work. Degrees of standardization in recited texts certainly should be debated.

50. For the main social levels of Old Testament cult and theology cf. Gerstenberger, *Theologies*; applied to the Psalms: Gerstenberger, *Psalms, Part 2*; Gerstenberger, "Theologies in the Book of Psalms."

51. Cf. van der Toorn, *Family Religion in Babylonia, Syria and Israel*.

52. Cf. Gerstenberger, *Yahweh the Patriarch*, 55–66.

53. The few occurrences of *teraphim* in narratives (Gen 31:19, 34, 35; Judg 17:5; 18:17–20; 1 Sam 19:16) are quite significant; they do betray a good bit of the functions of a domestic deity, cf. Moorey, *Idols of the People*.

environment or in relation to members of the household? We sure do not have full descriptions of cultic services administered in homes from the Old Testament. But closely related Babylonian incantations[54] should be indicative of alike ceremonies throughout the ancient Near East. What we call prayers of "individual complaint"[55] in Old Testament studies is matched by very similar supplications (in terms of form, structure, outlook) embedded in a framework of ritual prescriptions on the side of Babylonian incantations. This picture can be enlarged to include healing ceremonies within "primitive" peoples around the world, historically speaking or in terms of contemporary practices.

We are justified, therefore, to talk about domestic healing practices, conducted, as it were, by shamanistic mediators in order to heal and rehabilitate sick persons as being the *Sitz im Leben* for psalms of complaint (or: supplication), the most numerous category of prayers preserved in the Psalter. As to the administration of these psalms: Presumably, diseases and wounds always were treated within families with means and knowledge available through the experience of grandma and neighbors. Only if the treasure of "house drugs" was no longer sufficient to dominate the evil that had befallen the patient, outside help was sought after (2 Kgs 1:2). Shamanistic healers then would attend to the sick one and perform a ritual over him (2 Kgs 4:32-35; Isa 38:21; cf. Job 33:23-26). The expertise of performing powerful rites was, of course, a professional matter which ordinary people had to buy from the healer. This is exactly the situation of the *mašmašu*-priest in Babylonian incantations or the medicine man among North American Indian tribes.[56] A few Old Testament narratives suggest vaguely the domestic situation of healing rituals (2 Kgs 4; 5; Isa 38) while some others locate the saving intervention of a deity to a pilgrim's sanctuary, notably 1 Sam 1-2; 2 Kgs 14:1-3.

Looking at the persons involved in cultic rites destined to save the life of a single sufferer we should consider the participation of close family members in the ritual performances. Direct evidence in the Hebrew Scriptures is missing. Babylonian sources do not mention participants other than

---

54. Drawing on my habilitation thesis (*Der bittende Mensch*) I dare maintain the assertion: Babylonian prayers for divine help do generically employ the same functions as "complaints of the individual" in the Old Testament Psalter, cf. also Maul, *Zukunftsbewältigung*; Frechette, *Mesopotamian Ritual-Prayers of "Hand-lifting"*; Graham Cunningham, *Deliver Me from Evil*.

55. Psalm genres are briefly sketched in the introduction of my commentary: Gerstenberger, *Psalms, Part 1*, 5-22.

56. My own experience with "Navajo sings" (incantations) dates back to the early 1960s in Fort Defiance, Arizona.

priest and patient either. Contemporary anthropological research does meet with intimate circles supporting the patient which seems to be a very plausible arrangement given the strong bonds of solidarity among family groups. Perhaps the "friends" of Job and the "treacherous companions" within some complaint psalms do point towards the ideal institution of co-mourning with the sufferer.

Form-critical analysis of the large portion of individual complaints in the Psalter[57] has investigated the elements and motifs of the genre and scrutinized its overall structure: Every single psalm is composed in its own way, but all of them use similar basic elements. That means to say, the prayers are patterned according to their liturgical needs. They have been property of the professional healer who administered their use. The sequence of form-elements corresponds to the ceremony performed on behalf of the patient. Main sections are: There is a proper invocation of the deity, calling on her name, asking to be heard (initial plea: e.g., Pss 28:1-2; 102:2-3 [1-2]), mostly followed by a descriptive, reproachful, petitionary complaint, sometimes repeated in the course of the prayer (Pss 35:7, 11-16, 20-21; 38:3-15 [2-14]). Next may come—in accordance with the concrete case diagnosed by the healer—an assertion of innocence or a confession of sin (Pss 26:4-6; 38:19 [18]). This element is strongly attested also in Job 31 and in prayers of penitence like Ps 51. Affirmations of confidence do have an important role, they cling to former positive experiences with the God invoked (Pss 22:4-6, 10-11 [3-5, 9-10]; 71:5-7) and occasionally dominate a whole psalm (e.g., Pss 23; 62; 131).

The main thrust of individual complaints is with supplication for divine rescue, therefore petition looms large and can be implicitly intended also in other form elements (Pss 17:6-9; 35:1-3, 17, 22-24; 69:14-19 [13-18]). Imprecation against enemies is the other side of the coin: Most evil was considered mischief caused by malevolent persons or demons. Consequently, the sources of suffering had to be eliminated. The prayer usually ends with vow or pledge to give thanks (Pss 7:18 [17]; 56:10 [12]; 109:30). Thus situations of dire need and threatening death[58] would provoke domestic (or sanctuary-bound) ceremonies of supplication, casual worship-services, we might say. The prayer proper, only part of the ritual preserved in the OT Psalter, had to be spoken by the sufferer himself line by line prompted by the acting healer (in Babylonian texts: "let the patient recite . . ."). The vow at the end means to say: "If my God does hear my cries, I shall bring him/her a

---

57. About forty psalms are to be counted in this genre; cf. Gerstenberger, *Psalms, Part 1*, 14; Miller, *They Cried to the Lord*, 55-134.

58. Cf. Barth, *Die Errettung vom Tode* (1947), newly edited by Janowski (1997).

thanksgiving sacrifice..." (cf. Lev 7:11-21). This was an excellent occasion to celebrate a big feast with family, friends and neighbors, life-setting for the next genre of individual psalms. One narrative example in the Old Testament, by the way, is Absalom's return from exile, having been pardoned by his father (2 Sam 15:7-9).

Thanksgiving songs are attested also in narrative contexts, the most famous being the songs of Hannah (1 Sam 2), Jonah (Jonah 2), and Hezekiah (Isa 38). A programmatic poem, for the instruction of the community, about when thanksgivings are due is Ps 107.[59] The merry party spirit of a thanksgiving shines through in Ps 22:26: "The afflicted shall eat and be satisfied..." Anthropologists like E. E. Evans-Pritchard report that festive sacrifices are enjoyed by tribes people because of rich food and drink offered to the participants.[60] Thanksgiving psalms in the Psalter are reflecting exuberant joy of the healed or ones saved, who are able to share their experiences with the guest-crowd. A sacrificial formula seems to have been the pivotal moment in the ceremony: "I offer to you a thanksgiving sacrifice" (Ps 116:17). This so-called *todah*-formula marks the central act: the handing over of the animal to God.[61] The components of the obligatory prayer of the saved one include an *invitation to give thanks* to all present at the feast (Pss 30:2, 5 [1, 4]; 118:1-4), an *account of trouble and salvation* (Pss 32:3-5; 118:10-14), *praises of Yahweh* (Pss 18:47-49 [46-48]; 92:5-6 [4-5]), and the offertory formula already mentioned (Pss 118:21; 130:2; 138:1-2; Isa 12:1). In conclusion of the prayer *blessings* are invoked over participants, and sometimes an *exhortatory speech* may follow for the edification of the guests (Pss 41:2 [1]; 32:8-9; 118:8-9). Just like in the complaint genre we observe with thanksgiving psalms a neat correspondence of form elements with cultic procedure, even if the exact sequence of liturgies cannot be ascertained. In any case, complaints and thanksgivings for the individual and within the framework of the family group seem to constitute the main types of personal prayers (songs) preserved in the Old Testament Psalter.

We should, however, ask whether other possible life situations within the small group or relating to it gave rise to other types of psalms which then may be detected within the extant materials. Survival in times of crises certainly was an overriding interest of the small group so much depending on its own potentials to work and live together. An equally important area of concern—according to biblical narrative traditions—was the care for

---

59. Four exemplary life-situations (salvations from death) are presented as motivations to give thanks; cf. my exegesis of this psalm in Gerstenberger, *Psalms, Part 2*, 246-52.

60. Evans-Pritchard, *Nuer Religion*, 285-86 and passim.

61. Crüsemann, *Studien zur Formgeschichte*, 270-74.

progeny largely accredited to the charisma of house-wives. While there are some psalms taking up the topic of fertility and internal peace and strength (Pss 127; 128; 131; 133) they are designed purely from the patriarchal point of view, lauding the wife as the bearer and nurse of "his" children (Pss 127:3; 128:3; cf. also the eulogy Prov 31:10–31). Have there been no psalms for the specific use of women? Some experts answer in the positive,[62] but supplications, rituals, or ceremonies for women in travail—although female suffering to give birth is amply referred to (cf. Gen 3:16; 35:16–19; Jer 4:31; Isa 26:17)—have not entered the Hebrew Scriptures. Why is this the case? Babylonian (and other) omina and incantations in regard to complications in child bed have come down to us.[63] To take up another situation: The upbringing of children and the celebration of turning points in their lives is hardly made a topic in narratives, more so in wisdom tradition and law. Since *rites de passage*, however, are customarily held in all cultures we might expect some reflection on them in the psalms. Very little of such influence can be seen, perhaps the only instant is Ps 8, which I tentatively connected with puberty rites,[64] because of its euphoria in regard to the dominant position of humans in the world—much in contrast to rather humble assertions in other parts of the Scriptures (cf. Ps 144:3–4). If this be plausible we still may wonder why so many life-situations of family life, especially those celebrated with *rites de passage*, do not clearly show up in the sacred poetry of Israel nor in festive calendars. We do have only imperfect answers: The work of collecting the psalms in the post-exilic area did occur in line with the interests of the community of Yahweh-believers.[65] Much of family cult tradition may not have entered the community collection of prayers. Some texts we have in the Psalter, on the other hand, may have served *rites de passage* of individuals, but within the realm of community, not family life.

Village and Town

Human settlements of various families dedicated to common goals, turning reality because of agricultural progress since about 10,000 BCE in eastern Anatolia, do require a whole set of new paradigms in behavior, social adjustments, and religious beliefs. They get condensed also into cultic and legal

---

62. Cf., e.g., Miller, *They Cried to the Lord*, 233–43; Bail, *Gegen das Schweigen klagen*.

63. Cf. Reiner, "Babylonian Birth Prognoses"; Beckman, *Hittite Birth Rituals*; Stol, *Birth in Babylonia and the Bible*.

64. Gerstenberger, *Psalms, Part 2*, 67–72.

65. Cf. Gerstenberger, *Israel in der Perserzeit*, 272–78. (ET *Israel in the Persian Period*).

practice. We have to piece together how ancient Israelites lived in their villages and towns from the eleventh through the third centuries BCE in Palestine, as well as in various "foreign" regions like Babylonia and Egypt in order to get some reliable background for our quest for psalms coming out of this level of social organization.[66] Archaeological data from the ancient Near East help visualize the daily routine of these old Israelites. Legal regulations are most obvious from the Old Testament: The "Covenant Code" (roughly Exod 21–23) spells out rights and obligations among neighbors; juridical action was handled by heads of families (cf. Ruth 4).[67] Religious life of the community took place at the local *bamah* ("high place"), a sanctuary dedicated to the local deities (cf. Judg 6:11–32, reworked later; 1 Sam 9:10–14). What about the religious horizon and cultic performances of these villagers or towns-people? They were agriculturists, primarily concerned about their crops and herds. Family religion oriented towards basic necessities of individual life continued undisturbed in the village. But common interests of the community included favorable weather conditions in all seasons, protection against enemies and demonic forces, celebrations of harvests. Other deities than the personal gods of the family units were responsible for these regional issues. They resided at the local shrine, marked by Mazzebe and Asherah-pole (cf. Gen 28:18–22; Judg 6:25; 13:19). Seasonal feasts were characteristic for this cult of village and town. Psalms which originally belonged into this life-setting include hymns of annual thanksgiving, communal complaints and songs of salvation, ethical instruction on a local level.

To spell out a little more the psalm-types to be possibly connected with village cults at the "high places" of ancient Israel: some psalms are linked to harvest festivals, e.g., Ps 65 with its praise elements (v. 2–4 [1–3]), communal petition (v. 5 [4]), adoration of the creator and sustainer (v. 6–9 [5–8]), and thanksgiving (v. 10–14 [9–13]). In Ps 29, scholars agree, we meet an old Canaanite hymn to the weather God, while Ps 104 is a beautiful composition about the wondrous organization of nature based on Egyptian models of praising creation. These and other psalms may have been used at seasonal events of thanksgiving. Other hymns of the Psalter qualify as "communal thanksgivings" for non-seasonal celebrations or occasions.[68] Admittedly, the borderline between "hymns" and "thanksgivings" may shift, and seasonal versus ad hoc use may be a somewhat theoretical discussion.

---

66. See Gerstenberger, *Theologies*, 78–91, n44.

67. Cf. Köhler, *Der hebräische Mensch* (ET *Hebrew Man*).

68. Against scholarly denials of the existence of specific "communal thanksgivings" (in contradistinction to outright "hymns") for returning thanks in concrete cases of salvation, I like to maintain the category and nominate Pss 66; 67; 124; 129 as examples.

Times of communal mourning and supplication can easily be imagined. The common welfare, so much dependent on benevolent deities, needed to be repaired. Services of entreaty to the local Gods were held, and vestiges of collective complaining and imploring are present in the Psalter. They are fashioned more or less according to the individual complaint genre, but sometimes use explicitly the communal "we" when engaging in subjective discourse.[69] Sumerian city laments are a remotely related genre.[70] Numerous passages in the Old Testament do mention public calamities and deadly threats to agricultural communities, like droughts, diseases, plagues, invasions. References include ritual responses of the collective concerned, e.g., Jer 3:13–31; 14; Isa 63:7–64:11; Joel 1–2; Hos 6:1–3; Lam 1–2; 4–5; etc. Many of these "collective complaints" could be virtually incorporated into the Psalter.

Tribes and Tribal Alliances

Sociologists define tribes as loose alliances of family and clans for determined purposes: protection against foreign incursions, maintenance of cultural values including lineage systems, safeguarding regional economic interests. Political organization of tribes usually is weak, because heads of clans tend to cling to their particular chieftainships. An ancient Hebrew poem derides efforts to create a centralized monarchy in Israel which would mean total loss of clan autonomy (Judg 9:8–15). Old Testament references portray the pre-state tribal society almost exclusively in its warring capacities, e.g., in the book of Judges. Neighboring tribes, like Midianites or Amalekites are equally viewed as war faring entities. Juridical functions of the leaders are mentioned (Judg 4:4–5; 10:2–5) but not elaborated in tales.[71] Former theories about a central Yahwistic cult around the tribal religious symbol, the ark,[72] have been abandoned again. What remains of Israelite tribal cult in the Psalms are samples of victory songs, like Ps 68 with its generic parallel, Judg 5. From chance references in Exod 15:21; Judg 11:34; 1 Sam 18:7 we

---

69. Among others, Pss 44; 74; 79; 80; 83 certainly are communal complaints, although they already presuppose urban living and the existence of a Yahweh faith community. Still, they probably demonstrate the kind of lamenting common in pre-Yahwistic times.

70. Cf. Cohen, *The Canonical Lamentations of Mesopotamia*.

71. Judicial procedure administered by an "assembly" of tribes as in Judg 20–21 is a retrospective construction in the vein of deuteronomistic concepts; it cannot claim any historical authenticity.

72. In particular, Martin Noth's grand vision of a tribal amphictyony (see his *The History of Israel*) was not maintained by experts.

know that women would meet their returning troops with tambourines and chants of victory. This custom may constitute the beginning of the genre: Full-fledged victory songs narrate drastically and dramatically episodes of battle and praise the deity for his/her forceful intervention in favor of the fighting men.[73] Terrifying reports like the later description of bloody victorious Yahweh (Isa 63:1–6) are fully in line with old tribal victory songs. On the whole, we have to realize that the period of tribalism in Israel had already ended centuries before the active formation of traditions started, not to speak of the hot phase of collecting them into sacred books. Tribal structures only survived in collective memory and in an intricate system of genealogical ties.

Kingdoms

In a way, the premonition in regard to historical authenticity of tribal life also is valid over against monarchic traditions of Israel and Judah. The royal dynasties of the two states lasted roughly two and four centuries, respectively, which is a considerable amount of time. But the northern kingdom ended in 722 BCE, and the southern one was finally abolished in 587 BCE. Statehood and royal dynastic cult turned into memory and hope, they were no longer real when the composition of the Psalter took place. All the more astonishing is the fact that David was considered not only the great founder of the temple cult (cf. 1 Chr 16–17, etc.), but he was also made the poet and singer of psalms while his son Solomon was stylized into a lord of wisdom and architect of the temple. These two founding monarchs thus acquired a role of, so to speak, initiators and leaders of the Jewish community, and in some layers of tradition they also turned messianic figures. David was the ideal singer, and Solomon the sublime preacher and intercessor of Jewish community services, starting with the composition of the book of Kings and continuing with Chronicles. The fading away and reshaping of royal memories and the transformations of leadership roles naturally influenced the transmission of cultic heritages. We may assume that Israelite and Judean kings had taken part in a higher or lesser degree in the ancient Near Eastern patterns of divine commissioning. Now, after the demise of monarchy, they were "democratized" to act as leaders of the congregation of believers. Only in some messianic visions they kept a future function along the line of being son and vice-regent of Yahweh for the whole world.

Cultic enactments of dynastic claims did belong to any royal governance in the ancient Near East. Kingship "by the grace of a highest god" can

---

73. Becker-Spörl, *Und sang Debora an jenem Tag*; Dreher, *O Cântico de Débora*.

be maintained only by performing proper rites and services thus keeping the state deities on good terms with royal families and dependent nations. There are a good number of echoes coming from old monarchic ceremonies, e.g., coronation protocol and marriage rites (Pss 2; 110; 45), administration of justice and thanksgiving after victory (Pss 72; 18), divine guarantees for the dynasty (Ps 89; cf. 2 Sam 7), perhaps also intercession on behalf of the king (Pss 20; 21) and commemoration of his election (Ps 78:67–72). Dreams of universal reign exercised by Davidic monarchs, trust in their perfect administration of justice, hopes for their return at the end of time—these and other mythical exaggerations probably are later enlargements of historic figures and ideologies.

We will be able to reconstruct some authentic royal ceremony and project extant psalms texts back into monarchic times. But to which end did exilic/post-exilic communities of Yahweh worshippers still use psalmic elements inherited from past institutions and ritual? The difficult task will be to recognize more closely what intersections of bygone traditions and contemporary living and thinking did constitute meaningful nuclei of communal identity in emerging Judaism. It is this perspective on the "anachronistic" importance of kingship which should help us classify the so-called "royal hymns" of the Psalter. In reality, they are, in the late phase of the Old Testament no "royal" hymns at all, because they serve the Jewish community, not the Davidic dynasty any longer. Basically, the relevant psalms may either adopt some royalist motif to foster actual communal identity, or they project their past kings as coming saviors into the future. The Psalter does offer some examples for both interpretations. All texts counted, however, the royal overtones are not very frequent.

The historic Judean king (and possibly the monarchic structure of human society at large) does appear to the Jewish worshipper as the warrant for a divine world order (cf. Pss 18; 20; 21; 72) in which he wants to participate. The universal enthronement of a "son of God" (Pss 2; 110) he takes as a promise for the distant future. He may even consider a royal wedding song (Ps 45) as a prototype for his own happy feasting. In terms of genre classification, consequently, we should distinguish between old monarchic and new communitarian use of a Psalm or motif. True remnants of royal liturgies certainly may be called "coronation ritual," "marriage ceremony," or "intercession for the king." The later Jewish reading of royal psalms emphasized "community building," "justice and peace," "the future savior," etc., all in the context of the new congregation of faith. Genre classification in this life setting has still to be worked out satisfactorily because form critics have been too much impressed by an illusory royal metaphor.

Community of Faith

From what has been stated so far it may be easily deduced that the postexilic community was responsible for the collection and redaction of the psalms in accordance with the needs of its own life of worship and teaching.[74] Again we have to reconstruct the full range of ceremonial activities cultivated in various places of emerging Judaism to visualize the different life-settings for the genres of psalms used at the time. Biblical witnesses did not care to give us meticulous descriptions of their liturgical agendas, yet there are a good many valuable references in the texts. Torah-reading as depicted in Neh 8 apparently was the backbone of congregational worship, involving everybody: "both men and women and all who could hear with understanding" (v. 2). Some passages in historical narrative mirror that late torah-reading (e.g., Deut 29–31; Josh 24; Exod 24:3-4; Jer 26; 36; 44; etc.). Reading out aloud the revealed word of Yahweh was accompanied by some kind of interpretation (Neh 8:8), that means, the genre of "homily" was born in the context of emerging Judaism. The assembly of the whole congregation soon turned into a weekly worship service; the Sabbath receiving more and more attention in the contemporary literature.[75] But the central worship service was not the only communal celebration. Cultic calendars in the Old Testament (Exod 23:14-17; 34:18, 22-23; Deut 16; Lev 23; Num 28-29) betray a long and intricate history of religious feasting involving family homes, local and regional sanctuaries, and increasingly the temple of Jerusalem, Zion, the holy abode of Yahweh.[76] Pilgrimages to the spiritual capital are already reflected in the book of psalms (Pss 120-134). Furthermore, we can be sure that there have always been casual services, prayer times, meditations, incantations geared to the needs of individuals, small groups, special interests and life-situations.[77] The strict prohibition of mantic activities in Deut 18:9-14 and stories like that of the woman of Endor (1 Sam 28) give rise to the suspicion that there have been many more religious rites in Israel than attested in the Scriptures.

In any case, the cultic background for composition and use of the psalms was set in the formative period of Jewish history.[78] We may assume,

---

74. Cf. Gerstenberger, "Life Situations and Theological Concepts."

75. Cf. Haag, "Šabbat"; Lutz Doering, *Schabbat*; Alexander, *The Mystical Texts*.

76. Cf. Levine, *In the Presence of the Lord*; Day, ed., *Temple and Worship in Biblical Israel*.

77. Cf. Elbogen, *Der jüdische Gottesdienst*.

78. With good reasons, the period of Persian hegemony may be considered the most fertile phase of nascent Judaism; cf. Gerstenberger, *Israel in der Perserzeit* (ET *Israel in the Persian Period*).

then, that all the categories of psalms represented in the Psalter have been part of the faith community's spiritual life and cultic events. There practically were no psalms outside the religious sphere. We also may start from the hypothesis that genres unknown in previous social settings have to be attributed to the living conditions of the newly emerging Yahweh community. This is true in particular for the wide range of didactic psalms which give so much head ache to form-critical commentators of the Psalter. Lifelong exercise of faith in learning and debating the right ways of God has become the hallmark of early Jewish theology.

Along this line of thinking arrangement and classification of psalms within the life of post-exilic Jewish communities does not pose insurmountable difficulties. Each text would have to be discussed in particular. At this point we have to content ourselves with a short survey of the main genres. The large group of individual complaints, thanksgivings and hymns, inherited from family religion and amounting to more than one third of the Psalter continued to be used, very probably also in services of supplication and thanksgiving for special persons and their families. There are indications that older prayers were extended to include a plurality of sufferers, e.g., in Ps 12.[79] Sometimes explicit references to Zion or the congregation of Yahweh were added (e.g., Ps 102:13-23 [12-22])[80] in order to adjust the text to its new setting. Adaptations and variations of old cultic procedures may be assumed for the Jewish community of faith. Still, its members needed spiritual and medical attendance just like autonomous family groups had needed it before. With the concentration of religious life on the one and exclusive God of the ancestors and of Israel and strict prohibition of any other religious affiliation—this was at least the message of deuteronomistic preaching—the community had to offer those services formerly included in domestic ritual. Women, in this fashion, previously strong in the household lost control of their religious practices or their roles shifted e.g., to administering the Passover meal. Altogether, however, healing and rehabilitating psalms, as evidenced by their overwhelming presence in the Psalter, were kept in use. This is true even more so for old communal complaints and thanksgiving, which had to be changed very little to fit the concrete life conditions of the Torah community.

The second large group of songs found in the Psalter is linked with communal events like seasonal feasting, collective mourning and supplicating, historical commemorations, and—in an overall fashion—with

---

79. Cf. Gerstenberger, "Psalm 12: Gott hilft den Unterdrückten."

80. "The main problem of Ps 102 is the juncture of individual and communal elements ...": Gerstenberger, *Psalms, Part 2*, 211; the exposition of the whole psalm (210-15).

the building up and maintenance of a solid group identity. Many hymns, thanksgivings, memorial poems are to be considered here, another third of the whole Psalter. The calendar of feasts patently has been in flux over time. In the center we find three old harvest festivals (Exod 23:14-17; Deut 16:1-17; Lev 23), "unleavened bread" ("Passover")—"feast of weeks" (Pentecost)—"feast of booths" ("Atonement"). Quite a few of the psalms may belong to one or more of these festive occasions, exact attributions are impossible, just like the use of present-day church hymns cannot be tied down to exactly defined occasions. In the course of time and also with local differences the calendar of cultic events got modified and widened. Hebrew tradition points out new festivals to come into use: the "bewailing of virginity" (Judg 11:37-40), "Purim" (Esth 9:20-32), "dedication of the temple" (Ps 30:1), "fasting in memory of the destruction of the temple" (Zach 7:2-6; 8:18-19). The calendars themselves exhibit changes: Lev 23, presumably latest in line, places emphases on Sabbath and Day of Atonement unheard of in earlier lists, not to mention the new release and restitution regulations in Lev 25.[81] There is still much form-critical work to be done to get closer to early Jewish cultic practices, feasts, and commemorations that have used older psalms and produced new liturgical poetry for various occasions of congregational service to God.

The last group of psalms to be mentioned in regard to Jewish community life very likely is the most important one; it has been summarized under the rubric of "wisdom," "sapiential," "didactic" or "learned Psalms."[82] I do prefer the label "didactic"[83] because it is indicative of a creative communal teaching process and not tied to a particular profession or area of knowledge. The psalms in question exhibit a great variety of topics and speech forms. They agree in their intention to communicate sacred knowledge essential for the identity of the faith community and every member of it. Here are a few samples: A number of psalms give instruction about the sacred history (e.g., Pss 78; 105; 106; 136). A legitimate speaker takes the stage, addressing his "people":

---

81. For all references to the book of Leviticus, cf. Gerstenberger, *Leviticus*, and the mostly opposing views of Milgrom, *Leviticus*, 3 vols.

82. Gunkel and Mowinckel already labored to find a fitting *Sitz im Leben* for this genre, and later researchers were equally unhappy with it; cf. only Mowinckel, *The Psalms in Israel's Worship*, 2:104-25, he actually uses the designation "non-cultic" (111-14).

83. In my commentary (*Psalms, Part 1* and *Part 2*) I frequently employ the genre classification "Communal Instruction" (about eighty times!). Cf. also Gerstenberger, "The Psalms: Genre, Life-Situations, and Theologies."; Gerstenberger, "Communal Instruction."

> Give ear, O my people, to my teaching (*torah*);
>   incline your ears to the words of my mouth.
> I will open my mouth in a parable (*mašal*);
>   I will utter dark sayings (*hidah*) from of old,
> things we have heard and known,
>   that our ancestors have told us.
> We will not hide them from their children;
>   we will tell to the coming generation
> the glorious deeds of Yahweh, and his might,
>   and the wonders that he has done. (Ps 78:1–4)

The main concern is with transmission of ancient traditions, belonging to the community—note the plural "our ancestors" etc. Yahweh has constituted the group with no little travail, until he deposed northern leaders to elect his favorite David (vv. 56–72). All this is subject matter to learn, to heed, to live by, in order to avoid further annoyances of God. The speaker is teaching a powerful lesson from history. The paradigm of God's labor and Israel's constant deviations is very prominent in deuteronomistic literature. And this literature is part and parcel, in my opinion, of exilic/post-exilic times, when reconstitution and preservation of the religious community was the primary concern.

Another impressive example of didactic procedure is the "song of Moses." The liberator of Israel has to retell the whole Sinai experience, and every word Yahweh communicated to him on the holy mountain, all the precepts and admonitions, norms and rules for congregational life (Deut 12–26). After this "Torah" has been finished, properly put to writing and deposited with the ark as a covenant witness (Deut 31:24–26), a new effort is made to teach the people (Deut 32). The song, recited by Moses "to the very end" (Deut 31:30) is treated with equal reverence as the Torah. It is written down twice: Deut 31:19, 22; it is taught to the people and highlighted as extremely important: Deut 31:22; 32:44–47; it also serves as "witness" against an apostate people, that is, as a covenant reminder: Deut 31:21. Apparently, the "song" in itself is meant to be a manifestation of Torah; as such it is part and parcel of a worship liturgy, recited by a cantor to the congregation.

Didactic communication in the Hebrew Scriptures is expressed mainly by the verbs *yrh* (hiph.) "instruct"; *lmd* (piel) "teach"; *ydh* (hiph.) "let know." Allusions to ritual procedures around divine instruction are concentrated already in individual complaints of exilic or post-exilic provenance. Psalm 25, an acrostic poem, pleads for orientation in Yahweh's paths (vv. 4–5, 8–10). Psalms 27:8, 11 and 86:7, 11 are looking for clarifying, orienting words of God: Doing this they are close to Torah psalms (Pss 1; 19; 119) strongly testifying to the fact that Torah itself on the whole has been understood, at least in post-exilic contexts, as a proclamation of divine knowledge, or orientation for the congregation. Especially Ps 119, the largest of all psalmic texts, is replete with referring to the teaching process which Yahweh himself is conducting presumably by way of Torah services (cf. Deut 29–32). The burning question for us is: How do the Torah psalms, extolling the guidance of Yahweh through his Word, relate to the process of divine instruction? I do not believe that these texts were considered exact equivalents of the words of Torah, like some historical psalms have been. But they may have served as corollary texts to Torah readings, in that they portrayed the positive consequences of allegiance to Torah. Poems like Ps 119 are catechetical in character. They focus on those faithful who really live within the divinely illuminated space. As descriptive and acclaiming pieces of liturgy they may have well be used in the immediacy of Torah proclamation. Initial beatitudes of Ps 119:1–2 lend some strength to this argument.

If we acknowledge some sapiential psalms with didactic and liturgical qualities, then we may as well continue our search in the Psalter and find—surprisingly—also a few homiletical texts.[84] Prime examples are Pss 50; 75; 81; 95. A divine voice—represented by some unidentified preacher or liturgist in a congregational assembly—addresses the "people" of "Israel," the partners in covenant, the descendants of Jacob, the people which came out of Egypt and wandered through the wilderness—to ensure their loyalty over against Yahweh. This type of sermonizing definitely is exhortative in character, it does have didactic over- and undertones. Do homiletical psalms have anything to do with worship services of the time? Forms of speech as well as contents are all in favor of a quite tight relationship between the two. To some extent we may say that the direct, personal exhortations in the psalms in effect are proclamation of the will of God (cf. Pss 50:7, 15–18; 75:3–6 [2–5]; 81:7–17 [6–16]; 95:7–11). Torah in the beginning has been a more complex phenomenon than the final written form, the five scrolls connected with Moses, would suggest. It has been a vivid mixture of exhortative and homiletical genres, all destined to instruct the cultic community of the Second Temple.

And there are more topics clad into didactic forms which were possibly used in religious instruction: transience of life (Pss 39; 49; 90; 139) is one and another social justice or theodicy (Pss 9/10; 34; 37; 73; 94). In short, numerous psalms carry heavy loads of teaching very much tuned to the emerging Jewish communities in the post-exilic age. Torah was the center of the congregation's life and worship; Torah in itself was highly didactic in character; psalms of instruction supported and partially substituted Torah

---

84. Cf. Gerstenberger, "Höre, mein Volk, lass mich reden!"

in a variety of religious ceremonies. When and where regular Torah-worship was augmented by (or bifurcated into?) liturgy and study sessions ("houses of learning") we do not know. Didactic psalms have the potential to serve in both institutions.

Two more remarks: The available evidence of the Old Testament in my opinion is not sufficient to warrant the conclusion some canon-conscious colleagues are drawing: that the Psalter was used already that early (fifth through third centuries BCE) as a coherent written document for personal meditation and edification, as much later attested for Christian monastic orders. Second: Form-critical analyses leading to a stratification of life settings do carry also theological implications. Psalms originating from and being used in different strata of society will also develop concepts of God and human beings linked to and conditioned by their own environment.[85]

Psalm 22: Complaint and Thanksgiving

Structure (Preliminary View)

Reading carefully into this psalm so well known to Christians for its role in the passion story of Christ (Mark 15:34; Matt 27:46) we notice unusual breaks in style, addressees and emotional quality. The most severe rupture occurs in v. 22 [21]:[86] From dire complaints and desperate supplication characteristic for individual complaints the poem abruptly turns to thanksgiving, the exact Hebrew wording notwithstanding.[87] The MT may suggest a divine oracle answering positively to the pleas of the patient.[88] We do have two basic genres in one psalm: a first part is clearly complaint and supplication, the latter thanksgiving and praise. How can they be united under one heading? Would they have been recited in one and the same ceremony? Are we, by chance, dealing with two separate prayers accidentally copied together into one entity?—Looking at the two sections by themselves we see a certain oscillation of moods and expressions alternating between hope and despair in the front part, and addressing ever widening circles of listeners in the hind part. What can we make of such an irregular piece of poetry? A form-critical analysis of speech elements is necessary with constant lookout

---

85. Cf. Gerstenberger, *Theologies*.
86. Verses according to MT with following NRSV verse numbering in brackets [].
87. MT reads the last word of v. 22 [21] as "you have answered me," while LXX has "my poor soul" the Hebrew letters being very similar.
88. Miller extensively deals with the "divine response" to prayer: *They Cried to the Lord*, 135–77.

for the possible rootage of the genre in life and liturgy. Literary critical operations to distinguish stages of possible growth[89] are interesting but not too important: At the final stage this psalm still has been used in cultic ritual. Textual modifications may mark the transition of the prayer into communal liturgy.

Speech Forms

Individual complaints in the Psalter usually start with a proper "invocation" calling on the name of the deity and asking for audience (e.g., Pss 28:1-2; 88:2-3 [1-2]; 102:2-3 [1-2]) as etiquette over against God would require. The opening of our psalm (v. 2-3 [1-2]) is brusque and extremely urgent, crying out to the unnamed personal God[90] in a threefold staccato. Unusual is, as well, the initial lack of Yahweh's name which comes up only in v. 9 [8] and in the vocative only 22:20 [19]. This treatment of divine names and appellations may be already indicative of the psalm's origin in the domestic sphere, and its secondary adaptation to the Yahweh community. The vehemence of the invocation at hand has few parallels. Instead of pleading for admission to be heard by the deity the psalmist bellows out an accusatory complaint: "Why have you forsaken me?" This really is, according to ancient standards, an offensive articulation of utter frustration which has become a common literary expression by being quoted (and misinterpreted through the bystanders!) in the gospels. The second colon of v. 2 [1] may be understood as a continued question ("why are you . . .") or a statement ("you are far away . . ."), both readings intensify the accusation against the deity who has failed to help the client. "Physical absence" of God amounts to a main metaphor for abandonment and distress. Nearness, intimacy, on the other hand is the attribute of a personal protective deity who practically lives under the same roof.[91] The very first form element of Ps 22—a peculiar invocation or first plea to open up the individual complaint—draws us into the ambit of family religion, starting out with a desperate cry for help. Implied are disappointment, pain, reproaches—emotions run high. Still, we have to consider the genre of the prayer: It is not a unique momentary outburst of one determined person. All former efforts to understand psalms biographically, be it in regard to David (see superscription) or just an anonymous poet, have

89. Cf. Hossfeld and Zenger, *Die Psalmen 1–50*, 144–46.

90. Implications of this familial trait are generally ignored; cf. Gerstenberger, *Psalms, Part 1*, 109.

91. Cf. the relevant articles in the *ThWANT TDOT*. The concept of protective familial deity is elaborated in Gerstenberger, *Theologies*, 25–91.

been proven wrong by form-critical analysis. Psalms are standard prayers and songs to be used by many supplicants, and by subsequent generations of worshippers.

The following unit, clearly set apart from the opening element, is an "affirmation of confidence" quite essential for individual complaints. The sufferer, no matter how much he or she feels alienated from his God, preserves a string of trust with his or her protector. That much was already apparent in the opening cry "my God!" Now this *Urvertrauen* (basic confidence) is spelled out (vv. 4-6 [3-5]) directly aiming at God in pronounced second person singular pronoun. But what is the horizon of this trust statement? It does encompass all Israel (v. 4 [3]) the hymns of which constitute a sort of throne for the deity (no Yahweh-name!). The ancestors of v. 5-6 [4-5] are the founding fathers of Israel; we get the impression that the whole biblical history is looming behind. And the preceding reference to "praises" (*tehillot*)[92] of Israel may refer to the psalmic tradition. In any case, the horizon of this first affirmation of confidence, much in contrast to the second one (vv. 10-11 [9-10]) is definitely communal if not national in scope. Old domestic theology did not consider "Israel's" faith as its foundation. Are vv. 4-6 [3-5], then, another indication for the prayer's adaptation to congregational life?

To juxtapose to it the second affirmation of trust (vv. 10-11 [9-10]): Direct address of God, again beginning with emphatic personal pronoun "you," stresses all-inclusive reliance of supplicants since their mother's gestation on the protective deity—a very familial concept of God, who even is visualized as acting midwife (v. 10 [9]). The two theological conceptualizations are distinctly rooted in different social strata. But community life of the Yahweh fellowship in the post-exilic period brings them together. Familial and congregational (sometimes also obsolete national) traditions become interwoven in this period.[93] The term "trust," "confidence" (Heb. *bṭḥ*) is prominent in both elements, it probably has different connotations in each place, though.

Just as there are two affirmations of confidence the psalm offers two extensive complaint sections as well, but without any indication of social particularities. Both elements, vv. 7-9 [6-8] and vv. 12-19 [11-18] in rich poetic language describe the ill-fated patient as he/she is ailing and being mobbed by enemies. Everything said is conceived from the personal experiences of countless derelict persons seeking the help of the professional healer. This latter functionary, like any medicine man in tribal societies

---

92. LXX and some Heb. MS have the singular. The book of Psalms is distinctively denominated by the masculine plural *tehillim*.

93. Cf. Gerstenberger, *Theologies*, 207-72.

today, always has been an expert in human psyche, medical diagnosis, social disruptions and tensions. In short, healers over the millennia have been capable to administer a wholesome or integral kind of treatment including magical action (2 Kgs 4:32-35), medical attendance (Isa 38:21) and preformulated prayer[94] as extant in the complaint psalms for the individual. The description of own suffering, to be recited by the supplicant, next to the introductory parts was highly important for healing and rehabilitation. Looking around for alike forms in the Psalter we find a great number of astute, dramatic, and brutal pictures of patients struggling for life, cf. only Pss 35; 38; 55; 59; 69; 88; 102; 109; etc.[95] They all want to encourage the patient to realistically see his or her own situation ("I am a worm, and not human ..." (v. 7 [6]), "my heart is like wax ..." (v. 15 [16]), "I can count all my bones ..." (v. 18 [17]), and muster resoluteness to denounce the evildoers co-responsible for all the calamities (vv. 8 [7]: the mockers are even quoted verbatim, vv. 9 [8]; 13-14 [12-13]: "wild bulls"; 17 [16]: "dogs"). Thus, the complaint sections of the psalm are at the same time analyzing the situation: Not God (as suggested in the opening) but enemies did cause the sufferings, with a timid hint at God's collaboration in v. 16 [15]. They have to be identified, resisted, and defeated, which would eradicate the source of disease and persecution, bringing recovery to the miserable. Other complaint psalms modulate the degrees of responsibility. The supplicant may be partly or fully guilty of God's wrath, in that case he or she has to confess and atone for guilt (cf. Ps 51). Hostile persons or demons or both may be involved in the unbearable situation (cf. Ps 59), but also neighbors and friends sometimes are culpable (cf. Ps 55; 35; 41). In extreme cases, God is the one and only instigator of evil (cf. Ps 88) and we are reminded of Job (cf. Ps 73).

Petition puts all the underlying desires to the point (vv. 20-22 [19-21]). There need not be too many words urging God to intervene, because all the other elements by themselves are insinuating strongly that the deity alone is able to turn the tide.[96] Only now Yahweh is addressed directly by name and again by emphatic "you" (v. 20 [19]), a fact which does not change a bit the basic familial outlook of the supplicants nor the expected functions of the

---

94. This went together with small sacrificial gifts, purifications and exorcisms, according to the Babylonian incantations, see above pp. 56-60.

95. Gunkel's and Begrich's report on this form element is quite vivid, cf. their *Introduction to Psalms*, chap. 6. Also, Mowinckel's account of the situations is recommendable: *The Psalms in Israel's Worship*, vol. 2, chap. 8. Cf. also Gerstenberger, *Der bittende Mensch*, 98-101, 139-43.

96. Complaint psalms therefore may be named for their inner thrust: Prayers (songs) of petition or supplication, cf. Gerstenberger, *Der bittende Mensch*, 105-12.

protective deity.[97] Our present final petition explicitly wants God to return close to his or her adorer, and save him or her from sword, dogs, lions, bulls. Thus the last lines partially connect with former complaints. The imperative petitions straight forwardly ask for "rescue." Parallelism of vv. 21 and 22 [20-21] speaks for the LXX variant at the end of v. 22 [21]: "Save . . . my poor one." But MT has "you have answered me" instead, which should be heeded.

Turning to the thanksgiving hymn (vv. 24-32 [23-31]) we discover that it is not homogeneous either in terms of world views, concepts of God and humans, and literary style. Verses 23-27 [22-26] reflects the scenery of a thanksgiving party held by somebody saved from death (cf. Pss 30; 32; 116; 118), while vv. 28-32 [27-31] have a futuristic, globalizing vision, the addressees being "all the ends of the earth" (v. 28 [27]). Form critics nominate it "eschatological hymn of praise" like, e.g., Isa 12; 25:1-5; 26:1-6.[98] Again, the two "layers" of tradition come together, as it seems, within the congregational practice of worship in post-exilic times. This becomes obvious already in the first, down to earth section: The feast of salvation is heartily envisioned with good food and drink (v. 27 [26]), the invited guests are "brothers" in a merry "assembly" (v. 23 [22]).[99] But this group of participants is immediately specified along denominational, not familial, lines as descendant from Jacob and "house of Israel" (v. 24 [23]). And the name and confession of Yahweh now is pivotal in the thanksgiving announcement (vv. 24, 27 [23, 26]; cf. 28, 29 [27, 28]). This means to say: There is a good chance that the whole two-part thanksgiving hymn has been added at the congregational level to an original, "familial" complaint song. But to what end does an augmentation like this occur? On the other hand, some features are indicative of a liturgical unity of complaint and thanksgiving.

The Functioning of Psalm 22

The sequence of form elements in the complaint part of our psalm corresponds to the general pattern of the genre as outlined above. Complaints of the individual, whether in family or congregational realms, have been part and parcel of ancient healing or rehabilitation rituals. Some peculiarities have to be noted, however. The vehement opening of the prayer, its disregard

97. In ancient Near Eastern religious literature and iconography the (lower) protective deity often intercedes for the supplicant with the highest gods.

98. Joachim Begrich deals with them in chap. 9 titled "Prophetic Elements in the Psalms" in Gunkel and Begrich, *Introduction to Psalms*. The nature and scope of prophecy in Israel and the ancient Near East has to be re-evaluated, however, seventy-five years later.

99. Cf. the details of thanksgiving described above, pp. 56-61.

for cautious invocation of the deity, we assume, is indicative of grave cases of abandonment and desolation. Repetition of complaints proper as well as of affirmations of confidence, extensive and drastic descriptions of pains and attacks are liturgical redundancy which is to intensify the effect of the ritual.[100] At the end of the first part we find strong entreaties (vv. 20–22 [19–21]), but no customary vow, blessing, or exhortation. Instead, the major part of MT tradition abruptly comes to an end with: "You have heard me!" (v. 22 [21]). Is this statement hinting at a divine oracular (or liturgical) response? This problem has been discussed over decades.[101] We may cautiously reckon with the possibility that, indeed, there may have been voiced some assurances of being heard to the supplicant. Traces of this liturgical element can be found in Psalms and Second Isaiah.[102] Strangely enough, the Babylonian incantations in their elaborate ritual prescriptions do not mention words of absolution. They occur only in ancient Near Eastern prophetic texts.[103] Does the elaborated hymn of thanksgiving (Ps 22:23–32 [22–31]) take the place of compact vow or blessing? In any case, the juncture of a full-size complaint prayer with a (nearly) complete song of praise for being saved poses a serious problem.

Most commentators of Psalm 22 declare it to be a rather artificial and heterogeneous piece of literature put together by some canonical scribe for private lecture purposes.[104] I should like to consider some arguments in favor of a liturgical use of such composite texts, in analogy to those complaint psalms, already mentioned, which end in a vow of thanksgiving or a blessing to the participants of the service of supplication. We may call the use of a thanksgiving song as a liturgical close of entreaty for help an "anticipated praise." In terms of cultic procedure it is conditioned on the precondition of a realized salvation, thus putting more pressure on the deity to heed to the cries of the distressed person. In fact, in Isa 38 and Jonah 2 we find narrative contexts relating grave situations, threatening death, for the supplicants (Hezekiah and the prophet Jonah, respectively), with

---

100. Cf. repetitious elements in Pss 31; 35; 55; 59; 69; etc. in Gerstenberger, *Psalms, Part 1* and *Part 2*.

101. Since Joachim Begrich started the debate in 1934, many studies followed without coming to completely satisfying conclusions (e.g., Kirst, "Formkritische Untersuchung zum Zuspruch 'Fürchte dich nicht' im Alten Testament"; Schoors, *I am God your Saviour*.

102. Ps 35:3 is a request for divine assurance: "Say to me: I am your salvation!" Ps 91 contains two helpful or saving oracles, cf. v. 14: "Those who love me, I will deliver!" Cf. the fear-not-words in Isaiah (n101).

103. Cf. Miller, *They Cried to the Lord*, 147–53.

104. Cf., e.g., Hossfeld and Zenger, *Die Psalmen 1–50*, 144–51.

inserted hymns of thanksgiving. We would expect a clean cut complaint at this point, but the thanksgiving hymns seem to fulfil exactly the function of a strong entreaty.[105] Some more observations may strengthen the argument. Our particular song of thanksgiving is being introduced by: "I will tell your name to my brothers" (v. 23 [22]), the future aspect (imperfect/cohortative) corresponds to announcements of vows in regular complaint psalms (cf. Pss 7:18 [17]; 18:50 [49]; 43:4; 56:13-14 [12-13]; 59:18 [17]; 109:30-31; etc.). There are even small scale hymns firmly linked to complaints (e.g., Ps 31:20-25 [19-24]). And, significantly, the concrete "account of trouble and salvation," indispensable element of true thanksgivings offered after the salvation had occurred, is missing in Ps 22. There is only a reference to the pleas which will be certainly heard (v. 25 [24]). Otherwise, both parts of thanksgiving indulge in the description of jubilance of the congregation near and far, from the descendants of Jacob to the most remote adorers of Yahweh, which may have been quite an appropriate ending of a communal complaint service on behalf of individual sufferers.

Form-Critical Hermeneutics

To appreciate a given psalm, or, for that matter, any biblical passage, in its intimate context of ancient recitation and to make its original meaning dependent on the environment requires a special reflection on how to relate the text to our present day situation.[106] Inevitably, whoever rates ancient social conditionings so high in the process of biblical interpretation has to consider also the implications of modern societal and cultural influences on our exegetical efforts. While history at large, science, technology in particular are separating us from our biblical forbears, a linkage to certain levels of human existence may be much easier to achieve. Thus small group activities and concerns, in spite of dramatic changes over the centuries, possibly offer some common ground for ancient and modern experiences of God and the world.

The psalms of individual complaint were located with the smallest human social group, but noticeably moved into the congregational sphere during Old Testament times. How do they relate to piety, well-being, healthcare in our era? We know how much the parameters of individual and family

---

105. During my stay in Brazil (1975-1981) I always was impressed by a special category of private newspaper ads: pious people, on account of their previous vows, published the fact that they had been saved miraculously from evil and death by praying to certain saints or divine powers. They quoted the prayer itself, which was instrumental for divine intervention, and usually it was a short thanksgiving prayer, now recommended to readers for use in critical situations.

106. Cf. Gerstenberger and Schoenborn, eds., *Hermeneutik—sozialgeschichtlich*.

life have changed. Much of inner-circle activities have been "out-sourced," like work, education, medicine. The world views throughout society at large have changed deeply. We are living with a whole new, scientific set of logical interpretations of being, from microbes to outerspace. Still, significant parts of our existence resemble the ancient paradigms: self-consciousness, fears to live and to die, dependency on others (in spite of all autonomy achieved), solidarity and love, hate and animosities, pursuit of luck and power, etc. interconnect humans through the ages. Small wonder, then, that to a large extent we understand perfectly well what was going on in complaint ceremonies of old, in healing rituals or thanksgiving songs. Discrepancies between conceptualizations and realizations of Old Testament rites and our own schemes need to be recognized and clarified, the most serious problem being the treatment of the sources of evil, that is, enemies and demons in the psalms.[107]

The process of using the old complaint prayers, through a living dialogue with the ancient witnesses, in present-day life situations proves to be absolutely inspiring and enriching, as I can testify from my years as a parish minister and later on. The meaning of suffering, the roles of family and friends, significance of self and other, guilt and forgiveness, life and death become perspicuous. But also the nature of God is at stake. Dealing with the psalms we certainly have to move away from theological clichés. Formulas no longer help, all traditional definitions of God fall short of his/her reality to which the psalmists expose us. Old Testament complaints wrestle with God, in an almost suicidal way, at least running the risk of losing out.[108] The God of the small family group is by no means comparable to other theological concepts.[109] He/she is very close to the believers, not omnipotent and totally just but prone to error and wrath, just like an (oversize) human being. Starting by a conflictive encounter with Old Testament complaint psalms, considering present-day realities and experiences with the divine we may become enabled not only to come to grips with many a variety of human problems but also to compose new psalms of supplication and thanksgivings, as living congregations quite often have done.

---

107. Cf. Mowinckel, *Psalmenstudien*, vol. 1 (ET *Psalms Studies*, vol. 1, 1–174); Gerstenberger, "Enemies and Evildoers in the Psalms."

108. Cf., e.g., Pss 73; 88; Gen 32:23–33; the book of Job; Brueggemann, *Psalms and the Life of Faith*.

109. Gerstenberger, *Theologies*.

5

New Form Criticism

Psalm 55

ACTUAL OLD TESTAMENT EXEGESIS in all its variability of methods and theories betrays a tendency to reduce its ambit to a solipsistic discourse between reader and biblical texts. Small wonder in a world that is losing track of historical traditions and social relevance, placing the unrestricted and sometimes virtual "I" at the very top of human values! New form criticism could be a way to counteract such development.[1] This does not mean to return to the old glorification of texts as carriers of unchangeable, "objective," and everlasting truths. We have to acknowledge the productivity of reading brains that take part or even are mainly responsible for the creation of meaning. On the other hand, those eager subjects who look into the genesis and use of texts for their parts are products of historical and social conditions which cannot be separated from their views and evaluations. After all, every human grows out and acts within determined contexts that shape his or her opinions.

Hermann Gunkel defined his form-critical approach to biblical and other pre-literary texts as an investigation of modes or patterns of speech as they grow out of recurring (in anthropological terms: ritualized) human interaction. A third aspect for him were the "moods" (*Stimmungen*) of the participants in discourse. Thus he managed to link speech forms with social behavior maintaining a firm link between performed language and social reality. What could be guidelines of new form-critical research today after so many changes occurred on every level of thinking?[2]

---

1. Cf. Sweeney and Ben Zvi, eds., *The Changing Face of Form Criticism*; Buss, *The Changing Shape of Form-Criticism*; Boda et al., eds., *The Book of the Twelve*.
2. Cf. Eisen and Gerstenberger, eds., *Hermann Gunkel Revisited*.

"New Form Criticism" tries to adapt itself to new insights into the genesis and use of texts as well as the moods reflected by them.[3] Among other points being emphasized: "Form-critical scholars will come to terms with the perspectives of reader-response criticism, which demonstrates the fundamental role of the reader and the reader's or the readers' own socio-historical or literary contexts in the construction of the text that is read and reread."[4] The crucial points seem to be: Texts should not be considered autonomous, contingent entities. They grow out of and are tied into (ancient and modern!) social networks. Their nature thus can be described as truly "relational."[5] No individual methodological perspective may be denominated "form-critical."

Oral and Written Words

Ancient traditions have been preserved only by written sources and a whole range of archeological artifacts and leftovers. Since systems of writing were invented late in human cultural history we can easily conclude: There must have been long periods of oral transmission of texts before and probably also aside from literary fixations. Furthermore, ancient habits of writing and use of written materials do not necessarily correspond to modern literary ways of communication and performance. Studies in scope and purpose of ancient writing reveal close relationships with oral interchange. Written texts often support personal direct transmittance, being read to those who are illiterate. They show a serious lack of literacy in the population, an almost divine estimation of the art of writing, etc. With these conditions in mind it becomes clear that concepts and positions of authors in early antiquity diverge from ours. A general reading culture started to develop at the earliest in Hellenistic times and did not flourish in Europe until the late Enlightenment with the installation of public schools. The nature of communication has considerably changed by conserving statements over time and space. The culture of "Holy Books" later on became a theological fetish in some religious sectors.

Words and *Sitz im Leben*

Dealing with ancient texts, we have to rearrange our literary concepts of author, performer, user, generative forces in text-production, communicative

---

3. Cf. Sweeney and Ben Zvi, eds., *The Changing Face of Form Criticism*, 9–11.
4. Sweeney and Ben Zvi, eds., *The Changing Face of Form Criticism*, 10.
5. Buss, *The Concept of Form*, 73–112; Buss, *The Changing Shape of Form Criticism*.

action, etc. Most human utterances beyond emotive and involuntary sounds (like snoring, spontaneous laughter, etc.) imply a conscious will to communicate with others. So, from the very outset, words encompass social relations, while also referring back to determined circumstances (reality-context). Writing down texts may create the wrong impression as if the "materialized" discourse could emancipate itself from temporal and local bonds. Referential ties may shift, but they will not disappear, more precisely: As soon as a written text is being used again, let's say, if it is taken out of an archive or rediscovered by archaeologists, contextual conditions of some sorts immediately jump into action again. There is no "loss of life-setting," or "setting in the book." Words and texts are connected to senders and recipients, they belong to (changing) real or imagined cultural, historical, and religious situations; they need to fulfill their social mission of mediation, communication, denunciation, orientation, etc.[6]

Already on occasion of their first use words are products of human brains and tongues be they descriptive, demanding, denouncing or anything else. Written down, acoustic articulations become visually available for generations to come. Use and reuse of fixed words create new meanings coming, presumably, out of changed situations or interpretative angles. The creative reader, indeed, has a decisive part in this development. Nevertheless, a given, reported text interrelates with a socially conditioned responder (and vice versa). In this fashion, significance develops within an analogous, interactive spectrum of participants and dialogical patterns. Such development includes not only persons but also life conditions.

Psalms and Their Genres

The collection of Old Testament psalms (and equally, a host of similar ancient Near Eastern accumulations of religious poetry) may serve as a prime example of how the understanding of texts and text-users (composers) oscillates with changing basic parameters. Gunkel's masterful idea was this: With the absence of confirmed authors a piece of literature has to be valued by its linkage with "recurring situations of communication" which, in fact, are made co-responsible by him to have created the very psalms. This *Sitz im Leben* was taken to be the anchor of the text in social and religious reality. Modern psalm-exegesis to a large extent has shifted its approach-es (under the leadership of Brevard S. Childs, Gerald H. Wilson, Erich Zenger, Matthias Millard, and others) towards a secondary, that is, written state of

---

6. Cf. Gerstenberger, "Social Sciences and Form-Criticism"; Gerstenberger, "Vom Sitz im Leben zur Sozialgeschichte der Bibel"; Breed, *Nomadic Text*.

affairs: They postulate a predominant author–reader relationship in this poetry under canonical (dogmatic) perspective. Emphasis is on the final and canonized state of transmission: The book of Psalms is considered a wholesale literary product, and a certain hierarchical and doctrinal manifestation, notwithstanding former stages of oral, liturgical origin and use of individual psalms and smaller collections.[7] Granted, they formally stick to the concept of text–reader collaboration. But the tight relationship to various social communicative situations and the equivalence of both sides are dissolved. The canon gains supremacy and individual poetic units in their (theological) diversity are all but levelled out. Specific seasonal or other festivities (hymns), casual rites of supplication or fulfillment of promise (complaints; thanksgiving), self-reflective meditations on life and death, justice and culpability, sin and atonement (sapiential poems) all indicative of deep roots in a broad spectrum of real life situations are being set aside.[8]

In terms of an ancient Israelite history of literature "canonical" approaches seem to be grave misjudgments. "Reading" the psalms instead of using them in a variety of liturgical services very probably turned a custom only in later Christian monastic orders like that of St. Benedict of Nursia (fifth century AD). The Psalter's primary and abiding (to this day!) character as a collection of poems mostly for varied ritual use with the accompaniment of instruments and under the direction of liturgical specialists (masters of ceremony) is being disregarded and replaced by doctrinal considerations. Any kind of form-critical analysis of any given psalm would clearly lead to a classification in cultic terms.[9] Even "wisdom psalms" may have come out of meditative assemblies of early Jewish congregations. Along this line of argumentation, literary and doctrinal criticism could support the findings of form analysis. And there is ample evidence in Babylonian and other ancient Near Eastern cultures as well as in existing tribal societies of ritual or ceremonial use of prayers and hymns.[10]

Psalm 55 as an Example: Structural and Social-Critical Analysis

Psalm 55 is just one among some thirty specimens of "individual songs of complaint" ("persönliche Klage- und Bittgebete") of the Psalter. The genre

7. Cf. Hossfeldt and Zenger, *Psalms 51–100*, 26–35.
8. Cf. Gerstenberger, *Psalms, Part 1* and *Part 2*.
9. Meaning both temple and casual services; cf. Gerstenberger, "Non-Temple Psalms," 346–47.
10. Cf. Maul, *Zukunftsbewältigung*, 37–113; Gerstenberger, *Der bittende Mensch*, 6–11.

has its counterpart in Babylonian incantations: There they appear as "prayers of the patient" in the context of ritual ablutions, exorcisms, confessions, etc.[11] Such prayers certainly were sacred texts in the possession of shamanistic healers who made their patients recite them line by line at due points within extensive rituals.[12] There is a common basic pattern of individual complaints, a certain sequence of discourse-elements in approaching the deity, viz. "invocation; complaint; confession; supplication; affirmation of confidence; imprecation against enemies; vow; anticipated thanksgiving," etc. But every single psalm of this category has characteristics of its own, probably reflecting special diagnoses of the patient's condition.[13] A certain common pattern can be verified in cross-cultural comparison, although individual structures and wordings of petitionary prayers are quite distinct. The peculiarities of these texts, however, must not be counted as mere idiosyncrasies. Rather, since ritual petitions have been texts addressing the needs of specially diagnosed patients, they are administered and dosed like modern medicines on the basis of general symptoms and particular necessities.

Here, then, are some peculiarities of Ps 55: The speaking voice (who addresses whom?) sometimes is left in the dark. Is it the patient only who recites the psalm? Or does the ritual expert interfere here and there (cf. vv. 10a, 16, 20–23)? The sequence and frequency of form-elements (complaints: vv. 4–9, 10c–12, 20c–22; imprecation: vv. 10a–b, 16, 24a–d; contestation: vv. 13–15; affirmation of confidence: vv. 17–20b, 24e; exhortation of bystanders[?] or patient[?]: v. 23) do seem irregular. There are three complaints, three imprecations, two affirmations of confidence, and one contestation and exhortation each. Vow to bring sacrifices and (anticipated) thanksgiving are missing.[14] While literary and author-oriented studies envision the repetitious, performance-driven structure as purely poetic traits, form-critical analysis recognizes ceremonial or liturgical inducements. They would, of course, also imply participation of a ritual expert, most likely a priestly or shamanistic figure. Since Old Testament psalms give us little direct evidence of their handling complaint psalms, we have to refer to the mentioned Babylonian counterparts which, by their extensive ritual instructions, clearly

---

11. Cf. Maul, *Zukunftsbewältigung*, 67–71.

12. Cf. similar ceremonies of healing in some tribal societies of our era, e.g., Reichard, *Prayer*, 9–49.

13. Cf. Heeßel, *Babylonisch-assyrische Diagnostik*, 47–74.

14. Cf. structuring of the poem in Gerstenberger, *Psalms, Part 1*, 222–25.

illustrate the healing procedures.¹⁵ This line of analysis comes out of a long study of relevant matters; it is not a *petitio principii*.¹⁶

Among the agents starkly identified are the opponents of the supplicant. They are called by hostile names and attributed with the worst intentions against the speaking I: "enemies" (*'oyeb* אויב; vv. 4, 13), "godless, wicked" (*raša'* רשע; v. 4). Most despicable are the treacherous friends, formerly intimate companions (vv. 13–15, 21–22), who have turned to dangerous opponents. All these harbor deadly evil in their minds (cf. vv. 4b, 11–12, 13, 18, 21–22) and are plainly considered the instigators of all the evil that has befallen the supplicant. In vv. 10b–12 they apparently have demonic features or else they ally themselves with demons who circulate the city causing horror and destruction. Violence against the sufferer can be effected by mobbing and cursing alone (vv. 22; cf. Ps 5:10; 10:7; 50:19; 52:4; 57:5; 64:4; 109:2; 120:2–3; 140:4). Small wonder, that emotions run high against the evil-mongers. The imprecations v. 10a–b, 16, 24a–d are highly dangerous weapons of the ritual expert against the "enemies" (cf. Judg 17:2–3). Because the use of curses in rituals may have been restricted to the ceremonial experts (cf. Ps 109:6–20: a cursing litany of the supplicant or his healer) these "personal condemnations" indeed may have been spoken by the leader of ceremony.

The deity in petition rituals certainly is the most important agent. It is addressed in strong and direct pleas and praising or trustful affirmations (cf. Ps 55:2–3, 10, 16[?], 16–20 [3rd person], 24). Altogether, then, three parties interact in this prayer: The supplicant, speaking urgently in the first person singular to God, begging for his attention and help, describing his or her¹⁷ plight, emphasizing his or her confidence of being heard seems to be the dominant person. The "enemies" come next, especially those, or one of those, who had been former friends, being addressed even in the second person as if he were present ("But it is you, my equal, my companion, my familiar friend (אלופי ומידעי) with whom I kept pleasant company; we walked in the house of God with the throng," vv. 14–15). Last, but not least, there is God to whom all discourses are directed. He "will hear" the supplicant, "will humble" the adversaries (v. 20), "will cast them down into the lowest pit" (v. 24). The exhortation of v. 23 could possibly be an oracle of salvation or comfort from God, recited by the officiant. Stating this assumption we may go back to some former claims. The whole psalm most likely, on the evidence of its structure and characteristics and in the light of Babylonian

---

15. Cf. Maul, *Zukunftsbewältigung*, 37–66.
16. Cf. Gerstenberger, *Der bittende Mensch*, 93–160.
17. Cf. Bail, *Gegen das Schweigen*, 5–7.

counterparts, has originally been the work of a priestly, prophetic (cf. Elijah and Elisha and their healing activities) or other shamanistic curer who in ancient times would lead a full healing ritual in the midst of which the patient had to recite the prayer prepared by the liturgist for particular life-threatening dangers caused by hostile compatriots and possible demons.

For the rest, we may refine observations on Ps 55 and its *Sitz im Leben* (social setting) by pointing to the portrayed city-life (vv. 10b–12) sounding like the phobia of a country-dweller, counteracted by the supplicant's desire to "flee far away" to "lodge in the wilderness" (v. 8) "like a dove" (v. 7). Belief in demons (often animal-like; cf. v. 11; Ps 22:13–14, 17; 59:7–8, 15–16) has been very common in antiquity and far into the Christian era; in fact, the scientific age never eliminated completely the fear of ghostly forces. Ancient demonology is a vast field of research: Its influence on medical and incantational practice certainly is present in biblical and Christian literature and cult.

Psalm 55 lacks formal acknowledgment of customary sacrifice after salvation (cf. Ps 107) especially when vowed beforehand (cf. Pss 7:18; 13:7; 22:21b–27; 50:23; 52:11; 54:8–9; 56:13–14; 59:17–18; 61:9; etc.). Nevertheless, hope for salvation and restoration is quite present in this prayer (cf. vv. 17–20, 24). In all its parts the emotions go very strong, expressed in typical language of despair, anxiety, longing, feeling left alone and trusting in God's attention and readiness to help. Similar emotionality can be found in Babylonian counterparts. The assumption is, that the professional curer owned a collection of complaint and petitionary prayers. He would choose the appropriate text for each given case, and presumably, according to his experience, he also was free to modify it in line with initial diagnosis and further evaluations of each case. Each complaint psalm of the Psalter, in consequence, originated as a professional formulary of petition to be used by the patient at the discretion of the healer.

A recent study of Ps 55 takes the opposite view.[18] On the surface, the authors use text-pragmatic categories according to Christof Hardmeier.[19] But basically, they limit their vision to an autobiographical perspective of one author-poet who describes his or her personal fate. Thus the authors have to interpret the agitation of "enemies" being culminated by a mobbing attack of treacherous friends. They have to admit an audience, which is able to overhear the complaints of the sufferer, but they exclude a formal ritual procedure and the role of a shamanistic leader. The prayer of the patient remains a forlorn, solipsistic act in the face of a personal God. The text, for

---

18. Ruwe, *Du aber bist es*, 147–89.
19. Hardmeier, *Textwelten der Bibel entdecken*, vol. 1, 5–21.

Hardmeier and his pupils, remains a mystically closed unity. It does not open up to the generating social forces represented by the shaman-author and the spiritual community supporting him. Granted, the autonomy of the text can be defended by the notion that it is difficult for us to look "behind" ancient pieces of literature. Yet, we do have sufficient indications in the Psalter and impressive analogies outside its corpus that allow for plausible reconstructions of the prayers' ceremonial backgrounds. Reader-response theories have opened up the horizons to recognize not only individual producers and recipients of poems but also social implications. Ruwe and colleagues without legitimation take Ps 55 as the literary work of an individual sufferer.

My vision, on the contrary, is Ps 55 from of old being embedded in a healing ritual as described above. A shamanistic healer within the molds of the diviners, soothsayers, augurs, sorcerers, spell-casters, ghost-consultors, necromancers of Deut 18:10–11 would practice healing ceremonies on demand in pre-exilic times. Then, with the formation of the obedient Torah-community after the exile, in the Persian period, the whole gamut of shamanistic activities became outlawed. Who knows, however, how much of these vital curative functions and functionaries survived even at the time and level of the canonized text and orthodox synagogal life. First Samuel 28 may well tell of a post-exilic experience instead of being a story of King Saul. Sure, there very probably have occurred modifications of the genuine shamanistic complaint ritual. From the original shamanistic performance the complaint psalm came into the early Jewish community life with its Yahwistic and Torah-oriented liturgies, eliminating all polytheistic, demonic allusions.[20] Magical, incantational references were possibly purged from the rituals (but there remain a good number of allusions to demons and bad powers in the Psalter, as related above!). Yahweh-directed words took the place of incantations, or shamanistic magic was used under the new rubric of "prayer" (the compulsive word!) to Yahweh. Other examples of similar transitions in life-settings seem to prove, that much of earlier ritual traditions live on in the changed community framework. Thus ritual prayer and some pre-Yahwistic symbolic action were transplanted into congregational life (cf. Isa 38; Ps 12; 91; 102; 109). Even our own casual praxis still bears some witness to ancient predecessors in tribal traditions (e.g., exorcisms in Christian worship). Puristic reforms (cf. 2 Kgs 22–23, or Christian, Muslim, Hindu iconoclasms, for that matter) never achieve their goals thoroughly.

---

20. Cf. Deut 18:9–12; Gerstenberger, *Israel in the Persian Period*, 99–101, 353–60.

Ritual Performance and Socio-generic Forces in Literature

Whoever has witnessed some healing performances—e.g., in original tribal societies—will be impressed by the richness of liturgical ceremonies and the wealth of underlying thoughts, connotations, expertise, and theology.[21] It is important to state that healing rituals normally involve groups; require the leadership of specialists who interact with participants; conjure superhuman forces; and proceed through phases of purification, exorcisms, empowerment, rehabilitation, and healing. The communal or individual texts of prayer and dedication in all likelihood are property of the shamanic leader, but they are also products of the community in that they reflect necessities of the group—interactions with living situations.[22] Therefore, text-production as well as ceremonialism are not simply the work of the expert. They depend largely on communal experience and insight. Individual authorship of psalms cannot be measured by modern parameters of literary activity.

Catherine Bell summarizes common features of healing rituals from a global perspective.[23] If diagnosis, often by divination, has determined evil spirits as the cause of illness, the shamanistic expert selects rituals suited for the combat of the disorder, which "heal, exorcise, protect, and purify." "This takes the form of purging the body and mind of all impurities."[24] A first step of the healing procedure normally is determining the particular causes of the patient's ill fate. "Various divinatory techniques and skillful questioning of the client"[25] are in order. Therapy occurs within full family surroundings, including deceased ancestors and helpful spirits.[26] "Purification is a major theme within the rites of affliction,"[27] consisting of "physical and spiritual cleansing"; "fire and water are among the most common ritual agents of purification."[28] Besides their "psychotherapeutic effects," these rituals "hold all [the addressed] powers to some degree of accountability and service . . . they demonstrate that the human realm is not completely subordinate to the realms of spiritual power; these rites open up opportunities for redefining

---

21. Bell, *Ritual*, 115–20; Kluckhohn and Wyman, *Introduction*, 57–74.
22. Cf. Maul, *Zukunftsbewältigung*, 119–56.
23. Cf. Bell, *Ritual*, 115–20: "Rites of Affliction."
24. Bell, *Ritual*, 115.
25. Bell, *Ritual*, 116.
26. Cf. Bell, *Ritual*, 117.
27. Bell, *Ritual*, 118.
28. Bell, *Ritual*, 119.

the cosmological order in response to new challenges and new formulations of human needs."[29]

Anthropological and sociological considerations, in short, are opportune to widen the mere literary form-critical investigation of the text materials. This leads to a three-pronged interrelationship of text, professional expert (liturgist), and patient. The wicked opponents and the merciful deity are watching from the outside of the drama ready to interfere. This scheme, although amplified, is a truly form-critical set-up in the sense and, perhaps, to the liking of Hermann Gunkel and Sigmund Mowinckel. It does transcend the reader-response mechanisms of modern interpreters in that it is not constrained to a reading process but does include human action. Performative texts like the psalms need this extension. They have been composed and transmitted to serve a social, "ecclesiastic" function, until this very day. Private reading of psalms is a wonderful gift to literate and wealthy people, but it is a secondary mandate for performing texts.

Theological Implications; Transferability of Situations

Psalm interpretation today should abstain from narrow literary assumptions. The original use of some genres (mainly *complaints* and *thanksgivings*) was in the area of healing and rehabilitation. Theologically speaking, these psalms combat evil forces in the natural world and in society with the help of personal and higher gods. Enemies of various kinds have to be eliminated. Damage done has to be restored, life conditions to be amended. The patient's praise (and sacrifice) is a summons to and recompense for divine assistance. A similar backdrop can be surmised in today's different procedures in physical and psychic healing. Destructive powers are counteracted by remedies and psychological treatment. The saved person needs to be re-integrated into his/her social setting. Gratitude is considered a natural reaction to salvation and new life options (cf. testimonies of people who survived heart attacks, lethal injuries or infections, cancer, strokes, HIV/AIDS, etc.) The basic structure of diagnosis, healing, rehabilitation remains the same even in our secularized world. God is sometimes still involved in some anthropological or abstract ways as the ultimate healer or benign power. Theology has to recognize transformations of worldviews and thought patterns as well as present (so-called "scientific") models of reasoning and feeling. Some questions to wind up the foregoing deliberations are now in order.

29. Bell, *Ritual*, 97.

Crucial Points of Method and Hermeneutics

New Form Criticism uses refined methodological approaches to transmitted texts. It has discovered the interpreters' involvement in text-production, both in antiquity and present-day situations. Texts are no longer to be considered autonomous. In addition, they never have been final or canonical but always were subject to change, that is, to re-interpretation or re-creation. Exegesis therefore should, as it always has done, aim at speech patterns, literary forms, micro- and macro-text structures. But most of all it must not forget the roots of all communicative and performative discourse in real-life settings:

1. In the process of interpretation, a clarification of one's own standpoints and perspectives is necessary:[30] What is the general frame of our own understanding of ancient texts? Are we unwittingly applying our accustomed patterns of thinking to ancient living conditions? For example, do we exclusively count on reader–text relations so familiar to us in our literary environment?

2. Specifically: Are the psalms reflecting personal, biographical experiences or are they general statements, formulated for the use of individuals in their distress and joy? To what degree may they reflect liturgical performance embedded in more or less extensive rituals under the direction of experts (cf. Christian casual practice)? The vicinity of individual complaints to the congregational cult was already a hot issue of debate [*geistliche Nachdichtung*] between Gunkel and Mowinckel.

3. Liturgical (oral) beginnings of psalm poetry are almost uncontested in present research (references to ritual within the psalms; psalms in narrative contexts; Babylonian and other ritual instructions etc.). To what extent did the process of writing down and transmitting canonical texts change or amplify the original use? Is there some plausibility to the assumption that early Jewish, Torah-oriented communities continued to use, in slightly modified shapes, the shamanistic prayers of pre-exilic times, presumably in a remodeled, theologically "correct" form (cf. Ps 12 or the insertion of vv. 13–23 into Ps 102)?

4. How do we recognize formal modulations and secondary insertions of complaint psalms? Structural analyses of "minimal sequences" (on the basis of logical built-up?) are reasonable. Abrupt alterations of discourse (speaker, addressee, mood): Could they be evidence for ritual performance or literary insertion? Likewise, logical development of

---

30. Brown, *Handbook to Old Testament Exegesis*, 7–25.

thought, narrative, or situational plausibility—are they indications of scribal activity?

5. Do the language of psalm-poetry (rhythm, metaphors, semantics, theology, etc.), the superscriptions and recognizable collections of psalms, the comparable literature of the ancient Near East indicate anything about communal use of these prayers and hymns? One strong argument could be the I- and We-styles, much neglected in form-critical study. The plural form could often be indicative of communal singing or praying (cf. Pss 8:2, 10; 12:8; 28:8–9; 44; 46; 47; 48; 60; 65; 66:1b–12; 67; 68:20–21; 72:18; 74:1–11; 75:2; 79:8–13; 80; 81:2–4; 85:5–8; 90; 95; 99:5, 8–9; 100; 102:15, 29; 103:10–12; 106:6–7, 47; 108:12–14; 115; 117; 118:24–27; 123; 124; 126; 129:8; 132:6; 137; 147:1). The list of communal song or prayer is impressive, especially if one compares the rare examples in ancient Near Eastern cultic poetry. Very likely this fact reflects the "parochial" character of Jewish groups.

6. It is worthwhile to try to reconstruct further the real performance of psalm-liturgies in pre-canonical and canonical times. Who took part in the rituals? What were the roles of leader of ceremony, patients (individual supplicants and adorers of the divinity), community, bystanders, musicians, choirs? Unfortunately, there are some reports on communal festivities and their ceremonies, especially in Chronicles. Casual rites e.g., of diagnoses and healing procedures are rare (cf. 1 Kgs 14:1–16; 2 Kgs 4:8–37; 5; Isa 38 [with quoted prayer!]; Job 33:19–28; Num 5:11–28; etc.), as already pointed out.

7. Do comparisons with functionally related procedures (plea; thanksgivings; praise; meditation plus ritual prescriptions of cleansings, exorcisms, sacrifices, etc.) in tribal and other societies help us to understand psalmic texts? Is it legitimate to draw on such external evidence and postulate similar customs, institutions, personal among ancient Israelites? General considerations and more evidence from tribal cultures which can be observed *in situ* lend overwhelming strength to the argument in favor of comparability and virtual transfer of institutions. The latter would not have been identical, but analogous in their functions. Thus the ancient, most of all the Babylonian, texts on healing, including their spiritual power and theological conceptualizations, may serve as a type of models in Near Eastern healing ceremonialism.

8. The inclusion of life-settings in exegetical and theological scrutiny enables us to take seriously present-day social organization, in its text-and-ritual production from smallest units (family, neighborhoods,

congregations) to largest agglomerations (church-bodies, national/ international, and global networks). Their spiritual and theological needs are certainly different among the groups and in each period. Distinguishing them sociologically and theologically (that is, admitting different religious conceptualizations on each level) brings into the debate a plurality of religious ideas. Is it theologically legitimate to draw these conclusions? Are we leaving the monotheistic consensus of western civilizations when doing so?

New Form Criticism should not evaporate the social and performative dimensions of Old Testament psalms but uphold and strengthen the recognition of their performative use and social anchoring.[31] It also should liberate the sacred texts from their imprisonment in traditional doctrines of self-sufficiency.

---

31. Cf. Buss, *Changing Shape*, 155–214; Gerstenberger, "Social Sciences," 90–99.

6

Jeremiah's Complaints

Observations on Jer 15:10–21

THE BOOK OF JEREMIAH has always been regarded as particularly open for historical and psychological study. There seemed to be sufficient material at hand for the compilation of a biography of the prophet; his inner and outward life has even been made the subject of novels and plays.[1] The apparent abundance of data in Jeremiah has exercised an irresistible temptation on virtually all scholars and commentators regardless of their school of thought or method of approach[2] to focus their attention upon the prophet's curriculum vitae and experience. Jeremiah is looked upon as a religious genius, the champion of personal, inner, and spiritual religion.

The basic fallacy of this viewpoint is the presupposition that the "facts and figures" in Jeremiah are identical with "historical events," or that they, at least, permit easy access to that which "really happened" during Jeremiah's lifetime.[3] The ongoing discussion of what "history" is, and how it is

---

1. The most important scholarly monographs in English were written by T. K. Cheyne, *Jeremiah* (1888); John Skinner, *Prophecy and Religion* (1922); George Adam Smith, *Jeremiah* (1929); T. Crouther Gordon, *The Rebel Prophet* (1932); Adam C. Welch, *Jeremiah* (1955); J. Philip Hyatt, *Jeremiah* (1958); Sheldon H. Blank, *Jeremiah* (1961). Examples of a novel and a play are, respectively, Franz Werfel, *Hearken unto the Voice*; and Stefan Zweig, *Jeremiah* (1922).

2. Quite naturally psychologists of religion (cf. Hölscher, *Die Profeten*) are interested in biographical facts, as are literary critics (cf. Duhm, *Israels Propheten*). That adherents to a form-critical or traditio-historical approach (cf. von Rad, *Theology*, 2:203ff.; Nielsen, *Oral Tradition*, 64ff.) should so strongly focus on "accidental historical facts" seems strange, however; cf. von Rad, *Theology*, 2:204: "Each of these passages (confessions of Jeremiah) tells of a separate experience."

3. The protests of N. Schmidt ("Jeremia") and May ("Towards an Objective Approach") against such direct approach are in themselves very much caught up in historical thinking and have not convinced modern scholars; cf. Bright, "The Date of the

intertwined with, even sustained and created by, later interpretation[4] should make us wary of the great difficulties which lie in the path of any historical reconstruction on the basis of such collections of texts as that of Jeremiah. The fundamental insight of form-critical research, moreover, must not be forgotten: Any given text in the OT more likely than not has been cast into the mold of some conventional form of speech. Consequently it does not primarily reflect unique historical events but social and cultic habits and institutions.[5]

The proper way of interpreting a prophetic book, therefore, is to evaluate each layer of its tradition as a witness in its own right as well as a single voice within a choir. Besides looking for redactors and their theology one should carefully watch the small groupings of textual units and their growth and composition. We are not in a position to begin our work at the fountainhead of tradition, but we have to work upstream, closely noting the tributaries right and left. It may well be that the original fountain of one tradition becomes more remote in the process and shrinks in significance relative to the tributaries. Recognizing the multitude of voices in Jer does not diminish their quality as witnesses of God's actions, even if Jeremiah's biography should lose some of its familiar items.

I.

The passage Jer 15:10–21 in itself shows clear signs of long growth. The importance of its complex structure will become apparent when we cautiously try to understand the successive "editors" and "redactors," or, as they are better called, the "interpreters" and "expositors" of preceding witnesses. Form-critical observations may help us occasionally in restoring corrupted lines.

1. The most obvious secondary accretion in Jer 15:10–21 seems to be vv. 13–14. The sudden change of address from Israel to the prophet leads virtually all commentators to dismiss these verses as a mechanical insertion from Jer 17:3–4.[6] In refusing even to discuss these words as part of chap.

Prose Sermons of Jeremiah."

4. The old and new quests of the historical Jesus best illustrate the situation of modern scholarship; cf. the books of Schweitzer (*The Quest*) and Robinson (*A New Quest*) on that matter.

5. Gunkel, *Die Propheten*, 110 and 139, rightly warns against looking too soon for prophetic personalities behind prophetic forms. Baumgartner, *Die Klagegedichte des Jeremia*, by subtracting a standard form of complaint psalm from "Jeremiah's complaints," too easily arrives at the original prophesies of Jeremiah.

6. Bernhard Duhm, Friedrich Giesebrecht, Carl Heinrich Cornill, Paul Volz, Albert Condamin, Julius A. Brewer, Elmer A. Leslie, J. Philip Hyatt, Wilhelm Rudolph.

15 they show their disregard for the historical growth of the text. There are strong indications that vv. 13-14 were deliberately put into the context of the prophet's complaints.

The LXX translator,[7] it is true, was already "modern" enough to regard vv. 13-14 as a copy of parts of 17:3-4. He rendered the text as a threat against the people, thus announcing God's retaliation for their maltreatment of the prophet (cf. LXX in vv. 10-14). Most modern translations follow this version (cf. RSV). He, then, apparently omitted 17:1-4 altogether. Some Hebrew MSS follow the same line by reading in 15:14: "I will let you serve your enemies in a land unknown to you,"[8] a familiar prophecy of the exile (cf. Jer 5:19; Deut 28:36; also Jer 16:13; 22:28; 25:11; Deut 28:48, 64). This threat would show God's wrath against Israel in contrast to the favorable answer he bestows on his prophet (MT in v. 11; cf. KJV).

If this tradition of Jer 15:13-14 has a meaningful place within its present context, the unusual rendering of the first line in v. 14 presented by the bulk of Hebrew MSS deserves even closer attention. Instead of the root ʿbd hiph. ("to let serve") we find ʿbr hiph. ("to let pass"),[9] a form, which, furthermore, lacks the direct object "you." The MT thus exactly reverses the meaning: "I will let your enemies pass through (into)[10] a land unknown to you," proclaiming the banishment of the foe, and salvation for oppressed Israel. A peculiarity in vv. 13-14 supports this interpretation. Assuming our verses are in some way derived from a longer oracle such as Jer 17:1-4, it must strike us as significant that 17:1-2[11] and 17:4aα, namely, the indictment of Israel and the plain announcement that the people will "let go their

---

Commentaries from now on will be quoted only by author's name and page.

7. Verses 13-14 were in the present position already at that time. The LXX connects v. 12 with the beginning of v. 13, reading a Hebrew text *umaṣpon nḥšt hylk* (so W. Rudolph in *BH*) or *weṣpuy nḥšt hylk* (Duhm, 134); cf. the root *ṣph* (to overlay, plate), with LXX *peribolaion* (v. 12).

8. Biblical translations are my own unless otherwise stated.

9. LXX misread *daleth* for *resh*, as in v. 12: *ydʿ for yrʿ* (*rʿ*).

10. The preposition *b-* usually designates the area in which things happen (Gesenius, *Gesenius' Hebrew Grammar*, §119h); yet a sense of direction is quite often implied (§119k, l; Brockelmann, *Hebräische Syntax*, 96). ʿbr with a following *a* occurs, for instance, in Deut 2:30; 2 Sam 12:31; Ezek 14:15; 47:3-4; Ps 136:14; 2 Chr 30:5; 36:22; and in the technical phrase "to let go through the fire" (*bʾš*): Num 31:23; Deut 18:10; 2 Kgs 16:3; 17:17. The older translation of Jer 15:14a: "I will let you pass through with your enemies ..." (cf. W. Lowth [1719], 141; Freedman, 109; KJV) presupposes the suffix "you."

11. Rudolph, 96, suggests that 15:12 has, in a mutilated form, preserved 17:1-2 (cf. the word "iron" in both passages). This is possible, but unlikely, because of the exact correspondence of words wherever both texts coincide.

heritage," are left out in Jer 15. It seems, therefore, that 15:13–14 has been carefully remodeled into an oracle of promise which once may have read:

> Your wealth and treasures I give as spoil,
> as a price for all your sins throughout your land.
> The I will drive away your enemies into a land unknown to you,
> for a fire is kindled in my anger, which will burn forever.[12]

Israel's suffering under foreign intrusion is seen as atonement for her sins. Longing thoughts move beyond the plundering of the invaders: When, finally, will her overlords be defeated? When will Yahweh intervene for his people? This is the burden of our oracle. Its position between individual complaints betrays its late placement; so does its outlook on history. Suffering, redemption, liberation all appear in a well-proportioned, theological, and juridical balance. All indications would support the view that vv. 13–14 were formulated in the wake of Israel's total defeat in 587 BCE.[13]

What did the editor have in mind when he refashioned the text in this unexpected way? Several motives may have worked together. He wanted to reinterpret the term "enemy" in v. 11. Yes, Jeremiah's enemies deserved Yahweh's wrath! But now, in the editor's time, Israel's enemies are next in line for punishment. Israel's humiliation has lasted long enough. There is a point when even Yahweh's rightful punishment becomes intolerable. The faithful yearn for relief (cf. Hab 3:16 and the communal complaint-psalms) as the prophet does in vv. 10, 15–18. In the midst of such stress the editor wants God's reassuring and forgiving word to be heard, not only for the prophet of old (v. 11, MT) but for his whole people. He wants to counterbalance the harsh rejections (14:10; 15:1–4) of Israel's pleas and confessions of guilt (14:7–9, 19–22) with this word of hope. Yahweh confirmed the prophet against his enemies. Then and there, already, the restoration of Israel began. Now the time is ripe, after all the terrible judgments of history, for Israel's rehabilitation. The tension between the pronouncements of doom

---

12. Once the MT reading of v. 14a has been accepted, several adjustments have to be made in the text of vv. 13–14: (a) Instead of *lo' bmḥyr* the affirmative has to be read: Yahweh counts the spoil which he handed over to the enemies (cf. 2 Kgs 21:14; Isa 10:6; Ezek 7:21; 29:19) as a payment for Israel's sin; cf. Ps 44:13 and the presupposed transaction between God and the enemies in the stereotyped expression "Yahweh sold (Israel)," Judg 2:14; 3:8; 4:2; 10:7; 1 Sam 12:9; Isa 50:1; Ezek 30:12; Joel 4:8. Cf. especially Isa 42:22—43:4. This understanding requires (b) the omission of both conjunctions in v. 13b and (c) the reading *'ad 'olam* instead of *'lykm* in v. 14b (cf. 17:4; Duhm, 143–44; Rudolph, 96; Volz, 185).

13. In Pss 44; 74; 79; and 80 Israel tries to come to grips with the shock of foreign conquest. Our oracle could be understood as an answer to such a communal prayer (cf. Isa 43:3). If this holds true, the editor may have inserted vv. 13–14 as an analogy and continuation to the divine answer in vv. 11–12.

(in 14:1—15:9) and the proclamation of hope (30–31) finds a preliminary solution in 15:13–14.

Even if our understanding of vv. 13–14 is only approximately right, we have found in these two verses an example of how individual complaint and private oracle were augmented and thus actualized for the community of Israel.

2. Next we turn to vv. 19–21 because they stand out from their context as an emphatically introduced new oracle and because this personal word of assurance to the prophet seems to be a very well-preserved entity. Could we possibly look upon vv. 19–21 as another literary layer in the composition of Jer 15:10–21?

Verses 19–21, formally, are Yahweh's answer to the complaints in vv. 15–18. The "complainer" is rebuked, because his words are "worthless talk." He is first conditionally (19a), then without further discussion (19b, 20) reinstated in his office as Yahweh's mediator, as a bulwark against the rebellious people. The question is: Where do we find the original setting for such an oracle?

The introductory formula (v. 19: "Therefore, thus said the LORD")[14] unmistakably indicates that the following word is God's revealed judgment upon the matter. This introduction originally, being an integral part of the message itself, legitimatized a messenger.[15] Obviously this cannot be its present purpose at the beginning of this "private" oracle. Here *koh 'amar yhwh* no longer authorizes a person but solemnly emphasizes a divine revelation. The formula has been emptied of its previous meaning. Now it is a literary device, an abstract symbol of theological language, which marks the beginning of Yahweh's holy words.[16] Furthermore, this introductory

---

14. "Therefore" (*laken*) often marks the juncture between prophetic reflection and the divine word; cf. Wolff, "Die Begründungen," 2, 6; Westermann, *Grundformen*, 94, 107 (ET: *Basic Forms*). Jeremiah in particular abounds with "messenger formulas"; cf. Ross, "The Prophet as Yahweh's Messenger." They are often preceded by an emphatic *laken* (Jer 5:14; 6:21; 7:20; 9:6, 14; 11:11; 14:15; 18:13; 22:18; 23:2, 15, 30, 38; 25:8; 28:16; 29:32; 34:17; 35:17, 19; 36:30; 42:15; 44:11).

15. Cf. Jer 2:1–2, 4–5; 10:1–2; 21:3–4; 29:31; Gen 32:5; cf. especially Westermann, *Grundformen*, 70ff. (ET: *Basic Forms*).

16. Some commentators note the awkwardness of the messenger formula in the scheme of personal complaint and oracle (cf. Duhm, 136; Cornill, 198–99) without, however, realizing fully the implications of the transfer of this formula. Cf. the secondary, "theological" use of the phrase especially in Jer 6:9, 16; 11:21; 13:1; 17:19; 19:1; 22:1; 26:2; 27:2. One should compare this with the normal, conversational style of the prophetical, "autobiographical" dialogues (Jer 1:6, 7, 9, 11b, 12, 13b, 14; 11:5b, 6, 9; 13:6; 14:11, 13, 14; 15:1). Here the introductory words, *weyomer yhwh 'eli* and *we'amar*, are short and subordinate. Cf. also the third person "*memorabile*" Hos 1:2ff. (Wolff, *Hosea*, 7ff., 71–72).

formula does not indicate who is the recipient of Yahweh's word. Apparently its author already read Jer 15:19ff. in a larger context. Jeremiah 14:1, 11, and 15:1 which mention the prophet's name are sufficient for him to illuminate the situation in 15:19ff.

The first element of the oracle proper, the conditional reinstatement of the prophet (v. 19a), in view of its form and content seems to be a reflection of Jer 4:1-2. There the people are offered a blessed life, if they find their way back to Yahweh worship. The breaking of the covenant is not suggested in either passage.[17] This means that the people and/or the prophet are in a state of disgrace. Their apostasy has become manifest. The homiletical conclusion obviously is: one must preach "conversion" and offer the opportunity for return. In a number of parallel passages in Jeremiah, all of which have to be attributed to the deuteronomistic editor of the book, exactly the same situation is presupposed: Jer 7:5-7; 26:3; 27:17; 29:12-13; 35:15; 36:3. In numerous other sections, in a somewhat abstract way, the choice between "life and death" is set before the people. Our text (Jer 15:19-21) resembles deuteronomistic thinking not only in this evaluation of the present situation as the moment for decision and in its view of past history as a story of missed opportunities. It also has the characteristic emphasis on man's initial effort (*'im-tašuv*) to end the alienation from God, an effort which, however, is immediately and surprisingly superseded by God's validifying act (*weašivka*).[18]

This conditional acceptance of the prophet, considered proper by exilic theologians, may also appear in two other oracles (Jer 12:5 and 33:3), although the clear structure of an "if" clause with following promise is absent

---

17. Ultimately we have to see the homiletical form of "exhortation for conversion" derived from a legal background. Laws, treaties, and contracts were protected by heavy curses, which literally lay in wait for the potential transgressor (cf. Deut 27:15ff.). Apparently deuteronomistic theologians not only referred to the transgression of the law to explain the catastrophe of Jerusalem but also amplified the concept to include the counterpart of the curse, namely, the blessings of a life in obedience (cf. Deut 28:1ff.; 30:15ff.; Josh 24:15; 1 Kgs 8:31ff.; Jer 17:24ff.; 18:7ff.; 38:17ff.; 42:10ff.; and Noth, *Gesammelte Studien*, 155ff. The pure "conversion speech," then, would be an application of this theological system to the concrete situation of the people already under the curse: It need no longer refer to impending disaster but can look forward to a possible fulfillment of the blessing. Cf. Wolff, "Das Geschichtsverständnis," 230-31 n18. Earlier references to "conversion" are not yet so theologically formalized (cf. W. L. Holladay, *The Root Šûbh*, 120ff.).

18. We have to be careful not to identify the deuteronomistic *theologoumenon* about the necessity of conversion with our theological system of "works" and "grace." A short study of those wordplays which express the interaction between God and man shows the manifold layers of this concept: Jer 11:18; 16:21; 17:14; 20:7; 31:18. In all these cases Yahweh is the initiator as well as the one who warrants the described action. It seems, therefore, that one cannot take the *weašivka* in 15:19a as simply Yahweh's acknowledgment of man's initiative but as a creative act in itself.

in these cases. The characteristic theology underlying such a "reinstatement upon condition" finally becomes clear in a comparison with accounts of prophetic calls in the Old Testament. Man's refusal to take up God's mission is a standard part of some of these stories.[19] But nowhere is the prophet considered an apostate figure who has to return before he can be entrusted with his office. It seems that exilic theological anthropology, using the conditional promise of the homiletical address to the congregation, made possible this new concept. The prophet is man. In order to fulfill his holy mission, he, too, has to "turn around" towards Yahweh.[20]

The second, more elaborate part of the oracle, v. 19b–21, presents quite a changed picture of the prophet. It draws heavily on the formal language of the "prophetic call," thus justifying our comparison above. Yahweh, without further requirement, promises to be with the prophet, to "save and deliver" him (20b;[21] cf. Gen 28:15, 20; Josh 1:5, 9; Exod 3:12; Judg 6:16; Isa 41:10; Jer 1:8). God furthermore makes his prophet the pivot on which all of his plans for Israel turn. The prophet will be the man who accepts or rejects her supplications, will be the object of her scorn. An abstract theological air, akin to deuteronomistic thinking, pervades all of these statements. Detailed observations can only affirm this impression. The basic formula, "I am with you" (*'itka 'ani*, 20b), is expanded by a double verbal modification, both in the infinitive construct.[22] The full phrase which emerges as a result is unique to Jer (1:8, 19; 15:20b; 42:11; and 30:11, without the verb *nṣl*). Because it has persistently the same stereotyped form in these different passages[23] one feels compelled to attribute it to some editorial hand. The promise to "save and deliver" would in itself point to an exilic setting. The unexpected continuation of the wordplay on *šub* in v. 19b at the same time puts the prophet into the position of a decisive mediator and denies him the right to exercise his office. It fits equally well into the context of Jer 7:16; 11:14; 14:11; (37:3); (42:2, 20).[24] The notion of the fundamental and hitherto unbridgeable split

19. Cf. Exod 4:10; Judg 6:15; Jer 1:6; Zimmerli, *Das Buch Ezechiel*, 16ff. (ET *Ezekiel*).

20. Cf. the theology of the deuteronomist: Noth, *Überlieferungsgeschichtliche Studien*, 107ff. (ET *The Deuteronomistic History*); W. L. Holladay, *The Root Šûbh*, 127-28, 132, 153-54.

21. MT here has an elaborated text; cf. LXX.

22. The two verbs *yš'* hiph. and *nṣl* hiph., with occasional other synonyms, are a favorite expression in the language of prayer: Pss 7:2; 22:21-22; 31:3; 31:16-17; 34:18-19; 59:3; 71:2; 72:12-13. "Deliverance" becomes the most important theme for many exilic writers and preachers; cf. Ezek 13:21, 23; 34:10, 11ff.; Isa 43:1ff.; 50:1ff. A sophisticated theology of salvation originates only in these decades after the fall of Jerusalem.

23. It seems probable that Jer 1:17-19 is a late composition drawn in part from Jer 1:7-8, in part from 15:19-21.

24. Cf. Mowinckel, *Zur Komposition*, 37-38, for a sketch of the view that the

between God and his people, consequently also between the people and God's authoritative representative (v. 20), also conforms with the thinking of exilic Israel (cf. Jer 7:25-26, 27; 25:3ff.; 29:19; 35:15; 42:21; 44:4).[25]

Our oracle, Jer 15:19-21, then, shows a late mixture and transformation of elements of form. They are taken from various sources and are all used to express the new and exilic views of God, prophet, and people. The oracle responds to the complaint in vv. 15-18. Had it been united with the complaint when it appeared on the scene of Jer 15?

3. A few text-critical remarks have to be made before discussing vv. 15-18. The first two words in 15, "thou knowest," possibly were inserted after the Greek version had been made,[26] Jer 17:16 and 12:3 being the prototypes for this amendment. Baumgartner considers these words a possible opening phrase[27] rather than a secondary connection of the two complaints, Jer 15:10 and 15:18. The first possibility still seems to be the more likely solution.

The second textual difficulty in v. 15 is easier to handle. It is not the verb (*tiqqaheni*) which has to be eliminated in v. 15a (as LXX does), but the letters *l'rk*. They are a corrupted dittography of (*b*) or (*l*) *'pk* "(in) thy anger." This leaves us with the original text: "Do not, in thy anger, take me away..." just as in Pss 6:2; 27:9; 38:2. Apart from v. 16, which will be discussed presently, the text is fairly well preserved:

> Yahweh, remember me and visit me,
> and avenge me on my persecutors.
> Do not, in thy anger, take me away.
> Know that I bore reproach for thy sake.
> When thy words were found I ate them,
> and they became my joy and the delight of my heart,
> Because thy name was pronounced over me, Yahweh, God of hosts.
> I did not sit in merry company and enjoy myself.
> Under thy hand I sat alone because thou filled me with a curse.
> Why does my pain last endlessly,
> why is my wound incurable, resists to be healed?

---

deuteronomistic source in Jeremiah held in regard to the prophet. Mowinckel calls it unrealistic and abstract (37).

25. Cf. the figure hardening the face and heart of the people (Isa 48:4; Jer 6:28; Ezek 11:19; 36:26; Isa 6:10) and of the prophet (Ezek 3:8-9), which indicates the fundamental alienation of God's people.

26. Cf. the contrary opinion of Duhm, 135; Giesebrecht, 91; Rothstein, in Kautzsch, *Die Heilige Schrift*, 769; Volz, 171; Leslie, 143; Hyatt, 941.

27. Baumgartner, *Die Klagegedichte*, 33. Cf. Ps 139:1ff.; but we would expect a defining object, "Thou knowest *me*" or something similar (cf. Pss 10:14; 40:10; 69:6, 20; 142:4; 1 Chr 17:18; 2 Chr 6:30).

> Thou hast become to me like a deceptive water,
> which cannot be trusted. (15:15–18)

In judging its form and structure the strong resemblance of our text to the complaint-psalms has long been noted.[28] In the sequence of request, complaint, and reproach represented by vv. 15, 17, is each has its parallel in the psalms: Pss 6:2–3; 59:2–3; 106:4 and 44:23; 69:8; 89:51 are comparable to the two elements in v. 15; and Pss 55:13ff.; 88:9, 18; Job 19:13–19; 30:9–10 to v. 17.[29] The direct reproach against God (v. 18) is also found in Pss 89:39ff.; 88:7ff.; 44:10ff.; and Job 10:18. The one verse that cannot easily be fitted into this picture also presents the greatest textual difficulties; in LXX v. 16 continues 15b: "Know that for thee I bear reproach from those who despise thy words. Finish them up! But for me thy word shall be merriment and a heart's delight."[30] The theological concept of enemies despising God's words[31] seems to be more refined than MT's idea of a prophet eating God's words. Syntactically the MT avoids the long sentence structure. It furthermore offers the more difficult reading of the text, so it may be older than LXX. The vocabulary used in both versions seems very stereotyped.[32]

While the "eating of the divine word," described in MT, as well as the LXX's "contempt of God's word,"[33] still can be understood in the context of a complaint psalm, the individual's assertion in v. 16b, to have been taken into possession by Yahweh, certainly refers to a prophetic call. The evidence suggests that this formula in its theological meaning first was used in exilic and post-exilic times to express the enduring election of Israel and her peculiar

---

28. Cf. Baumgartner, *Die Klagegedichte*, 39–40: "The affinity to the structure of the complaint-song is obvious. The prophetic viewpoint comes out structurally in the oracle form, substantially in vv. 16, 17, 19, 20. The passionate reproach in v. 18b, too, would hardly be possible within the psalms." Cf. Hölscher, *Die Profeten*, 397; H. Schmidt, *Das Gebet des Angeklagten*, 272; Gunkel (introduction to H. Schmidt, *Die Schriften des Alten Testaments* 2:lxxii).

29. "Sitting alone" is a description of the seclusion that results from being punished by God (cf. Lam 1:1; Job 2:8; Lev 13:46). "Before your hand" does not imply a compulsion to prophesy as in Ezek 1:3; 3:14; it simply states that God is the author of the suffering (cf. Ps 32:4; Job 19:21; 23:2).

30. The Hebrew original which LXX may have used shows only three minor differences from MT. Cf. *apparatus criticus* of BH.

31. Cf. Ps 107:11; Isa 5:24; Jer 23:17 (LXX!); Jer 5:13; 6:10; 8:9.

32. "Joy and delight" (cf. Jer 7:34; 16:9; 25:10; 31:7, 13; 33:9, 11; Isa 22:13; 35:10; 51:3, 11; Ps 51:10; also Pss 4:8; 119:111); "called by thy name" (cf. Jer 7:10, 11, 14, 30; 32:34; 34:15; 14:9; 25:29; Amos 9:12; Deut 28:10; 1 Kgs 8:43; Isa 63:19; Dan 9:18–19; 2 Chr 7:14).

33. The word of God would be the favorable oracle a supplicant has received (Baumgartner, *Die Klagegedichte*, 35; cf. Ps 35:3). Duhm (135) views the MT reading as a shallow remembrance of Ezek 2:8ff.

relationship to God.³⁴ Later it would seem to have been used to indicate the individual's introduction into the community of the faithful (cf. Jer 15:16; Isa 43:7), although the evidence is scant.

If this assumption is correct, we have found a clue to the setting of vv. 15-18. A writer at home in prophetic theology probably augmented an older complaint psalm by inserting or rephrasing v. 16. Possibly it was the same hand that wrote vv. 19-21, augmented v. 16, and put the whole passage (vv. 15-21) into its present place. There is no doubt that this happened with a view towards the terrible doom announced in 14:1—15:4. The prophet's personal fate and suffering are drawn into the picture. More than that, the prophet's life is brought into relation with the people's sin and punishment. Their rebellion against Yahweh is the immediate cause of his distress. The prophet's suffering is representative of God's own suffering. So the complaint- and answer-liturgy in 14:7ff. and the complaint and oracle in 15:10ff. mark opposite but corresponding roles in one drama.

This does not exclude the possibility that Jer 15:10ff. may have been read later, as the insertion 13-14 suggests, as a communal complaint corresponding to the announcement of doom in 15:5-9.³⁵ Such an understanding of 15:10ff. could possibly arise in analogy to text compositions in which oracles of doom are followed by an added cry of anguish (cf. Jer 4:13-18, 19-21; 10:17-18, 19-21; Isa 21:2, 3-4; Hos 11:5-7, 8-9).

4. The last complex unit within our passage is vv. 10-12. Again we find two textual traditions, each of which permits numerous different interpretations. The crucial point is the reading of one single letter in the first word of v. 11. LXX apparently goes back to a Heb. *'amen*; MT on the contrary still shows in all old MSS uninfluenced by LXX *'amar* ("he spoke"). We consider the Hebrew text to be older than LXX and therefore understand vv. 11-12 as God's response towards the prophet's complaint.³⁶

---

34. The original juridic meaning is apparent in 2 Sam 12:28; Isa 4:1; Ezra 2:61. Calling out the name of a proprietor over his property has to be distinguished from the phrase, to "call somebody by his name" (cf. Isa 43:1; Gen 48:6; Deut 3:14). That Yahweh's name has been pronounced over Israel, the temple, the city becomes a fixed theological confession (*nqr' šm yhwh 'al*) in exilic times. The older tradition uses a similar formula only in regard to the ark (2 Sam 6:2).

35. So Barth, *Einführung in die Psalmen*, 22 (ET *Introduction to the Psalms*).

36. Most exegetes follow the LXX; cf. RSV. Too many arguments speak against its originality, however: (1) "Amen" is an individual (1 Kgs 1:36; Num 5:22; Jer 11:5; 28:6) or, more commonly, a communal liturgical response (cf. Deut 27:15ff.; Ps 106:48; Neh 5:13; 8:6; 1 Chr 16:36; Pss 41:14; 72:19; 80:53), a confirmation of an authoritative pronouncement. It cannot very well be considered a reaction to a confession of innocence (v. 10b). Sheldon Blank's line of argument (*Jeremiah*, 241), "Here the word would mean something like 'indeed,'" would better support our conclusion than his own. (2) A declaration of innocence itself can appear in the form of a conditional self-curse (Ps 7:4-6; Job

Oh me, my mother, that you bore me,
   a man of contention and strife for all the land.
I did not loan, nor did they lend to me;
   (yet) all are cursing me.
Yahweh said: I will set you free for good;
   I will intervene on your behalf,
   in time of trouble and distress, against the enemy.
Can one break iron, iron from the north, and bronze?[37]

LXX after misreading the *amar* interpreted the following conditional oath as a continuation of the declaration of innocence in accord with Jer 17:16; 18:20.

As it stands in Hebrew, our text gives no evidence whatsoever that it might be speaking about a prophet or prophetic office. Rather it seems to be a normal complaint with a following salvation oracle,[38] although v. 10, contrary to usual practice, is composed of a mourning cry,[39] a declaration of innocence (cf. Ps 26:4–6; Job 23:11–12), and a complaint about unjust treatment. The form elements in vv. 10 and 11–12 seem to be intricately connected. They probably came into writing as a unit. The lack of theological refinement and the brevity and compactness of our verses make them appear more archaic than their counterpart, vv. 15–21. So we may assume that in 10–12 we have finally reached the oldest elements in the composition of Jer 15:10–21, and the question that now arises, why and when vv. 10–12 came to Jer 15, is intimately tied up with the larger question of composition and purpose of the whole passage.

II.

To determine the present meaning of our whole passage we have to look for its position in its larger context. The arrangement of two complaints, plus an answer and the careful editing to fit the prophetic context especially of the second unit (15–21), should make it clear that Jer 15:10–21 was not placed

---

31:5–8, 9–10), but with a normal statement of consequence in case of perjury (Ps 7:6; Job 31:8, 10) and without the artificial "amen." (3) LXX is familiar with the liturgical "amen" and tends to read it into the Hebrew text (cf. Jer 3:19, LXX vs. MT).

37. Verses 11–12 are badly preserved. For the discussion of the text see the commentaries. Our translation follows mainly Baumgartner's, *Die Klagegedichte*, 61.

38. Cf. esp. Begrich, "Das priestliche Heilsorakel" in Gunkel and Begrich, *Einleitung in die Psalmen*, 246–47 (ET *Introduction to Psalms*).

39. Cf. the dirge style (Jahnow, *Das hebräische Leichenlied*, 83ff.) and Ps 120:5; Isa 6:5; 24:16; Jer 4:31; 10:19; 45:3.

there by accident, as some commentators seem to believe.[40] At least in the mind of some late editor the larger composition including our text is the combination of chaps. 14 and 15. The full revelation formula[41] occurs at the beginning of chap. 14. It is followed by a series of introductory expressions in simple narrative style (14:11, 14; 15:1). Only in 16:1 does the solemn formula, "the word of Yahweh came to me," begin a new section.[42] Although this division is clearly late, associated with the deuteronomistic edition of Jer,[43] it is confirmed by examination of the text itself. Chapter 13, as well as chap. 16, contains for the most part divine announcements, unilateral declarations of doom. Jeremiah 14–15, on the other hand, consists essentially of material in the form of a dialogue.

1. The basic material in 14:1—15:4 is in the form of two introductory laments and two complaints of the people. The laments describe, respectively, the devastating effects of a drought and the results of a military defeat (14:2-6, 17-18). Each of the complaints (14:7-9, 19-22) is complemented by an oracle (14:10; 15:1-4). Obviously, at least the answer to the second complaint is a later addition; in its introductory line ("the Lord said to me") it creates the false impression that the prophet had been speaking the preceding complaint.[44] But the use of the first person plural in 14:19-22 excludes this assumption. The oracle answer in itself is a complex unit,[45] consisting of a final rejection of the people's complaint (15:1; cf. Ezek 14:14), the people's inquiry about their way (15:2; cf. Jer 42:1ff.; Ezek 14:1ff.; 20:1ff.; 33:30ff.), and another pronouncement of doom on account of the sins of Manasseh (15:3-4; cf. Deut 28:25; 2 Kgs 23:20). For us it is important to note that the prophet throughout these verses is seen as the fully commissioned

---

40. Cf. Duhm, 134; Rudolph, 97.

41. In Jeremiah the revelation formula composed of some form of the verb *hayah* and the construct relationship *dabar YHWH* seems, as in Ezekiel, to divide the text material into revelatory acts. The formula is theologically charged when it describes the total prophetic activity (cf. Jer 25:1, 3). It occasionally refers to an individual revelatory act (cf. Jer 13:8; 28:12; 29:30). Cf. Grether, *Name und Wort Gottes*, 67ff., 84ff.

42. Both formulas, that of 14:1 and 16:1, are textually dubious: LXX translates more or less different formulations. We assume, however, that the MT tradition is older, and that LXX no longer understood the meaning of this systematization. In MT apparently Jer 2–6; 7–10; 11–12; 13; 16–17; 18–20; 21–23; 24; 25 are likewise considered "kerygmatic units" by the redactor. LXX betrays its lack of interest in this order by omitting the formula in 2:1 and 7:1.

43. Cf. Mowinckel, *Zur Komposition*, 31–32.

44. Cf. Duhm, 130-31. Does the editor look back to 14:17, regarding 17–22 as one prophetic announcement?

45. Hyatt, 936: "In its present form this passage is from the Deuteronomic editor." Cf. Rudolph, 95; Mowinckel, *Zur Komposition*, 22–23.

representative of Yahweh. We found the same image in 15:19-21. That the editor of this composition is not content with just describing the people's role is proven by an insertion which also regards the prophet as the decisive supplicant and mediator. The passage 14:11-16, clearly deuteronomistic in character and theme,[46] was drawn into this context precisely because of its understanding of the prophetic office as a mediatory one (cf. Jer 4:10; 7:16; 11:14; 42:2ff.). So we may say that in 14:1—15:4 the writer of Jeremiah adopts and reconstructs the well-known form of a complaint liturgy[47] and makes certain that the form is repeated once, perhaps because the twofold expression of complaint with an oracle answer was a standard one.[48] He places great emphasis on his concept of mediation. The prophet not only intercedes for the people but also executes Yahweh's will.

Most of the examples of a communal complaint liturgy preserved in the OT have favorable oracle answers. In Jer 14:1ff. the answer is unconditionally negative. Israel's complaints are not accepted. The prophet's intercession is refuted. This underscores the futility of Israel's hope. Even the rejection of the people's plea in Hos 6:4ff. does not match the harshness of our passage. Conceivably the unyielding judgment in Jeremiah shows or preserves the insight won after the fall of Jerusalem: supplication and intercession had not saved Israel, in spite of all covenant assurances.

Looking from Jer 14:1—15:4 to our passage 15:10-21 we can ascertain already the formal and substantial affinities between them. The communal complaint-answer dialogue corresponds to the prophet's complaints and the oracle answers in 15:10ff.; the introduction of the prophet in 14:11, 13, and 15:1-4 as an intercessor foreshadows his role in 15:19-21. Since the latest integral parts in the composition 14:1—15:4, namely, 15:1-4 (which only makes the "liturgy" complete) are definitely exilic, we have to conclude that the whole composition is of that date.[49] Consequently the final arrangement of 15:10-21, patterned as we shall see on 14:1—15:4, cannot be of an earlier date.

2. Jeremiah 15:5-9 does not seem to fit into this picture. The passage starts out as a lament in dirge style, spoken by Yahweh or the prophet for the desolate city of Jerusalem (v. 5; cf. Isa 51:19-20; Nah 3:7; Lam 1:2, 17; 2:15; Amos 5:2). But the rest of 15:5ff. is neither a lament nor a complaint.[50] In v.

---

46. Cf. Hyatt, 933; Mowinckel, *Zur Komposition*, 36ff.

47. Cf. Gunkel and Begrich, *Einleitung in die Psalmen*, 136ff., 408ff., 246-47 (ET *Introduction to the Psalms*).

48. Cf. Gunkel and Begrich, *Einleitung in die Psalmen*, 138 (ET *Introduction to the Psalms*); Gunkel, "Jesaia 33," 190ff., 194-95; Gunkel "The Close of Micah," 142ff.

49. Cf. Mowinckel, *Zur Komposition*, 22-23.

50. Cf. Jahnow, *Das hebräische Leichenlied*, 102-3, 168ff., 183ff. It would be

6 another element appears: Yahweh addresses himself directly to Jerusalem, first in an indictment (v. 6a), then in an affirmation of his punishment (6b). Verse 6 as a whole seems to be spoken in response to v. 5. The reason for the mourning in v. 5 is nothing but the deserved punishment from the Lord. The dialogue form, then, seems to be preserved in this unit, although the first part is no longer a complaint, but a *postfactum* lament. Verses 7–9 in a way seem to be patterned like 6b: Yahweh enumerates the punishments which he has already inflicted upon the people, and at the very end turns to even further threats against the remnant (9b; cf. 6b, "I am weary of relenting"). But vv. 7–9 lack the 2nd person address. They speak about the people rather than the city of Jerusalem. They also lack the response character of v. 6. So we may consider these verses as an expansion of the thoughts contained in v. 6.

Jeremiah 15:5–6 would then in a final dialogue (lament-answer) conclude and reinforce the picture of destruction painted in the liturgy of 14:1—15:4. The whole passage (15:5–9), dialogue plus expansion, speaks from the perspective of the completed devastation with some last catastrophes still to come. This sounds like a situation which might have existed after the first Babylonian conquest in 597 BCE. In this case it would be likely that the composer of the liturgy Jer 14:1ff. used old material to bring to a close his sketch about the futility of Israel's complaints.

3. Jeremiah 15:10–21 finally seems to be exactly modeled after the repentance liturgy in 14:1—15:4. According to our reconstruction of the text the same twofold cycle[51] of complaint and answer has become visible. Apparently the composer used one old unit (vv. 10–12) and augmented the words of another standard complaint by one line as well as by an oracle answer (vv. 15–21) in order to give his composition the standard two parts.[52] Since the oracle answer (vv. 19–21) proved to be of deuteronomistic character, we may even assume that the same hand which worked out the twofold liturgy in 14:1—15:4 completed the composition by adding the twofold complaint of the prophet himself. If this is correct—and the formal analysis of 15:10–21 would support such a view—then we have to ask for the meaning of this passage as it follows the people's complaint-liturgy. The composer,

---

profitable to distinguish between lament and complaint: a lament bemoans a tragedy which cannot be reversed, while a complaint entreats God for help in the midst of tribulation.

51. Cf. Gunkel and Begrich, *Einleitung*, 138 (ET *Introduction to the Psalms*).

52. Cf. Gunkel and Begrich, *Einleitung*, 409 (ET *Introduction to the Psalms*): The individual complaint-psalm cannot be considered the basis for liturgies of recurring complaint and answer. This observation seems to be confirmed in our text.

in taking such pains to demonstrate the parallelism between prophet and people, certainly saw a deep theological necessity for so doing.

Since the deuteronomist's view is most clearly expressed in his own additions to the composition, it is in the light of the concluding vv. 19-21 that we now have to interpret 15:10-21. Now all the attention is focused on the prophet and his relationship to the people. Neither the complaints in vv. 10, 15-18[53] nor the oracle answer in 11-12 (as far as it is recognizable) said anything like vv. 19-21 about the prophet himself. It is not so much "biographical" data that attracted the interest of the deuteronomist. The individual traits of the preceding complaints fade into the background (cf., e.g., 10b, 17a) and are not taken up in Yahweh's response. "Private" afflictions are no longer important. It is the divine office and Jeremiah, the authorized officeholder, that occupy the deuteronomist's mind (cf. especially v. 20a). The fate of Israel, according to the exilic view of history, has been decided by her hostile attitude to the prophetic office.[54] It had been the vessel of Yahweh's word; it had been authorized to grant salvation or reject the impenitent people (vv. 19b, 20a). It had been vested with Yahweh's own authority. No wonder that the officeholder can venture bitter castigations (cf. v. 18b: "Thou hast become to me like a deceptive water, which cannot be trusted") without being consumed by Yahweh's wrath. No wonder that he has to suffer in consequence of the people's rebellion against Yahweh's guidance (v. 20a). All the preceding complaints now have to be understood in the light of Israel's attack against the prophet. In all this the deuteronomist sees the prophetic commissioner involved in the controversy between Yahweh and his people (cf. 14:11ff.) but on Yahweh's side.

The divine office is, according to the deuteronomist, occupied by a weak mortal, who suffers, prays, loses the right track (cf. especially v. 19a). This is the reason why the deuteronomist introduces "prophetic" complaints (vv. 10, 15-18) in the same way he tells about the people's laments and complaints (14:2-9, 19-22). The "historical" Jeremiah, in his opinion, does not live up to the majestic task he is called to perform. In a sense he remains a member of these apostate people who lament, confess their sins—and are rejected (14:2ff.). Therefore, even the prophet has to be admonished to "turn back" (v. 19a; cf. 4:1-2).

But all we have said so far must be seen before a larger background. The deuteronomist does not confine himself to presenting to his reader a divine office and a prophet struggling to fill it. The ultimate concern of our

---

53. Verse 16 is an exception because it was reformulated by the deuteronomist.

54. Cf. the similar position of the prophet in deuteronomistic historical writings; Noth, *Überlieferungsgeschichtliche Studien*, 78ff. (ET *The Deuteronomistic History*).

final editor rests with the people. He wrestled with the problem of their election and rejection in 14:2—15:9. Historical events had demonstrated that the incomprehensible could happen: God had put Israel out of his sight (15:1). Prophetic intervention had been useless (14:11ff.). Was this the absolute end for Yahweh's people? The deuteronomist answers "no," because the prophet himself, as a member of this weak and unreliable Israel, becomes a paradigmatic figure of salvation. "I am with you to save and deliver you" (v. 20b) is the final pronouncement over the prophet. Thus Jer 14–15 ends on a more hopeful note. One man has found grace with Yahweh.[55] This is a ray of light that shines out in the darkness of the unconditional doom expressed in 14:2—15:9.

III.

Our literary and form-critical analysis attempted to show that Jer 14–15 is an organic textual unit composed over a long period of time. The central theme of the whole passage is the suffering of the people and Yahweh's response to their cry, be it the communal laments in chap. 14 or the individual's complaints in 15:10ff. The linking together of lament or complaint and divine oracle certainly reflects the liturgical pattern of prayer and oracle answer although it is by no means clear whether such "prophetic liturgies" had been "performed" in actual worship or whether they were only literary products.

The dating of a complex unit like Jer 14–15 poses great difficulties. In its final form the composition was finished in exilic times. Deuteronomistic thinking has left its impression on it. The original cycle (Jer 14:2—15:9) with its grim outlook into the future could possibly go back to a time before the fall of Jerusalem. More probably it reflects the sentiment after the fall of the city. It is a deuteronomistic rationalization that nothing could in the end prevent the final destruction because of the "sin of Manasseh" (cf. 15:4; 14:11ff.).

The deuteronomist has had a similarly decisive influence on the following passage. This second, "prophetic" round of complaint and answer, which mirrors the structure of the preceding communal part, was not completed until late exilic times. There are good reasons to believe that the deuteronomist can be credited with the composition of 15:10-21, in contrast to 14:2—15:9 where deuteronomistic passages seem to have been inserted into an already existing liturgy.

---

55. Some Jeremiah narratives (cf. chaps. 26; 28; 37; 38) also could be called stories of paradigmatic salvation rather than "passion stories" (cf. Kremers, "Leidensgemeinschaft mit Gott").

Of course, this sketch of the literary development of Jer 14–15 does not say very much about the authors of its individual literary components. Answers to direct questions in this regard must be extremely hypothetical. The individual words are not signed by any writer, nor does the fact that we find them collected in a book ascribed to the prophet Jeremiah guarantee their "authenticity." There is a slight possibility that the oldest parts of the first cycle (14:10; 15:5–9) are Jeremianic, because they contain prophesies similar to those in Jer 2; 4–6; and 8–9, which have the best claim to have originated with the prophet himself. Even the oldest part of the second cycle (15:10–11) hardly betrays any prophetic origin.

Our main concern has been to trace the growth of Jer 15:10–21. To summarize the results: The oldest layer within this passage is vv. 10–11, an individual complaint with a priestly oracle of assurance. This unit has been incorporated into Jeremiah probably because the editor, knowing already about the sufferings of Jeremiah from the "biographical" narratives, saw in them an analogy to the agony of the people (chap. 14). It was possibly the same deuteronomistic editor who augmented this first complaint-answer dialogue with a second one (vv. 15–21) and so completed the cultic pattern. By doing so he also intended to make plain the crucial role Jeremiah played for the people of Israel. We noticed the strong deuteronomistic coloring of all the concepts involved. At a third stage of growth another hand inserted vv. 13–14 to turn attention back to Israel in her distress. This last editor not only refers us back to the central theme of the composition Jer 14–15. He also makes it explicit that the whole kerygmatic unit ends in a veiled promise for Yahweh's people. So he is justified in announcing an end of Israel's oppression and the dispersal of her enemies.

Among the many questions that remain unsolved, one of the most urgent is this: Can the other individual complaints in Jeremiah also be explained as compositive elements in some larger textual unit? Can the complaints in Jeremiah thus be shown to be later insertions into an existing collection of prophesies?

7

Elusive Lamentations

What Are They About?

Difficulties

IRONICALLY A PIECE OF the Hebrew Bible so neatly constricted, so poetically refined, and seemingly so transparent in its literary fiber is at the same time awfully renitent when determining its genre and use in real life. Sibylline answers given to painstaking inquiries oscillate between "artful poetry" and "efficient liturgy" putting the five more or less acrostic chapters of Lamentations into the brackets either of pure literature in the modern sense to be savored by the wise and gifted, academic teachers and students or of mourning rituals performed during large commemorative popular festivals. The case for the first option can be argued on the basis of the artificial acrostic setup, as well as the lack of proper complaint elements (invocation, initial plea, affirmation of confidence, concrete petitions, vow, praise, etc., as in Pss 44 and 89). Furthermore, there seems to linger around these texts—besides the shocks of traumatizing horrors—an air of reflection and rationalizing past experience better suited for intellectuals and academic circles than worshiping congregations. The other option leads into the communal world of regular mourning rites.[1] The poems become elements of worship and importune style and form are forgotten.

---

1. Jahnow, *Das hebräische Leichenlied*.

Sitz im Leben

It may be advisable then to discuss first some basics of the practical use of the five poems before entering formal analyses. The attribution to the prophet Jeremiah, reluctant and lamenting commissioner of YHWH's words (cf. Jer 15:10-21; 20:7, 18), seems to have been triggered by 2 Chr 35:2-5: "Jeremiah also uttered a lament for Josiah ... recorded in the Laments." Later Jewish and Christian interpretation stuck to this identification, leaving aside, however, the more general reference in that same verse to "male and female singers" (!) and the mourning customs in early Jewish communities (cf. also Zech 7:3; 8:19). Only the rise of "enlightened" critical scholarship in modern times cut the umbilical cord to the historical prophet for good, and also moved away from the date of Josiah's death (609 BCE). Instead, most specialists on the book of Lamentations now consider it the work of various unknown poets "singers" who in retrospect wrestle with the dreadful collective memory of Jerusalem's destruction and downfall in the wake of Babylonian conquest (597 to 587 BCE).[2] Avoiding an exclusive focus on the siege and fall of Jerusalem, we may think of more general and long-ranging war experiences of ancient Near Eastern populations, which have been worked into poems of lament. Destructions and forced migrations, after all, were common throughout the history of that region.[3] Development of trauma theories in recent years has fostered this kind of interpretation, which seems to be essentially correct. No matter what exact relationship may have existed between historical events, authors, and audiences, texts like Lamentations are never mere horror fiction or mythological imagination, but preserve in some way or another collective memories of "real," man-made catastrophes. Such lamenting discourses, furthermore, should be considered as therapeutic means to overcome historical trauma, most probably in some ceremonial, commemorative practice.[4] Days of mourning and/or of victory celebrations until our own time serve the same functions. This should be the first insight to be gained from the texts. Closer analyses must follow.

---

2. Cf. Westermann, *Klagelieder* (ET *Lamentations*); Lee, *The Singers of Lamentations*; O'Connor, *Lamentations and the Tears of the World*.

3. Michalowski, *Lamentation over the Destruction of Sumer and Ur*; Pham, *Mourning in the Ancient Near East and the Hebrew Bible*.

4. Linafelt, *Surviving Lamentations*.

Literary Forms and Structures

Studies of poetic and stylistic articulations in Lamentations are most important. Yet they do not seem to lead very far, because they do not tell us the ways and locales of presentation.

> Formally the five chapters share their predilection for the Hebrew alphabet: Lamentations 1 and 2 display 22 three-line units and Lamentations 4 an equal number of two line strophes which start out with subsequent letters. Lamentations 3 even has each individual score of its three-liners commence with the same character while Lamentations 5 contents itself by sticking to the mere number of 22 verses.[5]

This close entanglement with—perhaps a sort of addiction to—written media certainly points, in terms of authorship, to literary elites. But it does not preclude, in my opinion, communal use of the poems. Acrostic poems also loom fairly large in the Psalter (cf. Pss 9/10; 25; 34; 37; 111; 112; 119; 145) and are common in ancient Near Eastern Wisdom literature. For more illumination of the mysteries involved, commentators have tried to identify speakers in the dramatic plot unfolding in Lam 1–5.[6] On the whole, we meet five alternating voices: 1) a neutral speaker, mostly describing the sad state of conquered, maltreated, despised Jerusalem (cf. Lam 1:1–9; 2:1–10, 17–19; 4:1–16); 2) the desecrated "dame" Zion/Jerusalem herself;[7] 3) possibly God in person, deploring the misery of his "daughter" (cf. Lam 2:11–16);[8] 4) an individual supplicant (Lam 3:1–39, 49–66); and 5) a community or congregation, using the first person plural (cf. Lam 3:40–48; 4:17–20; 5:1–22). Some short quotations of still other "participants" may be left aside at this point. While each one of those voices demands comments, the communal "We," it seems to me, is the most conspicuous and usually overlooked one. Possibly the author, speaker, or liturgist at given moments incorporates him- or herself into a real or imagined audience.

Even if the author did this only virtually, writing away at a desk and fancying a listening crowd, the fact in itself would be significant if the text of Lamentations did not come about without the real or ideal presence of

---

5. Meyer, "Die Klagelieder," 479.

6. Cf. Berlin, *Lamentations*; O'Connor, *Lamentations and the Tears of the World*.

7. Lam 1:9 quotes her briefly: "Look Yahweh, at my affliction, for the enemy has triumphed." Then, in Lam 1:11–22 (except v. 17), Jerusalem complains directly to God: "Look, Yahweh, and see, how worthless I have become . . ."; cf. Lam 2:20–22 (prayer style).

8. The narrator or liturgist, cited under 1) may have been imbued with the task of communicating divine speech.

community, more precisely, of a responsive congregation. In the Psalter, this phenomenon of "We" passages also has drawn scholarly attention.[9] The numerous witnesses of ancient Near Eastern prayer ceremonies in the complaint and lamentation genres hardly provide any evidence that communal groups—whether ideal or real—by way of leading speakers or in common recitation/response took active part in religious ritual.[10] This near lack of "We" speech in religious literature among Israel's neighbors certainly does not prove the absence of such patterns in real life, but it may testify to the fact that religious lay organization on a communitarian basis has been a peculiarity in exilic/post-exilic Israel. To our knowledge, the predominating way of organizing religious faith in Egypt and the ancient Near East was either in the realm of family and clan-structures or on an official state level. Both modes of organization offer little opportunity to use communal "We" discourse.[11] A comparable structure of community life as found in exilic/post-exilic Israel may have existed in early Zoroastrian faith, extant in the oldest layers of the Avesta.

Returning to the book of Lamentations, we elaborate the evidence of "We" discourse by observing an interesting increase of first-person plural statements from Lam 3–5. The first incident of "We" speech (Lam 3:40–47) is inserted into an overwhelmingly clear-cut "complaint of the individual"—in terms of form-elements and general structure.[12] "Let us test and examine our ways, and return to Yahweh" (v. 40) abruptly opens the communitarian section (cf. Hos 6:1–3; Jer 9:18–20; 14:7–9; Isa 64:4–11; Ezra 9:6–15; Ps 106:6, 47, etc.). The very existence of the "We"-block apparently makes the whole chapter a "communal" voice, the predominant first person singular, then, representing the individual member of the congregation. That is to say, the community is speaking in the first person plural as in so many other Old Testament congregational laments and complaints. But the collective

---

9. Cf., e.g., Pss 90; 95; 100. See also Scharbert, "Das 'Wir' der Psalmen"; Seybold, "Das 'Wir' in den Asaph-Psalmen."

10. Sumerian literature provides some instances of "We" discourse, cf. ETCSL: 1.2.1, lines 1–3 ("Enlil and Ninlil"); ETCSL 2.2.3, lines 225–242 ("Lament for Sumer and Urim"); ETCSL 4.07.9, lines 22–25; 2.4.4.3, lines 18–20; possibly in a hymn to Bau: ETCSL 4.02.1, Segm. B, line 8, Segm. C, lines 4, 10.

11. In complaints of the individual, the supplicant is the principal agent after the professional healer (cf. Gerstenberger, *Der bittende Mensch*. State rituals did rarely include the worshipping crowd concentrating on priests and kings as protagonists (cf., however, n4 above).

12. More form-critical definitions may be found in Gerstenberger, *Psalms, Part 1*, esp. 9–21. Lamentations 3 is almost universally considered a true "individual" prayer; cf. Berges, *Klagelieder*; Dobbs-Allsopp, *Lamentations*; Gerstenberger, *Psalms, Part 2*, 492–97 (emphasis on the communal aspects in vv. 37–47).

dimension also comes to the fore through the individual sufferer: "I am one who has seen affliction under the rod of God's wrath . . ." (Lam 3:1). Every one of the afflicted community testifies to the common ordeal. The language is stereotyped, not specific to one exclusive situation, a truism for all laments and complaints, as well as for other prayers and liturgical pieces. But in the present context of "We" affirmations, the singular discourse clearly is embedded in community life becoming a communal lament. The same phenomenon transpires in Lam 4. The explicitly communal part of vv. 17–20 sets the parameter for the entire chapter, because first person plural discourse is the more unlikely, therefore more authentic, mode of speech revealing a social body of equals as the agents. Finally, Lam 5, from the first lines of invocation through lament and on to regular petition (vv. 21–22), features "We" speech throughout: "Remember, O Yahweh, what has befallen us . . ." (v. 1); "Restore us to yourself, O Yahweh, that we may be restored . . ." (v. 21). This chapter is obviously the final "song" or "prayer" in the series and beyond doubt betrays a congregational setting.

Grammatical and poetic devices (meter, strophes, alliteration, assonance, metaphors, etc.) are still being pondered in the exegesis of Lamentations together with structural, historical-critical, and literary analyses,[13] to mention a few typical fields of research. The art of alphabetic and acrostic composition naturally is discussed in all recent studies.[14] Comparison with Akkadian sapiential literature is mandatory, but, as a rule, there are no social or liturgical consequences to be drawn from this artful design. The question of the *qinah*-line has caught the attention of commentators ever since Marburg professor Karl Budde identified the 3 + 2 meter as a typical dirge pattern.[15] His thesis was almost universally accepted, with some adaptations along the way.[16] Hedwig Jahnow links the "hobbling" meter with the mood of mourning: "The hopelessness of dirges was perfectly expressed by this irregular, limping rhythm sounding as if the female singer was unable to properly conclude the second part of the line because of her deep emotional involvement."[17] The literary analysis of the individual chapters and in the book as a whole has been in vogue over the past decades. Literary critics from their estimation of the individual author lay open different layers of

---

13. Renkema, *Lamentations*; Bergant, *Lamentations*; Diller, *Zwischen YHWH-Tag und neuer Hoffnung*; Salters, *Lamentations*.

14. Cf. Paul, "Mnemonic Devices"; Pinker, "Nahum 1."

15. Budde, "Das hebräische Klagelied."

16. E.g., Dobbs-Allsopp emphasizes literary cadences that transcend the single line ("enjambment"), in *Weep, O Daughter of Zion*; Dobbs-Allsopp, *Lamentations*.

17. Cf. Jahnow, *Das hebräische Leichenlied*, 92.

composition thus emphasizing originally independent sub-units.[18] Structuralists, and poetologists, on the other hand, tend to discover important internal cohesions in individual chapters and in the book as a whole (inclusions, chiasms, concentricity, etc.).[19] The terminology of Lamentations is under constant scrutiny, in particular its metaphorical language of suffering and warfare. A special point of concern, also prompted by feminist readings of the Bible, is the figure of the lamenting "lady" or "daughter" Jerusalem and her progeny.[20]

In general, however, exegetes have shifted attention from small details of the composition to comprehensive literary themes, inherent ideas and mentalities, and, not to be underestimated, to spiritual values and theological concepts that can be connected to present-day thinking. As Adele Berlin puts it: "The focus now is on the broader aspects of the meaning of the whole rather than on its parts."[21] She concentrates on three main concepts of Lamentations: "the paradigm of purity, the political paradigm, and the concept of mourning," and to her, "the most central theme of Lamentations is mourning."[22] Kathleen O'Connor stresses the poetic voices in Lamentations "bringing pain to speech"; they "are acts of survival; they express resistance to death and a resilient grasp on life."[23] From here, she draws conclusions about the *Sitz im Leben* of the poems: "I imagine the book as a public performance of speakers in which survivors stand up, each in turn, to tell of their particular pain and to demand God's attention. Together the voices possess only the raw harmony of common wounds, even as they offer competing and irreconcilable opinions of the disaster."[24]

Nancy C. Lee, from the start of her doctoral work,[25] has been thinking in broad terms of human suffering. In due course, she followed up her exegetical studies of Lamentations with a Society of Biblical Literature workgroup on "Ancient and Contemporary Cultural Contexts"[26] and a moving anthology of the poetry of distress from around the world.[27] The vivid

---

18. Cf. Jahnow, *Das hebräische Leichenlied*, 168–91.
19. Cf. Dobbs-Allsopp, *Lamentations*; Berges, *Klagelieder*.
20. Cf. O'Connor, *Lamentations and the Tears of the World*; Dobbs-Allsopp, *Weep, O Daughter of Zion*.
21. Cf. Berlin, "On Writing a Commentary on Lamentations," 5.
22. Berlin, "On Writing a Commentary on Lamentations," 6, 8.
23. O'Connor, "Voices Arguing about Meaning," 28.
24. O'Connor, "Voices Arguing about Meaning," 28.
25. Lee, *The Singers of Lamentations*.
26. Cf. Lee, "The Singers of Lamentations."
27. Lee, *Lyrics of Lament*.

experience of recent Balkan wars and traditional Balkan oral poetry[28] led her to accent the strong popular influences of unwritten laments eventually forming the book of Lamentations. Female voices beyond that of "daughter Zion" are recognizable, she insists.[29] Carleen Mandolfo in her published dissertation[30] defends—on the basis of Mikhail Bakhtin's linguistic theories— a "dialogic biblical theology"[31] that counts on partnership with God and "makes demands on God" to the effect "that as surely as God authors us, we author God."[32] In this fashion, the book of Lamentations becomes a dissenting voice against prophetic condemnation of female Israel (cf. Hos 1–3; Jer 3; Ezek 16; 23). Now, in Lamentations, the congregation recovers its self-esteem, argues for God's solidarity, leniency, and active support. An interesting variant of the "dissent" paradigm is Robert Williamson's "Lament and the Arts of Resistance,"[33] building on James C. Scott's distinction of "public" vs. "hidden" transcripts.[34] According to Williamson, Lam 5:22 is the outburst of a maltreated people contradicting "public transcripts" of submission and pretended harmony. But do the forms of collective complaint betray appeasing demeanor to begin with?

Given the large number of "holistic" interpretations of Lamentations, all aiming at making connections to our present world of pain and destruction, we rightly should marvel at the enduring dynamics of this age-old poetry. All the exemplary designs of a lasting lament tradition cited above laud its poetic achievement. In doing so, they acknowledge the origin and bearing of the written words in human experience. The connection of exegesis and theology with discomforting realities in and around our lives is a necessary one. It should include the awareness that much of traumatic suffering in antiquity was treated in communal ceremonies and rituals. A mere literary approach to Lamentations after all these incisive studies seems out of the question.

Factual and Spiritual Issues

We may now try to undergird our proposition that Lamentations grew out of communal interaction with God, not primarily out of a poet's endeavors to

28. Cf. Lord, *The Singer of Tales*.
29. Lee, "The Singers of Lamentations," 39.
30. Mandolfo, *Daughter Zion Talks Back to the Prophets*.
31. Cf. also Mandolfo, "Talking Back," 52; and Boase, *The Fulfillment of Doom?*
32. Mandolfo, "Talking Back," 55.
33. Williamson, "Lament and the Arts of Resistance."
34. See Scott, *Domination and the Arts of Resistance*.

satisfy intellectual or aesthetic desires. Supportive evidence comes, perhaps, from different perspectives of investigation. Hermann Gunkel stressed that each genre presupposes a "common set of moods."[35] Today, we may want to focus not so much on emotions but on agreed upon "values, outlooks, mental and social patterns," even "rituals" or the like, which make a given genre a recognizable, cohesive (oral or written) text. What, then, are these configurations of lament within the book? And are they compatible more with individual, communitarian, or state structures?

There is neither space nor time to take up all relevant items. We may concentrate on the central experience: that of physical violence, hunger, helplessness, forsakenness, etc., which the citizens of Jerusalem had to suffer at undetermined historical occasions. I repeat my contention that Lamentations does not exclusively relate to one determined defeat and sacking of the holy city, but to an accumulated ensemble of defeats and humiliations, sufferings, and frustrated hopes. In this context, hardships, misery, threatening death, with the seeming exception of Lam 3, are depicted in typical communal dimensions, not in the obligatory individual molds. To be more specific: "Woman" Jerusalem bewails the fate of her many "children" who fell in battle, were massacred by the invaders, or are starving to death in the aftermath of defeat. All the descriptions of violence and death relate in the first place to the group, not to individual agonies. They carry a certain statistic quality, not the horror of individual persons regardless whether standardized or not. A comparison with descriptive lament in individual complaints may immediately exhibit the difference: Psalms 22, 38, and 69 describe, although in stereotyped images, the personal suffering at the hand of brutal, unrelenting foes.

The enemies are crowds too. Their disdain impacts the community as a whole, not as individual persons. Interestingly, not even the kings of Israel or Judah are mentioned by name in this cumulative lament.[36] All citizens suffer the brunt of hostilities, repressions, and mockeries; leaders of the community being "elders," "princes" (*śarim*), "counts" (*nezirim*), "priests," and "prophets." Allusions to their social ranking are vague; they have been debased.[37] The sins, which have irritated YHWH, are the transgressions of the community, not of individuals, prominent as they once may have been. Petitions are not for the restoration of personal happiness, but for a functioning community. In short, the communal dimension prevails throughout

---

35. Gunkel, *The Psalms*, 10.

36. References to a "king" (Lam 2:2, 6, 9) are reminiscences of past times. There is one occurrence of the "anointed of Yahweh" (Lam 4:20), possibly a signal of emerging messianism.

37. Former glory and actual degradation are vividly picked; e.g., Lam 4:5, 7–8.

all the chapters, even Lam 3. The "mood" or common sense in Lamentations is perfectly tied to an intermediate social organization ("congregation"? the terminology is missing!), not toward smaller or larger groupings. The catastrophes that hit the community are viewed and described from the outside, seemingly by eyewitnesses, sometimes personified as "virgin" or "mother" Zion/Jerusalem, in reality by the narrator or liturgist. Lamentations 3, the personal complaint of a sufferer, fits into the picture. As already indicated, the complaining "I" uses vocabulary and images of individual suffering to demonstrate human "affliction": "He [God] has made my flesh and my skin waste away, and broken my bones . . ." (Lam 3:4; cf. Pss 22:15–16 [14–15]; 38:6–8 [5–7]). The sufferer, clearly a member of the congregation, takes on an almost vicarious or scapegoat role for his group: "I have become the laughingstock of all my people, the object of their taunt-songs all day long."[38]

It would be worthwhile to investigate related mental configurations like the concepts of locals (Zion; Jerusalem; foreign territory); history (former and actual state of affairs; transgression and punishment); social stratification; enemy constellations; etc. in order to detect specific community relations as juxtaposed to family or state organization. There is a great chance, in my opinion, that underlying orientations, i.e. patterns of thinking, evaluation, and worldview, point to that particular form of social life produced by a religious community occupying a sphere between family/clan and state organization.[39] The peculiarity of a faith organization, on the one hand, is its thoroughly spiritual dimension, and on the other, its non-political character.

(Non-) Topics

Taking a look at the themes selected in Lamentations may supplement the investigation of "moods" and "configurations." This tradition-historical perspective basically leads to far-reaching comparisons with Sumero-Akkadian lament literature, about which we cannot follow up at the moment.[40] But a glance at our text reveals a significant absence of military terminology and references. There are, to be sure, a few allusions to the defeat of the city's own forces:

---

38. Lam 3:14; cf. Ps 69:8–13, and the servant of YHWH in Isa 52:13—53:12. The "Joban" tone of Lam 3:1–18 is also to be noted.

39. Cf. Gerstenberger, *Theologien* (ET *Theologies*).

40. Cf. Cohen, *The Canonical Lamentations of Ancient Mesopotamia*; Michalowski, *The Lamentation over the Destruction of Sumer and Ur*; Dobbs-Allsopp, *Weep, O Daughter of Zion*; Löhnert, *"Wie die Sonne tritt heraus!"* Five Sumerian texts and translations are given in ETCSL nos. 2.2.2–2.2.6.

> The LORD has rejected
>> all my warriors in the midst of me,
> he proclaimed a time against me
>> to crush my young men;
> the Lord has trodden as in a winepress
>> the virgin daughter Judah. (Lam 1:15)[41]

But in general, lamenting goes on in civil ways—mother Jerusalem weeping over her children, the congregation describing its fate under foreign domination thus, Lam 5:1–16, part of which runs like this:

> Our inheritance has been tamed over to strangers,
>> our homes to aliens (v. 2)
>
> We have become orphans, fatherless;
>> our mothers are like widows (v. 3)
>
> We must pay for the water we drink;
>> the wood we get must be bought (v. 4)
>
> Our ancestors sinned; they are no more,
>> and we bear their iniquities (v. 7)
>
> Slaves rule over us;
>> there is no one to deliver us from their hand (v. 8)
>
> Our skin is black as an oven
>> from the scorching heat of famine (v. 10)
>
> Women are raped in Zion,
>> virgins in the towns of Judah (v. 11)
>
> Princes are hung up by their hands;
>> no respect is shown to the elders (v. 12)
>
> Young men are compelled to grind,
>> and boys stagger under loads of wood (v. 13)
>
> The old men have left the city gate,
>> the young men their music ... (v. 14)

The overall picture is that of a relatively small group of people, living in saddening conditions, but having no recollection of military triumph, pride in statehood and dynasty, power over neighboring peoples, etc. Even the deportations are not focused upon but mentioned in passing (cf. Lam 1:3, 6–7, 18). For a contrast, we may compare the so-called victory songs (Judg 5;

---

41. Further instances with military connotations include, e.g., Lam 2:2–3; 4:9, 12; 5:16.

Pss 18; 68; Isa 63:1–6) and even those collective laments, which seem to be closer to the times of monarchy (cf. Pss 44; 89; 137).

We may follow a similar line of argument in regard to priestly influence on Lamentations. The topic of destroyed temple and destitute priests and prophets plays a large role in the book. Still, their importance is a long way off the central attention priests and purity receive in some sections of the Pentateuch. Confessions of sin do not loom large in Lamentations,[42] and the few relevant passages do not spell out very clearly what the trespasses have been in the past. They seem to fall into deuteronomic categories of disobedience rather than impurity (cf. Lam 1:8, 20; 3:42; 4:13) although torah is not explicitly mentioned except in Lam 2:9: "her king and princes are among the nations; guidance (Heb. *torah*) is no more." This fact brings to mind that Lamentations also does not give any hints as to the "classical" history of Israel with its God YHWH, as narrated in the Pentateuch or the histories of the monarchies, be they transmitted by Deuteronomists or Chroniclers.

All this means to say that the authors, transmitters, and users of the book of Lamentations selected their own themes and materials in composing the extant texts. The five chapters concentrate on the deplorable destiny of the Jerusalem congregation after the Babylonian occupation (and in exile?), commemorating its downfall and pleading for mercy.

Core Theology and Community

It is my conviction that concepts of God—besides being results of traditional developments—also reflect in one way or another the social group and organization that bring about such theological ideas. Nomadic people, in fact, nurture different notions of the divinity than farming folks, citizens of urban centers believe in another way than villagers. Do the theological concepts in Lamentations reveal anything about the community we are trying to understand?

First of all, we may register those theological traits we do not find in Lamentations: YHWH here is not, as already pointed out, the God from Egypt, who liberated Israel out of bondage, gave it his ordinances, and led it into the promised land. Nor is this the God of Second Isaiah and the Babylonian congregation eagerly waiting for release from captivity. This is, most of all, the God who dwelled on Zion. Metaphorical discourse of marriage

---

42. Cf. Boda, "The Priceless Gain of Penitence." Boda places Lamentations between "communal lament" and "penitential prayer." For a discussion of genres, cf. Gerstenberger, *Psalms, Part 2*.

bonds between God and people (Hos 1–3; Ezek 16; 23) may have had some impact on Lamentation's theological ideas. God destroyed his temple and town, permitting his people to be shamed and taken captive.[43] He has "poured out his wrath" (cf. Lam 4:11) over his community, utterly destroying it. YHWH himself is the agent of all evil, notwithstanding Jerusalem's guilt that triggered the catastrophe. "From on high he sent fire . . ." (Lam 1:13); "My transgressions were bound into a yoke . . . They weigh on my neck" (Lam 1:14); "The Lord has trodden as in a wine press the virgin daughter Judah" (Lam 1:15; cf. 2:1–8). That enemies were involved in the downfall of the city does not counteract YHWH's responsibility; on the contrary, it may be a synonymous expression of his brutal punishments (cf. Lam 2:17, 22).

Where is such a destructive deity to be located? It certainly is not a concept of family religion we meet here. Isaiah 63:7—64:11 implores the furious deity by his familiar epithet "father" (63:16; 64:7) and by conjuring up the salvation history of Moses (63:7–14). In Ps 44, it is the help that the people have received from God and his covenant with Israel that are the points of reference for complaint, reproach, and petition (cf. vv. 2–4, 18 [1–3, 17]). Not so in Lamentations. The concept of the furious deity punishing even his own clientele seems to be a general Mesopotamian concept extant in old city laments. There are no explicit theological configurations of alliances or generic affiliations between deity and people recognizable in Mesopotamian sources aside from the frequent claim that one determined god or goddess establishes a certain temple in a given city. Lamentations seems to presuppose, along this same line, a close (marital!) relationship of YHWH to Zion and Jerusalem, but nothing more. We have to learn, then, that Israel's theological concepts were not uniform in the sixth to fourth centuries BCE. Lamentations does not draw on covenant theology nor on familial traditions to articulate its grave concerns over against the dreadful God of destruction. Therefore, the final verse, Lam 5:22, need not be a gross deviation from otherwise deferential attitudes over against YHWH. In the same vein, there is no refined theory of sin or repentance or perhaps impurity apparent in Lamentations, although such priestly or Deuteronomistic vocabulary does occur (for "sin," cf. Lam 1:8, 14, 18; 3:42; 4:13, 22; 5:7; for "impurity," Lam 1:9, 17; 3:45; 4:1, 14–15).

Secondly, the social structure of the community shines through here and there. The (Judean) king is gone (Lam 2:9, cf. vv. 2, 6). Present offices in

---

43. Cf. Lam 1:5, 12–15; 2:1–8 (esp. v. 6: "He has broken down his booth like a garden, he has destroyed his tabernacle . . ." Verse 7: "Yahweh has scorned his altar, disowned his sanctuary; he has delivered into the hand of the enemy the walls of her palaces . . ."); Lam 2:17; 4:11: "Yahweh gave full vent to his wrath; he poured out his hot anger, and kindled a fire in Zion that consumed its foundations."

the community include "princes" (*śarim*, Lam 1:6; 2:2, 9; 5:12), "prophets" (Lam 2:9, 14, 20; 4:13), "priests" (Lam 1:4, 19; 2:6, 20; 4:13, 16), and "elders" (Lam 1:19; 2:10, 21; 4:16; 5:12, 14). As *śarim* is a general expression for "leader" including community foremen, the terminology is not a royalist one. Rather, it betrays "civilian" traits: prophets and priests certainty belong to the pillars of the exilic/post-exilic congregation. And the "elders" fit into this spectrum (cf. Ezek 8:1, 11, 12; 14:1; 20:1). They became the most important lay instrument of community organization. Furthermore, the "people" visible in Lamentations are composed most of all of women (mothers) and children, some young females, a generic group of youngsters and elderly, with the men of valor killed in the war or deported and therefore all but missing (cf. Lam 1:15, 18; 2:21; 5:13, 14). Interestingly, some late texts of the Hebrew Bible stress the presence of women and children at Torah gatherings (cf. Neh 8:2; Deut 31:12–13; 2 Chr 34:30). So we are probably close to the first person plural voice in Lamentations indicating the contours of a religious community that wrestles with its patron God because of its dire situation of violence, hunger, discrimination, etc.

Practical Use and Place in Canon

The question of *Sitz im Leben* to my mind is of highest importance in biblical interpretation.[44] If we refrain from heeding it, Lamentations becomes a literary composition blown by the winds.

My general assumption is that most of biblical literature was composed or revised in the Persian period within the process of emerging Judaism. The community produced literary agendas for its various ceremonies. The material, collected into the Hebrew canon, was part and parcel of worship services, festive celebrations, rites of passage, etc. The canon was not created as a volume for private reading and individual edification. It came about as the book of a community of believers to be used in manifold communal rites and stayed on this track to our own days. That private reading became another option for encountering the Bible is due to various factors favoring the development of literary cultures.

In the case of Lamentations, we should certainly search for particular "communicative actions" or "special worship-rituals" that gave rise to such exquisite poetic texts. Fortunately, there are some traces of exilic/post-exilic mourning rites in Hebrew Scriptures. Psalm 137 mentions songs in memory of Jerusalem performed by exiles in Babylonia and denouncing the Edomites (v. 7; cf. Lam 4:21) who took part in the city's sacking. Zechariah

---

44. Cf. Gerstenberger, "Social Sciences and Form-Criticism."

7:2–7 and 8:19 testify to annual commemorations of the fall of Jerusalem. The question is raised: Should these days of mourning be continued or abolished, apparently in the light of the rebuilding of the temple (cf. Ezra 6:13, 15)? Mourning in these instances goes hand in hand with fasting. Such realizations (implicitly a therapy against trauma suffered) seem to belong to the exilic and post-exilic period. To be sure, we do not have direct evidence for a linkage of Lamentations to those commemorations. Fasting and mourning rites are not referred to in Lamentations. But there is a certain plausibility for just this possibility. Lamentations and the fasting days of Zechariah belong into the same period; they both focus on the ill fate of Jerusalem, and they are in a broad stream of ancient Near Eastern mourning habits. Poetic artistry is no argument against the hypothesis, because public ritual certainly demands refined language.

The book of Lamentations is an enigmatic pamphlet and offers sufficient points for discussion. In my view, it should be assessed primarily as a piece of liturgical art, originating in mourning rituals of old and being used to this day in synagogue worship for the Ninth of Av. The booklet has been a powerful mediator to understand modern collective trauma (and vice versa). Its position in the festive scroll of Megilloth has supported its ceremonial function, while the LXX (Septuagint)/Christian (Protestant) placement after the prophet Jeremiah fostered an individualistic and prophetic interpretation.

Bibliography

Abusch, I. Tzvi. "The Promise to Praise the God in Šuilla Prayers." In *Biblical and Oriental Essays in Memory of William L. Moran*, edited by Agustinus Gianto, 1–10. Biblica et Orientalia 48. Rome: Pontifical Biblical Institute Press, 2005.

Abusch, I. Tzvi, and Daniel Schwemer. *Corpus of Mesopotamian Anti-Witchcraft Rituals*. Ancient Magic and Divination 8/1. Leiden: Brill, 2011.

Albertz, Rainer. "Der sozialgeschichtliche Hintergrund des Hiobbuches und der 'Babylonischen Theodizee.'" In *Die Botschaft und die Boten: Festschrift für Hans Walter Wolff zum 70. Geburtstag*, edited by Jörg Jeremias und Lothar Perlitt, 349–72. Neukirchen-Vluyn: Neukirchener, 1981.

———. *A History of Israelite Religion in the Old Testament Periods*. 2 vols. Translated by John Bowden. Louisville: Westminster John Knox, 1994.

Alexander, Philip S. *The Mystical Texts: Songs of the Sabbath Sacrifice and Related Manuscripts*. Companion to the Qumran Scrolls 7. London: T. & T. Clark, 2005.

Allen, Leslie C. "The Value of Rhetorical Criticism in Psalm 69." *JBL* 105 (1986) 577–89.

*Alonso Schökel, Luis. *A Manual of Hebrew Poetics*. Subsidia Biblica 11. Rome: Pontifical Biblical Institute Press, 1988.

Alt, Albrecht. "The Origin of Israelite Law." In *Essays in Old Testament History and Religion*, 81–132. Translated by R. A. Wilson. Garden City, NY: Doubleday, 1966.

*Ambos, Claus. "Ritual Healing and the Investiture of the Babylonian King." In *The Problem of Ritual Efficacy*, edited by William S. Sax et al., 17–44. Oxford Ritual Studies. New York: Oxford University Press, 2010.

Anderson, Gary A. "The Praise of God as a Cultic Event." In *Priesthood and Cult in Ancient Israel*, edited by Gary A. Anderson and Saul M. Olyan, 15–33. JSOTSup 125. Sheffield: JSOT Press, 1991.

Augustine. *Enarrationes in Psalmos*. Corpus Christianorum X/2. Series Latina 38, 39, 40. Turnhout: Brepols, 1956.

Bail, Ulrike. *Gegen das Schweigen klagen: Eine intertextuelle Studie zu den Klagepsalmen Ps 6 und Ps 55 und der Erzählung von der Vergewaltigung Tamars*. Gütersloh: Kaiser, 1998.

Barth, Christoph. *Einführung in die Psalmen*. Biblische Studien. Neukirchen-Vluyn: Neukirchener, 1961.

———. *Die Errettung vom Tode: Leben und Tod in den Klage- und Dankliedern des Alten Testaments.* 1947. Reprint, edited by Bernd Janowski. Stuttgart: Kohlhammer, 1997.

———. *Introduction to the Psalms.* Translated by R. A. Wilson. New York: Scribner, 1966.

Baumgartner, Walter. *Die Klagegedichte des Jeremia.* BZAW 32. Gießen: Töpelmann, 1917.

Becker, Joachim. *Israel deutet seine Psalmen.* 2nd ed. SBS 18. Stuttgart: Katholisches Bibelwerk, 1967.

Becker-Spörl, Silvia. *Und sang Debora an jenem Tag: Untersuchungen zu Sprache und Intention des Deboraliedes (Ri 5).* European University Studies, Series XXII: Theology, 620. Frankfurt: Lang, 1998.

Beckman, Gary M. *Hittite Birth Rituals.* 2nd ed. Wiesbaden: Harrossowitz, 1983.

Begrich, Joachim. "Das priestliche Heilsorakel." *ZAW* 52 (1934) 81–92. Reprinted in Begrich, *Studien zu Deuterojesaja.* Edited by Walther Zimmerli. Theologische Bücherei 20. Munich: Kaiser, 1965.

Bell, Catherine. *Ritual: Perspectives and Dimensions.* New York: Oxford University Press, 1997.

Benetti, Santos. *Salmos al derecho y al revés.* Madrid: Paulinas, 1977.

———. *Salmos para vivir y morir: Ensayo sobre la paradoja humana.* Madrid: Paulinas, 1978.

Ben Zvi, Ehud, and Michael H. Floyd, eds. *Writings and Speech in Israelite and Ancient Near Eastern Prophecy.* SBL Symposium Series 10. Atlanta: SBL, 2000.

Bergant, Dianne. *Lamentations.* Abingdon Old Testament Commentaries. Nashville: Abingdon 2003.

Berges, Ulrich. *Klagelieder.* Herders Theologischer Kommentar zum Alten Testament. Freiburg: Herder, 2002.

Berlin, Adele. *Lamentations: A Commentary.* Old Testament Library. Louisville: Westminster John Knox, 2002.

———. "On Writing a Commentary on Lamentations." In *Lamentations in Ancient and Contemporary Cultural Contexts,* edited by Nancy C. Lee and Carleen Mandolfo, 3–11. SBL Symposium Series 43. Atlanta: SBL, 2008.

Blank, Sheldon H. *Jeremiah: Man and Prophet.* Cincinnati: Hebrew Union College Press, 1961.

Blenkinsopp, Joseph. *Geschichte der Prophetie in Israel: Von den Anfängen bis zum hellenistischen Zeitalter.* Translated by Erhard S. Gerstenberger. Stuttgart: Kohlhammer, 1998.

———. *A History of Prophecy in Israel.* Rev. ed. Louisville: Westminster John Knox, 1996.

Boase, Elizabeth. *The Fulfillment of Doom? The Dialogic Interaction between the Book of Lamentations and the Pre-exilic/Early-exilic Literature.* LHBOTS 437. London: T. & T. Clark, 2006.

Boda, Mark J. "The Priceless Gain of Penitence: From Communal Lament to Pennitential Prayer in the 'Exilic' Literature of Israel." In *Lamentations in Ancient and Contemporary Cultural Contexts,* edited by Nancy C. Lee and Carleen Mandolfo, 81–101. SBL Symposium Series 43. Atlanta: SBL, 2008.

Boda, Mark J., et al., eds. *The Book of the Twelve and the New Form Criticism.* Ancient Near Eastern Monographs. Atlanta: SBL, 2015.

Boecker, Hans Jochen. *Redeformen des Rechtslebens im Alten Testament*. 2nd ed. WMANT 14. Neukirchen-Vluyn: Neukirchener, 1970.
Borger, R. "Šurpu II, III, IV und VIII in 'Partitur.'" In *Wisdom, Gods and Literature: Studies in Assyriology in Honor of W. G. Lambert*, edited by A. R. George and Irving L. Finkel, 15–90. Winona Lake, IN: Eisenbrauns, 2000.
Breed, Brennan W. *Nomadic Text: A Theory of Biblical Reception History*. Indiana Series in Biblical Literature. Bloomington: Indiana University Press, 2014.
Brewer, Julius A. *The Book of Jeremiah in the King James Version*. 2 vols. Harper's Annotated Bible 5–6. New York: Harper, 1951–1952.
Bright, John. "The Date of the Prose Sermons of Jeremiah." *JBL* 70 (1951) 15–35.
Brockelmann, Carl. *Hebräische Syntax*. Neukirchen: Verlag der Buchhandlung des Erziehungsvereins, 1956.
Brown, William P. *A Handbook to Old Testament Exegesis*. Louisville: Westminster John Knox, 2017.
Brueggemann, Walter. *The Psalms and the Life of Faith*. Edited by Patrick D. Miller. Minneapolis: Fortress, 1995.
Budde, Karl. "Das hebräische Klagelied." *ZAW* 2 (1882) 1–52.
Burkhardt, Jakob Chr. *The Civilization of the Renaissance in Italy*. Vienna: Phaidon, 1937.
Buss, Martin J. *Biblical Form Criticism in Its Context*. JSOTSup 274. Sheffield: Sheffield Academic, 1999.
———. *The Changing Shape of Form Criticism: A Relational Approach*. Hebrew Bible Monographs 18. Sheffield: Sheffield Phoenix, 2010.
———. *The Concept of Form in the Twentieth Century*. Sheffield: Sheffield Phoenix, 2008.
Câmara, Hélder. *A Thousand Reasons for Living*. Edited by José de Broucker. Translated by Alan Neame. Philadelphia: Fortress, 1981.
Caplice, Richard I. *The Akkadian Namburbi Texts*. Sources from the Ancient Near East 1/1. Los Angeles: Undena, 1974.
Carmichael, Calum M. *Illuminating Leviticus: A Study of Its Laws and Institutions in the Light of Biblical Narratives*. Baltimore: Johns Hopkins University Press, 2006.
Cheyne, T. K. *Jeremiah: His Life and Times*. Men of the Bible. London: Nisbet, 1888.
Childs, Brevard S. *Old Testament Theology in a Canonical Context*. Philadelphia: Fortress, 1985.
Clark, W. Malcolm. "Law." In *Old Testament Form Criticism*, edited by John H. Hayes, 99–139. Trinity University Monograph Series in Religion 2. San Antonio: Trinity University Press, 1974.
Coats, George W. *Genesis: With an Introduction to Narrative Literature*. FOTL 1. Grand Rapids: Eerdmans, 1983.
———. *Saga, Legend, Tale, Novella, Fable: Narrative Forms in Old Testament Literature*. JSOTSup 35. Sheffield: JSOT Press, 1986.
Cohen, Mark E. *The Canonical Lamentations of Ancient Mesopotamia*. 2 vols. Potomac, MD: Capital Decisions, 1988.
Condamin, Albert. *Le livre de Jérémie*. Études bibliques. Paris: Gabalda, 1920.
Cornill, Carl Heinrich. *Das Buch Jeremia*. Leipzig: Tauchnitz, 1905.
Crüsemann, Frank. *Studien zur Formgeschichte von Hymnus und Danklied in Israel*. WMANT 32. Neukirchen-Vluyn: Neukirchener, 1969.
Cunningham, Graham. *Deliver Me from Evil: Mesopotamian Incantations, 2500–1500 BC*. Studia Pohl: Series Minor 17. Rome: Pontifical Biblical Institute Press, 1997.

Daube, David. *Studies in Biblical Law*. Cambridge: Cambridge University Press, 1947.
Day, John, ed. *Temple and Worship in Biblical Israel*. LHBOTS 422. London: T. & T. Clark, 2005.
Deist, Ferdinand E. "The Prophets: Are We Heading for a Paradigm Shift?" In *Prophet und Prophetenbuch: Festschrift für Otto Kaiser zum 65. Geburtstag*, edited by Volkmar Fritz et al., 1–18. BZAW 185. Berlin: de Gruyter, 1989.
de Melo Neto, João Cabral. *Tod und Leben des Severino*. Uppertal: Dia, 1985.
Diller, Carmen. *Zwischen YHWH-Tag und neuer Hoffnung: Eine Exegese von Klagelieder 1*. Arbeiten zu Text und Sprache im Alten Testament 82. St. Ottilien: EOS, 207.
Dobbs-Allsopp, F. W. *Lamentations*. Interpretation. Louisville: Westminster John Knox, 2022.
———. *Weep, O Daughter of Zion*. Biblica et Orientalia 44. Rome: Pontifical Biblical Institute, 1993.
Doering, Lutz. *Schabbat : Sabbathalacha und -praxis im antiken Judentum und Urchristentum*. Texte und Studien zum antiken Judentum 78. Tübingen: Mohr Siebeck, 1999.
Dreher, Carlos A. *O Cântico de Débora—Juízes 5: Conflito social e teologia num episódio da história do Israel pré-estatal*. São Leopoldo: Escola Superior de Teologia, 1984.
Duhm, Bernhard L. *Israels Propheten*. 2nd ed. Lebensfragen 26. Tübingen: Mohr Siebeck, 1922.
———. *Das Buch Jeremia*. Kurzer Hand-Commentar zum Alten Testament 11. Tübingen: Mohr Siebeck, 1901.
Ebeling, Erich. *Die akkadische Gebetsserie "Handerhebung."* Berlin: Akademie, 1953.
Eisen, Ute E., and Erhard S. Gerstenberger, eds. *Hermann Gunkel Revisited: Literatur- und religionswissenschaftliche Studien*. Exegese in unserer Zeit 20. Berlin: Lit, 2010.
Eißfeldt, Otto. *Einleitung in das Alte Testament*. 3rd ed. Tübingen: Mohr Siebeck, 1964.
———. *The Old Testament: An Introduction*. Translated by Peter Ackroyd. New York: Harper & Row,
Elbogen, Ismar. *Der jüdische Gottesdienst in seiner geschichtlichen Entwicklung*. 3rd ed. 1931. Reprint, Hildesheim: Olms 1967.
ETCSL. Electronic Text Corpus of Sumerian Literature. Edited by Jeremy Black et al. Oxford, 1996–2006. http://etcsl.orinst.ox.ac.uk.
Evans-Pritchard, E. E. *Nuer Religion*. Oxford: Clarendon, 1956.
Falkenstein, Adam, and Wolfram von Soden. *Sumerische und akkadische Hymnen und Gebete*. Die Bibliothek der alten Welt: Der alte Orient. Zürich: Artemis, 1953.
Flint, Peter W., and Patrick D. Miller. *The Book of Psalms: Composition and Reception*. VTSup 99. Leiden: Brill, 2005.
Fohrer, Georg. *Einleitung in das Alte Testament*. 11th ed. Heidelberg: Quelle & Meyer, 1969.
———. *Introduction to the Old Testament*. Translated by David Green. Nashville: Abingdon, 1968.
Frechette, Christopher G. *Mesopotamian Ritual-prayers of "Hand-lifting" (Akkadian Šuillas). An Investigation of Function in Light of the Idiomatic Meaning of the Rubric*. AOAT 379. Münster: Ugarit-Verlag, 2012.
Furht, Borko, ed. *Encyclopedia of Multimedia*. New York: Springer, 2006.
Gelbard, Izabela. [poem]. In *Hiob 1943: Requiem für das Warschauer Getto*, edited by Karin Wolff, 153–54. Neukirchen-Vluyn: Neukirchener, 1983.
———. *Pieśni żałobne getta*. Warsaw: Rok, 1946.

Gerstenberger, Erhard S. *Der bittende Mensch*. WMANT 51. Neukirchen-Vluyn: Neukirchener, 1980. Reprint, Eugene, OR: Wipf & Stock, 2010.

———. "Canon Criticism and the Meaning of 'Sitz im Leben.'" In *Canon, Theology, and Old Testament Interpretation*, edited by Gene M. Tucker et al., 20–31. Philadelphia: Fortress, 1988.

———. *Charting the Course of Psalms Research: Essays on the Psalms Volume 1*, edited by K. C. Hanson, 74–86. Eugene, OR: Cascade Books, 2022.

———. "Communal Instruction: Origin and Purpose of 'Sapiential Psalms.'" Paper presented at Society of Biblical Literature annual meeting, Atlanta, 2003.

———. "Covenant and Commandment." *JBL* 84 (1965) 38–51.

———. "Enemies and Evildoers in the Psalms: A Challenge to Christian Preaching." *Horizons in Biblical Theology* 4/5 (1982/83) 61–77.

———. "Höre, mein Volk, lass mich reden! (Ps 50:7)." In *Bibel und Kirche* 56 (2001) 21–25.

———. *Israel in der Perserzeit: 5. Und 4. Jahrhundert v. Chr.* Biblische Enzyklopädie 8, Stuttgart: Kohlhammer, 2005.

———. *Israel in the Persian Period: The Fifth and Fourth Centuries B.C.E.* Translated by Siegfried Schatzmann. Biblical Encyclopedia 8. Atlanta: Society of Biblical Literature, 2012.

———. *Leviticus*. Alte Testament Deutsch 6. Göttingen: Vandenhoeck & Ruprecht, 1993.

———. *Leviticus: A Commentary*. Translated by Douglas W. Stott. Old Testament Library. Louisville: Westminster John Knox, 1996.

———. "Life Situations and Theological Concepts of Old Testament Psalms." *Old Testament Essays* 18/1 (2005) 82–92.

———. "The Lyrical Literature." In *The Hebrew Bible and Its Modern Interpreters*, edited by Douglas A. Knight and Gene M. Tucker, 409–44. Philadelphia: Fortress, 1985.

———. "Non-Temple Psalms: Their Cultic Setting Revisited." In *The Oxford Handbook of Psalms*, edited by William P. Brown, 338–49. New York: Oxford University Press, 2014.

———. "Proverbia." In *Theologische Realenzyklopädie*, 27:583–90.

———. "Psalm 12: Gott hilft den Unterdrückten." In *Anwalt des Menschen*, edited by Bernhard Jendorff and Gerhard Schmalenberg, 83–104. Gießen: Fachbereich Theologie 1983.

———. "Psalms." In *Old Testament Form Criticism*, edited by John H. Hayes, 179–223. Trinity University Monograph Series in Religion 2. San Antonio: Trinity University Press, 1974.

———. "The Psalms: Genres, Life-Situations, and Theologies—Towards a Hermeneutics of Social Stratification." In *Diachronic and Synchronic: Reading the Psalms in Real Time. Proceedings of the Baylor Symposium on the Book of Psalms*, edited by Joel S. Burnett et al., 81–92. LHBOTS 488. London: T. & T. Clark, 2007. Reprint in Gerstenberger, *Charting the Course of Psalms Research: Essays on the Psalms volume 1*, edited by K. C. Hanson, 74–86. Eugene, OR: Cascade Books, 2022.

———. *Psalms, Part 1: With an Introduction to Cultic Poetry*. FOTL 14. Grand Rapids: Eerdmans, 1988.

———. *Psalms, Part 2, and Lamentations*. FOTL 15. Grand Rapids: Eerdmans, 2001.

———. "The Psalter." In *The Blackwell Companion to the Hebrew Bible*, edited by Leo G. Perdue, 402–17. Blackwell Companions to Religion 3. Oxford: Blackwell, 2001.

———. "The Religion and Institutions of Ancient Israel." In *Old Testament Interpretation: Past, Present, and Future*, edited by James L. Mays et al., 261–76. Nashville: Abingdon, 1995.

———. "Social Sciences and Form Criticism: Towards the Generative Force of Life-Settings." In *Relating to the Text: Interdisciplinary and Form-Critical Insights on the Bible*, edited by Timothy J. Sandoval and Carleen Mandolfo, 84–99. JSOTSup 384. London: T. & T. Clark, 2003.

———. *Theologie des Lobens in sumerischen Hymnen: Zur Ideengeschichte der Eulogie*. ORA 28. Tübingen: Mohr Siebeck, 2018.

———. *Theologien im Alten Testament*. Stuttgart: Kohlhammer, 2001.

———. "Theologies in the Book of Psalms." In *The Book of Psalms: Composition and Reception*, edited by Peter W. Flint and Patrick D. Miller, 603–25. VTSup 99. Leiden: Brill, 2005.

———. *Theologies in the Old Testament*. Translated by John Bowden. Minneapolis: Fortress, 2002.

———. "Vom Sitz im Leben zur Sozialgeschichte der Bibel: Hermann Gunkel, ein zeitgebundener Visionär. Was macht seine Exegese heute noch aktuell?" In *Kontexte: Biografische und forschungsgeschichtliche Schnittpunkte der alttestamentlichen Wissenschaft: Festschrift fur Hans Jochen Boecker zum 80. Geburtstag*, edited by Thomas Wagner et al., 157–70. Neukirchen-Vluyn: Neukirchener, 2012.

———. *Wesen und Herkunft des 'apodiktischen' Rechts*. WMANT 20. 1965. Reprint, Eugene, OR: Wipf & Stock, 2009.

———. *Yahweh the Patriarch: Ancient Images of God and Feminist Theology*. Translated by Frederick J. Gaiser. 1996. Reprint, Eugene, OR: Wipf & Stock, 2021.

Gerstenberger, Erhard S., and Ulrich Schoenborn, eds. *Hermeneutik—sozialgeschichtlich: Kontextualität in den Bibelwissenschaften aus der Sicht (latein)amerikanischer und europäischer Exegetinnen und Exegeten*. Exegese in unserer Zeit 1. Münster: Lit, 1999.

Gesenius, Wilhelm. *Gesenius' Hebrew Grammar*. Edited by E. Kautzsch and A. E. Cowley. Oxford: Clarendon, 1910.

Giesebrecht, Friedrich. *Das Buch Jeremia*. Handkommentar zum Alten Testament. Göttingen: Vandenhoeck & Ruprecht, 1894.

Girard, René. *Violence and the Sacred*. Translated by Patrick Gregory. Baltimore: Johns Hopkins University Press, 1977.

Gordon, T. Crouther. *The Rebel Prophet: Studies in the Personality of Jeremiah*. New York: Harper, 1932.

Grätz, Sebastian, and Bernd U. Schipper, eds. *Alttestamentliche Wissenschaft in Selbstdarstellungen*. Uni-Taschenbücher 2920. Göttingen: Vandenhoeck & Ruprecht, 2007.

Grether, Oskar. *Name und Wort Gottes im Alten Testament*. BZAW 64. Gießen: Töpelmann, 1934.

Gunkel, Hermann. "The Close of Micah." In *What Remains of the Old Testament?*, 115–50. Translated by A. K. Dallas. 1928. Reprint, Eugene, OR: Wipf & Stock, 2016.

———. *The Folktale in the Old Testament*. Translated by Michael D. Rutter. Historic Texts and Interpreters in Biblical Scholarship 5. Sheffield: Almond, 1987.

———. *Genesis*. 3rd ed. HKAT. Göttingen: Vandenhoeck & Ruprecht, 1910.

———. *Genesis*. Translated by Mark E. Biddle. Mercer Library of Biblical Studies. Macon, GA: Mercer University Press, 1997.

———. "Die israelitische Literatur." In *Kultur der Gegenwart: Ihre Entwicklung und ihre Ziele*, I/VII, 51–102. Leipzig: Teubner, 1906. 2nd ed., 1925, 53–112. Reprint, Darmstadt: Wissenschaftliche Buchgesellschaft, 1963.

———. "Jesaia 33, eine Prophetische Liturgie." *ZAW* 42 (1924) 177–208.

———. "The Literature of Ancient Israel." Translated by Armin Siedlecki. In *Relating to the Text: Interdisciplinary and Form-Critical Insights on the Bible*, edited by Timothy J. Sandoval and Carleen Mandolfo, 26–83. JSOTSup 384. London: T. & T. Clark, 2003.

———. *Das Märchen im Alten Testament*. Religionsgeschichtliche Volksbücher für die deutsche christliche Gegenwart. Tübingen: Mohr Siebeck, 1921.

———. *Die Propheten*. Göttingen: Vandenhoeck & Ruprecht, 1917.

———. *Die Psalmen*. HKAT. Göttingen: Vandenhoeck & Ruprecht, 1926.

———. *The Psalms: A Form-Critical Introduction*. Translated by Thomas M. Horner. Facet Books: Biblical Series. Philadelphia: Fortress, 1967.

———. "Ziele und Methoden der alttestamentlichen Exegese." In *Reden und Aufsätze*, 11–29. Göttingen: Vandenhoeck & Ruprecht, 1913 (orig. essay 1904).

Gunkel, Hermann, and Joachim Begrich. *Einleitung in die Psalmen: Die Gattungen der religiösen Lyrik Israels*. HKATErg. Göttingen: Vandenhoeck & Ruprecht, 1933.

———. *Introduction to Psalms: The Genres of the Religious Lyric of Israel*. Translated by James D. Nogalski. 1998. Reprint, Eugene, OR: Wipf & Stock, 2020.

Gunn, Joshua. *Modern Occult Rhetoric: Mass Media and the Drama of Secrecy in the Twentieth Century*. Rhetoric, Culture, and Social Critique. Tuscaloosa: University of Alabama, 2005.

Haag, Ernst. "Šabbat." In *TWAT* 7 (1993) 1047–57 = *TDOT* 14 (2004)

Hallo, William W. *The World's Oldest Literature: Studies in Sumerian Belle Lettres*. Culture and History of the Ancient Near East 35. Leiden: Brill, 2010,

Hardmeier, Christof. *Erzähldiskurs und Redepragmatik im Alten Testament*. Forschungen zum Alten Testament 46. Tübingen: Mohr Siebeck, 2005.

———. *Texttheorie und biblische Exegese*. Beiträge zur evangelischen Theologie 79. Munich: Kaiser, 1978.

———. *Textwelten der Bibel entdecken: Grundlagen und Verfahren einer textpragmatischen Literaturwissenschaft der Bibel*. 2 vols. Textpragmatische Studien zur Literatur- und Kulturgeschichte der Hebräischen Bibel 1. Gütersloh: Gütersloher, 2003, 2004.

Hawking, Stephen. *A Brief History of Time: From the Big Bang to Black Holes*. New York: Bantam, 1988.

Hayes, John H., ed. *Old Testament Form Criticism*. Trinity University Monograph Series in Religion 2. San Antonio: Trinity University Press, 1974.

Hayes, John H., and Carl H. Holladay. *Biblical Exegesis: A Beginner's Handbook*. 3rd ed. Louisville: Westminster John Knox, 2007.

Heeßel, Nils P. *Babylonisch-assyrische Diagnostik*. AOAT 43 Münster: Ugarit-Verlag, 2000.

Heiler, Friedrich. *Das Gebet: Eine religionsgeschichtliche und religionspsychologische Untersuchung*. Munich: Reinhardt, 1923. Reprint, 1969.

Herman, David, ed. *The Cambridge Companion to Narrative*. Cambridge Companions to Literature. Cambridge: Cambridge University Press 2007.

Hermann, Siegfried. *Die prophetischen Heilserwartungen im Alten Testament*. BWANT 85. Stuttgart: Kohlhammer, 1965.

Herms, Eilert. "Herder, Johann Gottfried." In *Theologische Realenzyklopädie*, edited by Gerhard Krause und Gerhard Müller, 15:70–96. Berlin: de Gruyter, 1986.

Holladay, William L. *The Root SUBH in the Old Testament with Particular Reference to Its Usages in Covenantal Contexts*. Leiden: Brill, 1958.

Hölscher, Gustav. *Die Profeten: Untersuchungen zur Religionsgeschichte Israels*. Leipzig: Hinrichs, 1914.

Hossfeld, Frank-Lothar, and Erich Zenger. *Die Psalmen 1–50*. Die Neue Echter Bibel: Altes Testament. Würzburg: Echter, 1993.

———. *Psalms 2: A Commentary on Psalms 51–100*. Translated by Linda M. Maloney. Hermeneia. Minneapolis: Fortress, 2005.

———. *Psalms 3: A Commentary on Psalms 101–150*. Translated by Linda M. Maloney. Hermeneia. Minneapolis: Fortress, 2011.

Howard, Thomas A. *Religion and the Rise of Historicism: W.M.L. de Wette, Jacob Burckhardt, and the Theological Origins of Nineteenth-Century Historical Consciousness*. Cambridge: Cambridge University Press, 2000.

Huffmon, Herbert B. "The Covenant Lawsuit in the Prophets." *JBL* 78 (1959) 285–95.

Hyatt, J. Philip. *Jeremiah: Prophet of Courage and Hope*. New York: Abingdon, 1958.

Jahnow, Hedwig. *Das hebräische Leichenlied im Rahmen der Völkerdichtung*. BZAW 36. Gießen: Töpelmann, 1923.

Janzen, Waldemar. *Mourning Cry and Woe Oracle*. BZAW 125. Berlin: de Gruyter, 1975.

Jaques, Margaret. *Mon dieu qu'ai-je fait? Les diĝir-ša-dab-ba et la piété privée en Mésopotamie*. Orbis Biblicus et Orientalis 273. Göttingen: Vandenhoeck & Ruprecht, 2015.

Kautzsch, Emil. "Jeremia." In *Die Heilige Schrift des Altes Testaments*. 4th ed.

Keel, Othmar. *Feinde und Gottesleugner: Studien zum Image der Widersacher in den Individualpsalmen*. Stuttgarter biblische Monographien 7. Stuttgart: Katholisches Bibelwerk, 1969.

Kirst, Nelson. "Formkritische Untersuchung zum Zuspruch 'Fürchte dich nicht' im Alten Testament." PhD diss., University of Hamburg, 1968.

Klopfenstein, M. A. *Scham und Schande nach dem Alten Testament*. Abhandlungen zur Theologie des Alten und Neuen Testaments 62. Zürich: Theologischer Verlag, 1972.

Kluckhohn, Clyde, and Leland C. Wyman. *An Introduction to Navaho Chant Practice: With an Account of the Behaviors Observed in Four Chants*. Memoirs of the American Anthropological Association 53. Menasha, WI: American Anthropological Association, 1940.

Knierim, Rolf. *Die Hauptbegriffe für Sünde im Alten Testament*. Gütersloh: Gütersloher, 1965.

Koch, Klaus. *The Growth of the Biblical Tradition: The Form-Critical Method*. Translated by Susan M. Cupitt. Scribner Studies in Biblical Interpretation. New York: Scribner, 1969.

———. *Die Priesterschrift von Ex 25 bis Lev 16*. FRLANT NF 53. Göttingen: Vandenhoeck & Ruprecht, 1959.

———. "Propheten/Prophetie II. Israel in seiner Umwelt." In *TRE* 17:477–99.

———. *Was ist Formgeschichte?* Neukirchen-Vluyn: Neukirchener, 1964.

Köckert, Matthias, and Martti Nissinen, eds. *Propheten in Mari, Assyrien und Israel*. FRLANT 201. Göttingen: Vandenhoeck & Ruprecht, 2003.

Köhler, Ludwig H. *Der hebräische Mensch: Eine Skizze*. Tübingen: Mohr Siebeck, 1953.

———. *Hebrew Man*. Translated by Peter R. Ackroyd. London: SCM Press 1956.
Kremers, Heinz. "Leidensgemeinschaft mit Gott im Alten Testament: Eine Untersuchung der "biographischen" Berichte im Jeremiabuch." *Evangelische Theologie* 13 (1953) 278–96.
Lang, Bernhard. *Die weisheitliche Lehrrede*. SBS 54. Stuttgart: Katholisches Bibelwerk, 1972.
Lee, Nancy C. *Lyrics of Lament: From Tragedy to Transformation*. Minneapolis: Fortress, 2010.
———. *The Singers of Lamentations: Cities under Siege, from Jerusalem to Sarajewo*. Biblical Interpretation Series 60. Leiden: Brill, 2002.
———. "The Singers of Lamentation: (A)Scribing (De)Claiming Poets and Prophets." In *Lamentations in Ancient and Contemporary Cultural Contexts*, edited by Nancy C. Lee and Carleen Mandolfo, 33–46. SBL Symposium Series 43. Atlanta: SBL, 2008.
Lenzi, Alan. *Reading Akkadian Prayers and Hymns: An Introduction*. Ancient Near East Monographs 3. Atlanta: SBL, 2011, 56.
Leslie, Elmer A. *Jeremiah: Chronologically Arranged, Translated, and Interpreted*. New York: Abingdon, 1954.
Levine, Baruch A. *In the Presence of the Lord: A Study of Cult and Some Cultic Terms in Ancient Israel*. Studies in Judaism in Late Antiquity 5. Leiden: Brill, 1974.
Linafelt, Tod. *Surviving Lamentations: Catastrophe, Lament, and Protest in the Afterlife of a Biblical Book*. Chicago: University of Chicago Press, 2000.
Lohfink, Norbert. *Lobgesänge der Armen*. SBS 143. Stuttgart: Katholisches Bibelwerk, 1990.
———. *Option for the Poor: The Basic Principle of Liberation Theology in the Light of the Bible*. Translated by Linda Maloney. Edited by Duane L. Christensen. 2nd ed. N. Richland Hills, TX: Bibal, 1995.
Lohnert, Anne. "*Wie die Sonne tritt heraus!*" *Eine Klage zum Auszug Enlils mit einer Untersuchung zu Komposition und Tradition sumerischer Klagelieder in Altbabylonischer Zeit*. AOAT 365. Münster: Ugarit-Verlag, 2009.
Longmire, Linda, and Lisa Merrill, eds. *Untying the Tongue: Gender, Power, and the Word*. Contributions in Women's Studies 164. Westport CT: Greenwood, 1998.
Lord, Albert B. *The Singer of Tales*. New York: Atheneum, 1968.
Luther, Martin. *Psalmenauslegung*. Vol. 2. Edited by Erwin Mühlhaupt. Göttingen: Vandenhoeck & Ruprecht, 1962.
Mandolfo, Carleen. *Daughter Zion Talks Back to the Prophets: A Dialogic Theology of the Book of Lamentations*. Semeia Studies 58. Atlanta: SBL, 2007.
———. "Talking Back: The Perseverance of Justice in Lamentations." In *Lamentations in Ancient and Contemporary Cultural Contexts*, edited by Nancy C. Lee and Carleen Mandolfo, 47–56. SBL Symposium Series 43. Atlanta: SBL, 2008.
Maul, Stefan M. *"Herzberuhigungsklagen": Die sumerisch-akkadischen Eršaḫunga-Gebete*. Wiesbaden: Harrassowitz, 1988.
———. *Zukunftsbewältigung: Eine Untersuchung altorientalischen Denkens anhand der babylonisch-assyrischen Löserituale (Namburbi)*. Baghdader Forschungen 18. Mainz: von Zabern, 1994.
Mauss, Marcel. *The Gift: Form and Reason for Exchange in Archaic Societies*. Translated by W. D. Halls. New York: Norton, 2000.
May, Herbert G. "Towards an Objective Approach to the Book of Jeremiah: A Biographer." *JBL* 61 (1942) 139–55.

McCarthy, Dennis J. *Treaty and Covenant: A Study in Form in the Ancient Oriental Documents and in the Old Testament*. 2nd ed. Analecta Biblica 21. Rome: Biblical Institute Press, 1978.

Mendenhall, George E. "Ancient and Biblical Law." *Biblical Archaeologist* 17 (1954) 26–46.

———. *Law and Covenant in Israel and the Ancient Near East*. Pittsburgh: Biblical Colloquium, 1955.

Meyer, Ivo. "Die Klagelieder." In *Einleitung in das Alte Testament*, edited by Erich Zenger, 478–83. 5th ed. Stuttgart: Kohlhammer, 2004.

Michalowski, Piotr. *The Lamentation over the Destruction of Sumer and Ur*. Mesopotamian Civilizations 1. Winona Lake, IN: Eisenbrauns, 1989.

Milgrom, Jacob. *Leviticus*. 3 vols. Anchor Bible 3, 3A, 3B. Garden City, NY: Doubleday, 1991, 2000, 2001.

Miller, Patrick D. *"They Cried to the Lord": The Form and Theology of Biblical Prayer*, Minneapolis: Fortress, 1994.

Monod, Jacques. *Chance and Necessity: An Essay on the Natural Philosophy of Modern Biology*. New York: 1970.

Moorey, Peter R. S. *Idols for the People: Miniature Images of Clay in the Ancient Near East*. Schweich Lectures 2001. Oxford: Oxford University Press, 2003.

Mowinckel, Sigmund. *Le Décalogue*. Paris: Alcan, 1927.

———. *Psalmenstudien*. 6 vols. 1921–1924. Reprint, Amsterdam: Schippers, 1961.

———. *Psalm Studies*. 2 vols. Translated by Mark E. Biddle. SBL History of Biblical Studies 2, 3. Atlanta: SBL Press, 2014.

———. *The Psalms in Israel's Worship*. 2 vols. Translated by D. R. Ap-Thomas. 1962. Reprint, with foreword by James L. Crenshaw. Grand Rapids: Eerdmans, 2004.

———. *Religion and Cult: The Old Testament and the Phenomenology of Religion*. Edited by K. C. Hanson. Translated by John Sheehan. Eugene, OR: Cascade Books, 2012.

———. *Religion und Kultus*. Göttingen: Vandenhoeck & Ruprecht, 1953.

———. *Zur Komposition des Buches Jeremia*. Videnskapsselskapets skrifter. II., Hist.-filos. klasse 1913 no. 5. Kristiania: Dybwad, 1914. Reprint, Eugene, OR: Wipf & Stock, 2012.

Murphy, Roland E. *Wisdom Literature*. FOTL 13. Grand Rapids: Eerdmans, 1981.

Nielsen, Eduard. *Oral Tradition: A Modern Problem in Old Testament Introduction*. Studies in Biblical Theology 1/11. London: SCM, 1954.

Noth, Martin. *The Deuteronomistic History*. JSOTSup 15. Sheffield: Sheffield Academic, 1981.

———. *Gesammelte Studien zum Alten Testament*. Theologische Bücherei 6. Munich: Kaiser, 1957.

———. *The History of Israel*. Translated by Peter R. Ackroyd. New York: Harper, 1960.

———. *Überlieferungsgeschichtliche Studien*. 2nd ed. Tübingen: Niemeyer, 1957.

O'Connor, Kathleen. *Lamentations and the Tears of the World*. Maryknoll, NY: Orbis, 2002.

———. "Voices Arguing about Meaning." In *Lamentations in Ancient and Contemporary Cultural Contexts*, edited by Nancy C. Lee and Carleen Mandolfo, 27–32. SBL Symposium Series 43. Atlanta: SBL, 2008.

Olyan, Saul M. "Honor, Shame, and Covenant Relations in Ancient Israel and Its Environment." *JBL* 115 (1996) 201–18.

Paul, Shalom M. "Mnemonic Devices." In *Interpreter's Dictionary of the Bible: Supplementary Volume*, edited by K. R. Crim, 600–602. Nashville: Abingdon, 1976.

Pham, Xuan Huong Thi. *Mourning in the Ancient Near East and the Hebrew Bible*. JSOTSup 302. Sheffield: Sheffield Academic, 1999.

Pinker, Aron. "Nahum 1: Acrostic and Authorship." *Jewish Bible Quarterly* 34 (2006) 1–8.

Placencia, Maria Elena, and Carman Garcia, eds. *Research on Politeness in the Spanish-Speaking World*. Mahwah NJ: Erlbaum, 2007.

Pritchard, James B., ed. *Ancient Near Eastern Texts Relating to the Old Testament*. 3rd ed. Princeton: Princeton University Press, 1969.

Rad, Gerhard von. *Das formgeschichtliche Problem des Hexateuch*. BWANT 78. Stuttgart: Kohlhammer, 1934. Reprinted in von Rad, *Gesammelte Studien zum Alten Testament*, 9–86. Munich: Kaiser, 1965.

———. *The Problem of the Hexateuch and Other Essays*. Translated by E. W. Trueman Dicken. London: Oliver & Boyd, 1966.

———. *Theologie des Alten Testaments*. Vol. 2: *Die Theologie der prophetischen Überlieferung*. Munich: Kaiser, 1957.

———. *Old Testament Theology*. Vol. 2: *The Theology of Israel's Prophetic Traditions*. Translated by D. M. G. Stalker. New York: Harper & Row, 1965.

———. *Weisheit in Israel*. Neukirchen-Vluyn: Neukirchener, 1970.

———. *Wisdom in Israel*. Translated by James D. Martin. Nashville: Abingdon, 1972.

Reichard, G. A. *Prayer, the Compulsive Word*. Monographs of the American Ethnological Society 7. New York: Augustin, 1944.

Reiner, Erica. "Babylonian Birth Prognoses." *ZA* 72 (1982) 124–38.

———. *Šurpu: A Collection of Sumerian and Akkadian Incantations*. AfO.B 11. Graz: self-published, 1958.

Rendtorff, Rolf. *Das überlieferungsgeschichtliche Problem des Pentateuch*. BZAW 147. Berlin: de Gruyter 1977.

Renkema, Johan. *Lamentations*. Historical Commentary on the Old Testament. Kampen: Kok, 1998.

Reventlow, Henning Graf. *Liturgie und prophetisches Ich bei Jeremia*, Gütersloh: Gütersloher, 1963.

Richter, Horst Eberhard. *Der Gotteskomplex: Die Geburt und die Krise des Glaubens an die Allmacht des Menschen*. Reinbek, 1979.

Robinson, James M. *A New Quest of the Historical Jesus*. Studies in Biblical Theology 1/25. London: SCM, 1959.

Römer, Willem H. Ph. *Hymnen und Klagelieder in sumerischer Sprache*. AOAT 276. Münster: Ugarit-Verlag 2001.

Ross, James F. "The Prophet as Yahweh's Messenger." In *Israel's Prophetic Heritage: Essays in Honor of James Muilenburg*, edited by Bernhard W. Anderson and Walter Harrelson, 98–107.

Rudolph, Wilhelm. *Jeremia*. Handbuch zum Alten Testament 1/2. 2nd ed. Tübingen: Mohr Siebeck, 1958.

Ruwe, Andreas, ed. *Du aber bist es, ein Mensch meinesgleichen (Psalm 55:14)*. Biblisch-theologische Studien 157. Neukirchen-Vluyn: Neukirchener, 2016.

Ryan, Marie-Laure. *Narrative as Virtual Reality: Immersion and Interactivity in Literature and Electronic Media*. Parallax. Baltimore: Johns Hopkins University Press, 2001.

Salters, Robert B. *A Critical and Exegetical Commentary on Lamentations*. International Critical Commentary. London: T. & T. Clark, 2010.

Scharbert, Joseph. "Das 'Wir' in den Asaph-Psalmen auf dem Hintergrund altorientalischen Betens." In *Freude an der Weisung des Herrn: Beiträge zur Theologie der Psalmen: Festgabe zum 70. Geburtstag von Heinrich Gross*, edited by Ernst Haag et al., 297–324. Stuttgart: Katholisches Bibelwerk, 1986.

Schipper, Bernd U., ed. *Apokalyptik und kein Ende?* Biblisch-theologische Schwerpunkte 29. Göttingen: Vandenhoeck & Ruprecht, 2007.

Schmidt, Hans. *Das Gebet des Angeklagten im Alten Testament*. BZAW 49. Gießen: Töpelmann, 1928.

———. *Die Schriften des Alten Testaments*. 2nd ed. Göttingen: Vandenhoeck & Ruprecht, 1920.

Schmidt, N. "Jeremia." In *Encyclopaedia Biblica* 11:2372ff.

Schoors, Antoon. *I Am God Your Savior: A Form-Critical Study of the Main Genres in Isaiah 50–55*. Vetus Testamentum Supplements 24. Leiden: Brill, 1973.

Schweinhorst-Schonberger, Ludger. "Präskriptive Texte." In *Lesarten der Bibel: Untersuchungen zu einer Theorie der Exegese des Alten Testaments*, edited by Helmut Utzschneider and Erhard Blum, 117–26. Stuttgart: Kohlhammer, 2006.

Schweitzer, Albert. *The Quest of the Historical Jesus: A Critical Study of Its Progress from Reimarus to Wrede*. Translated by W. Montgomery. 3rd ed. New York: Macmillan, 1959.

Scott, James C. *Domination and the Arts of Resistance: Hidden Transcripts*. New Haven: Yale University Press, 1990.

Seybold, Klaus. *Introducing the Psalms*. Translated by R. Graeme Dunphy. Edinburgh: T. & T. Clark, 1990.

———. *Poetik der Psalmen*. Poetologische Studien zum Alten Testament 1. Stuttgart: Kohlhammer, 2003.

———. "Das 'Wir' in den Asaph-Psalmen." In *Neue Wege der Psalmenforschung: Für Walter Beyerlin*, edited by Klaus Seybold and Erich Zenger, 143–55. HBS 1. Freiburg: Herder, 1994.

Seybold, Klaus, and Erich Zenger, eds. *Neue Wege der Psalmenforschung: Für Walter Beyerlin*. HBS 1. Freiburg: Herder, 1994.

Skinner, John. *Prophecy and Religion: Studies in the Life of Jeremiah*. Cunningham Lectures 1920. Cambridge: Cambridge University Press, 1922.

Smith, George Adam. *Jeremiah: Being the Baird Lecture for 1922*. 4th ed. New York: Doran, 1929.

Smith, Morton. *Palestinian Parties and Politics That Shaped the Old Testament*. 2nd ed. London: SCM, 1987.

Steck, Odil Hannes. *Exegese des Alten Testaments*. 12th ed. Neukirchen-Vluyn: Neukirchener, 1989.

———. *Old Testament Exegesis*. 2nd ed. Translated by James D. Nogalski. Resources for Biblical Study 39. Atlanta: Scholars, 1998.

Steible, Horst. *Rimsin, mein König: Drei kultische Texte aus Ur mit der Schlussdoxologie dri-im-dsin lugal-mu*. Freiburger altorientalische Studien 1. Wiesbaden: Steiner, 1975.

Stol, Marten. *Birth in Babylonia and the Bible: Its Mediterranean Setting*. Cuneiform Monographs 14. Groningen: Styx, 2000.

Sweeney, Marvin A. "Formation and Form in Prophetic Literature." In *Old Testament Interpretation: Past, Present, and Future*, edited by James Luther Mays, 113–26. Nashville: Abingdon, 1995.
Sweeney, Marvin A., and Ehud Ben Zvi, eds. *The Changing Face of Form Criticism for the Twenty-first Century*. Grand Rapids: Eerdmans, 2003.
Toorn, Karel van der. *Family Religion in Babylonia, Syria and Israel: Continuity and Change in the Forms of Religious Life*. Studies in the History and Culture of the Ancient Near East 7. Leiden: Brill 1996.
Tucker, Gene M. "Prophecy and Prophetic Literature." In *The Hebrew Bible and its Modern Interpreters*, edited by Douglas A. Knight et al., 325–68. Philadelphia: Fortress, 1985.
———. "Prophetic Speech." *Interpretation* 32 (1978) 31–55.
Utzschneider, Helmut, and Erhard Blum, eds. *Lesarten der Bibel: Untersuchungen zu einer Theorie der Exegese des Alten Testaments*. Stuttgart: Kohlhammer, 2006.
Volz, Paul. *Der Prophet Jeremia*. Kommentar zum Alten Testament 10. Leipzig: Deichert, 1928.
Vorländer, Hermann. *Mein Gott: Die Vorstellungen vom persönlichen Gott im Alten Orient und im Alten Testament*. AOAT 23. Kevelaer: Butzon & Bercker, 1975.
Wagner, Andreas. *Prophetie als Theologie: Die 'so spricht Jahwe-Formeln' und das Grundverständnis*. FRLANT 207. Göttingen: Vandenhoeck & Ruprecht, 2004.
Welch, Adam Cleghorn. *Jeremiah: His Time and His Work*. Oxford: Blackwell, 1955.
Werfel, Franz. *Hearken unto the Voice*. New York: Viking, 1938.
Westermann, Claus. *Der Aufbau des Buches Hiob*. Beiträge zur historischen Theologie 23. Tübingen: Mohr Siebeck, 1956.
———. *Basic Forms of Prophetic Speech*. Translated by Hugh Clayton White. 1967. Reprint with a new Forward by Gene M. Tucker. Louisville: Westminster John Knox, 1991.
———. *Gewendete Klage: Eine Auslegung des 22. Psalms*. Biblische Studien 8. Neukirchen-Vluyn: Kreis Moers, Erziehungsverein, 1955.
———. *Grundformen prophetischer Rede*. 2nd ed. Munich: Kaiser, 1964.
———. *Die Klagelieder*. Neukirchen-Vluyn: Neukirchener, 1990.
———. *Lamentations: Issues and Interpretation*. Translated by Charles A. Muenchow. Minneapolis: Fortress, 1994.
———. *Das Loben Gottes in den Psalmen*. 4th ed. Göttingen: Vandenhoeck & Ruprecht, 1968.
———. *Praise and Lament in the Psalms*. Translated by Keith R. Crim and Richard N. Soulen. Atlanta: John Knox, 1981.
———. *The Praise of God in the Psalms*. Translated by Keith R. Crim. Richmond: John Knox, 1965.
———. *The Psalms: Structure, Content and Message*. Translated by Ralph D. Gehrke. Minneapolis: Augsburg, 1980.
———. *Der Psalter*. 2nd ed. Stuttgart: Calwer, 1967.
———. "The Role of Lament in the Theology of the Old Testament." *Interpretation* 28 (1974) 20–38.
———. *The Structure of the Book of Job: A Form-Critical Analysis*. Translated by Charles A. Muenchow. Philadelphia: Fortress, 1981.
———. "Struktur und Geschichte der Klage im Alten Testament." *ZAW* 66 (1954) 44–80.
Whedbee, J. William. *Isaiah and Wisdom*. Nashville: Abingdon, 1971.
Wilcke, C. "Gebet." In *RlA* 3 (1964) 141–77.

———. "Hymne." In *RlA* 4 (1973) 539–44.
Williams, Jerome D. et al., eds., *Diversity in Advertising*. Mahweh, NJ: Erlbaum, 2004.
Williamson, Robert, Jr. "Lament and the Arts of Resistance: Public and Hidden Transcripts in Lamentations 5." In *Lamentations in Ancient and Contemporary Cultural Contexts*, edited by Nancy C. Lee and Carleen Mandolfo, 67–80. SBL Symposium Series 43. Atlanta: SBL, 2008.
Wilson, Robert R. *Prophecy and Society*. Philadelphia: Fortress, 1980.
Wolff, Hans Walter. "Die Begründungen der prophetischen Heils- und Unheilssprüche." *ZAW* 52 (1934) 1–21.
———. "Das Geschichtsverständnis der alttestamentlichen Prophetie." *Evangelische Theologie* 5 (1960) 218–35.
———. *Hosea*. Biblischer Kommentar 14/1. Neukirchen-Vluyn: Neukirchener, 1961.
———. *Hosea: A Commentary on the Book of the Prophet Hosea*. Translated by Gary Stansell. Hermeneia. Philadelphia: Fortress, 1974.
Yupanqui, Atahaulpa. In *Cantaré: Songs aus Lateinamerika*, edited by Carlo Rincón and Gerda Schattenberg-Rincón, 21–22. Dortmund: Weltkreis, 1980.
Zenger, Erich, ed. *Ritual und Poesie: Formen und Orte religiöser Dichtung im Alten Orient, im Judentum und im Christentum*. HBS 36. Freiburg: Herder, 2003.
Zgoll, Annette. "Audienz—Ein Modell zum Verständnis mesopotamischer Handerhebungsrituale: Mit einer Deutung der Novelle vom Armen Mann von Nippur." *Baghdader Mitteilungen* 34 (2005) 181–203.
———. "Für Sinne, Geist und Seele: Vom konkreten Ablauf mesopotamischer Rituale zu einer generellen Systematik von Ritualfunktionen." In *Ritual und Poesie: Formen und Orte religiöser Dichtung im alten Orient, im Judentum und im Christentum*, edited by Erich Zenger, 25–46. Freiburg: , 2003.
———. *Die Kunst des Betens: Form und Funktion, Theologie und Psychagogik in babylonisch-assyrischen Handerhebungsgebeten zu Ištar*. AOAT 308. Münster: Ugarit-Verlag, 2003.
Zimmerli, Walther. *Das Buch Ezechiel*. Biblischer Kommentar 13. Neukirchen-Vluyn: Neukirchener, 1969.
———. *Ezekiel: A Commentary on the Book of the Prophet Ezekiel*. Translated by Ronald E. Clements. 2 vols. Hermeneia. Philadelphia: Fortress, 1979–1983.
Zweig, Stefan. *Jeremiah: A Drama in Nine Scenes*. New York: Seltzer, 1922.

Author Index

Abusch, I. Zvi, 3, 6, 10
Albertz, Rainer, 37, 51
Alexander, Philip S., 65
Allen, Leslie C., 33
Alt, Albrecht, 50
Anderson, Gary A., 12
Augustine, 27

Bail, Ulrike, 60, 83
Barth, Christoph, 3, 29, 58, 100
Baumgartner, Walter, 46, 92, 98–99, 101
Becker, Joachim, 29
Becker-Spörl, Silvia, 63
Beckman, Gary A., 60
Begrich, Joachim, 28, 46–48, 51, 53, 73–75
Bell, Catherine, 5, 86
Benetti, Santos, 20
Ben Zvi, Ehud, 48, 52, 78, 79
Bergant, Dianne, 112
Berges, Ulrich, 111, 113
Berlin, Adele, 110, 113
Blank, Sheldon H., 91, 110
Blenkinsopp, Joseph, 52
Boase, Elizabeth, 114
Boda, Mark J., 78, 118
Boecker, Hans Jochen, 50
Bohr, Niels, 17
Borger, R., 3
Bousset, Wilhelm,
Breed, B. W., 80
Brewer, Julius A., 92

Bright, John, 91
Brockelmann, Carl, 93
Brown, William P., 88
Brueggemann, Walter, 77
Budde, Karl, 112
Bultmann, Rudolf, 46
Burkhardt, Jakob Chr., 44
Buss, Martin J., 44, 45, 78, 79, 90

Câmara, Hélder, 26
Caplice, Richard I., 28
Carmichael, Calum M., 50
Cheyne, T. K., 91
Childs, Brevard S., 39, 80
Clark, W. Malcolm, 50
Coats, George W., 49
Cohen, Mark E., 62, 116
Condamin, Albert, 92
Cornill, Carl Heinrich, 92, 95
Crüsemann, Frank, 29, 59
Cunningham, Graham, 3, 6, 57

Daube, David, 50
Day, John, 65
de Melo Neto, João Cabral, 20
de Wette, Wilhelm M. L., 45
Deist, Ferdinand E., 52
Dibelius, Martin, 46
Diller, Carmen, 112
Dobbs-Allsopp, F. W., 111–13, 116
Doering, Lutz, 65
Dreher, Carlos A., 63

AUTHOR INDEX

Duhm, Bernhard, 45, 52, 91–95, 98–99, 101–2

Ebeling, Erich, 28
Eichhorn, Karl Albert, 45
Einstein, Albert, 17
Eisen, Ute E., 78
Eissfeldt, Otto, 48
Elbogen, Ismar, 65
Evans-Pritchard, E. E., 59

Falkenstein, Adam, 2
Floyd, Michael H., 52
Fohrer, Georg, 48
Frechette, Christopher G., 3, 57
Furht, Borko, 47

Garcia, Carman, 47
Gelbard, Izabela, 16–17
Gerstenberger, Erhard S., 2–3, 6–7, 8, 10, 13, 27–29, 34, 37, 39, 50–52, 54–56, 58–61, 65–67, 69–73, 75–78, 80–83, 85, 90, 111, 116, 118, 120
Gesenius, Wilhelm, 93
Giesebrecht, Friedrich, 92, 98
Girard, René, 23
Gordon, T. Crouther, 91
Grätz, Sebastian, 55
Gressmann, Hugo,
Grether, Oskar, 102
Gunkel, Hermann, 28, 45–49, 53, 67, 73–74, 78, 80, 87–88, 92, 99, 101, 103–4, 115
Gunn, Joshua, 47

Haag, Ernst, 65
Hallo, W. W., 3, 5, 7
Hardmeier, Christof, 48, 84–85,
Hawking, Stephen, 17
Hayes, John H., 48
Heeßel, Nils P., 4, 8, 82
Heiler, Friedrich, 2
Herman, David, 49
Herrmann, Siegfried, 51–52
Herms, Eilert, 45
Holladay, Carl H., 48
Holladay, William L., 96–97

Hölscher, Gustav, 91, 99
Hossfeld, Frank-Lothar, 29, 71, 75, 81
Howard, Thomas A., 44
Huffmon, Herbert B., 51
Hyatt, J. Philip, 91, 93, 98, 102–3

Jahnow, Hedwig, 46, 53, 101, 103, 108, 112–13
Janzen, Waldemar, 52
Jaques, Margaret, 3

Kautzsch, Emil, 98
Keel, Othmar, 19, 34
Kirst, Nelson, 75
Klopfenstein, M. A., 22, 34
Kluckhohn, Clyde, 86
Knierim, Rolf, 31
Koch, Klaus, 47, 50–52
Köckert, Matthias, 52
Köhler, Ludwig H. 61
Kremers, Heinz, 106

Lang, Bernhard, 51
Lee, Nancy C., 109, 113–14
Lenzi, Alan, 1
Leslie, Elmer A., 92, 98
Levine, Baruch A., 65
Linafelt, Tod, 109
Lohfink, Norbert, 38
Löhnert, Anne, 116
Longmire, Linda, 47
Lord, Albert B. 114
Luther, Martin, 27

Mandolfo, Carleen, 114
Maul, Stefan M., 3–5, 57, 81–83, 86
Mauss, Marcel, 36
May, Herbert G., 91
McCarthy, Dennis J., 51
Mendenhall, George E., 51
Merrill, Lisa, 47
Meyer, Ivo, 110
Michalowski, Piotr, 109, 116
Milgrom, Jacob, 67
Miller, Patrick D., 58, 60, 70, 75
Monod, Jacques, 18
Moorey, Peter R. S., 56

AUTHOR INDEX

Mowinckel, Sigmund, 28, 46, 48, 50–51, 53, 67, 73, 77, 87–88, 97–98, 102–3
Murphy, Roland E., 51

Nielsen, Eduard, 91
Nissinen, Martti, 52
Noth, Martin, 50, 62, 96–97, 105

O'Connor, Kathleen, 109–110, 113
Olyan, Saul M., 34

Paul, Shalom M., 112
Pedersen, Johannes, 49
Pham, Xuan Huong Thi, 109
Pinker, Aron, 112
Placencia, Maria Elena, 47
Pritchard, James B., 28

Rad, Gerhard von, 50–51, 91
Reichard, Gladys A., 1, 5, 6, 82
Reiner, Erica, 4, 60
Rendtorff, Rolf, 50
Renkema, Johan, 112
Reventlow, Henning Graf, 52
Richter, Horst Eberhard, 15
Ritschl, Albrecht, 45
Robinson, James M., 92
Römer, Willem H. Ph., 9
Ross, James F., 95
Rudolph, Wilhelm, 92–94, 102
Ruwe, Andreas, 84–85
Ryan, Marie-Laure, 49

Salters, Robert B., 112
Scharbert, Josef, 111
Schipper, Bernd U., 52, 55
Schmidt, Hans, 30, 46, 99
Schmidt, N., 91
Schoenborn, Ulrich, 54–55, 76
Schoors, Antoon, 75
Schweitzer, Albert, 92
Schwemer, Daniel, 3, 6
Schwienhorst-Schonberger, Ludger, 50

Scott, James C., 114
Seybold, Klaus, 39, 111
Skinner, John, 91
Smith, George Adam, 91
Smith, Morton, 38
Smith, W. Robertson, 49
Soden, Wolfram von, 2
Steck, Odil Hannes, 47
Steible, Horst, 10
Stol, Marten, 60
Sweeney, Marvin A., 48, 52, 78, 79

Toorn, Karel van der, 56
Tucker, Gene M., 52

Utzschneider, Helmut, 48

Volz, Paul, 92, 94, 98
Vorländer, Hermann, 37

Wagner, Andreas, 52
Weiß, Johannes, 45, 46
Welch, Adam Cleghorn, 91
Wellhausen, Julius, 45
Werfel, Franz, 91
Westermann, Claus, 8, 51, 95, 109
Whedbee, J. William, 51
Wilcke, C., 2, 9
Williams, Jerome D., 47
Williamson, Robert, Jr., 114
Wilson, Gerald H., 80
Wilson, Robert R., 52
Wolff, Hans Walter, 51, 95, 96
Wrede, William, 46
Wundt, Wilhelm, 49
Wyman, Leland C., 86

Yupanqui, Atahaulpa, 16, 23

Zenger, Erich, 28, 29, 38, 71, 75, 80, 81
Zgoll, Annette, 6, 10, 11
Zimmerli, Walther, 97
Zweig, Stefan, 91

Scripture Index

Old Testament

Genesis

3:16	60
8:20–21	21
28:15	97
20	97
28:18–22	61
31:5	56
31:19	56
31:34	56
31:35	56
31:42	56
32:5	95
32:23–33	77
35:16–19	60
48:6	100

Exodus

3:12	97
4:10	97
15	13
15:21	62
20:12–17	50
21–23	61
21–22	50
21:6	56
21:37—22:8	30
22:17	6
23:1–8	50
23:14–17	65, 67
24:3–4	65
32:12	33
32:19	42
32:32–33	35
34:18	65
34:22–23	65

Leviticus

1–9	7
5	31
7:11–21	59
11–15	50
13–16	7
13:45–46	39
13:46	99
18	50
18:24–25	33
19:13	30
23	65, 67
25	67
26	50

Numbers

5:11–28	7, 89
5:22	100
28–29	65
31:23	93

Deuteronomy

2:30	93
3:14	100
7:17–26	33
12–26	68
15:4	40
16	65
16:1–17	67
17–19	50
18:9–14	6, 65
18:9–13	7, 30
18:9–12	85
18:10–11	85
18:10	93
21:1–9	7
28:1ff.	96
27–28	50
27:15ff.	96, 100
28:10	99
28:25	102
28:36	93
28:48	93
28:64	93
29–32	69
29–31	65
30:15ff.	96
31:12–13	120
31:21	68
31:22	68
31:24–26	68
31:30	68
32	68
32:44–47	68

Joshua

1:5	97
1:9	97
7:20	31
24	65
24:15	96

Judges

2:14	94
3:8	94
4:2	94
4:4–5	62
5	62, 117
6:11–32	61
6:15	97
6:16	97
6:22	5
6:25	61
9:8–15	62
10:2–5	62
10:7	94
11:34	62
11:37–40	67
13:19	61
14:6	42
15:18	5
17:2–3	83
17:5	56

1 Samuel

1–2	57
2	59
2:15	5
4–5	22
9:10–14	61
11:6–7	42
12:9	94
15:24	31
15:30	31
18:7	62
19:16	56
22:2	40
28	65, 85
28:3–9	7
28:7–25	6

2 Samuel

7	64
7:20	30
12:13	31
12:28	99
12:31	93
15:7–9	59
19:21	31
24:10	31
24:17	31

1 Kings

1:36	100
8:31ff.	96
8:39	30
8:43	99
14:1–16	89
14:1–3	30
14:2–3	18
17:19–22	7

2 Kings

1:1–2	30
1:2	18, 57
4	57
4:2	18
4:8–37	89
4:21–25	30
4:32–35	57, 73
5	57
7:3–10	39
14:1–3	57
16:3	93
17:17	93
18:33–35	22
21:14	94
22–23	85
23:20	102

1 Chronicles

16–17	63
16	13
16:36	100
17:18	32, 98
25	13

2 Chronicles

6:30	30, 98
7:14	99
20:18–30	13
29:27–30	13
30:5	93
30:21	13
34:30	120
35:2–5	109
35:15	13
36:22	93

Ezra

2:61	99
6:13	121
6:15	121
9:6–15	111

Nehemiah

5:13	100
8	55, 65
8:2	65, 120
8:6	100
8:8	65
9:10	30
12:27–43	13

Job

1–2	32
2:9	21
3:2–6	20
10:18	99
19:6–22	20
19:13–22	32
19:13–19	99
23:11–12	101
30:9–10	99
30:9	32
30:17	99
31	58
31:5–8	100
31:8	100
31:9–10	100
31:10	100
33:14–28	7
33:19–28	89
33:23–26	57

Psalms

1	68
2	13, 64, 64
3–7	6

Psalms (continued)

3:4	21
4:2	29, 32
4:8	99
5:2–3	29
5:4	7
5:9–11	34
5:10	83
6	29
6:2–3	99
6:2	31, 98
6:7	7
6:10	32
7:2	29, 35, 97
7:4–6	30, 100
7:6	35, 100
7:18	13, 58, 76, 84
8	13, 60
8:2	89
8:10	89
9/10	38, 39, 69, 110
10:4–11	24
10:7	83
10:14	98
11	6
12	29, 40, 66, 85, 88
12:8	89
13	6
13:6	21
13:7	84
14	25
14:2	37
14:14–15	22
15	13
17	6
17:1	30, 32
17:6–9	58
18	64, 118
18:47–49	59
18:50	76
19	68
20	64
21	64
22	6, 70–77
22:2–3	71
22:2	19, 71
22:4–6	58, 72
22:4	72
22:5–6	72
22:6–7	
22:7–9	72
22:7	73
22:8–9	19
22:8	73
22:9	19, 71, 73
22:10–11	58, 72
22:10	72
22:12–19	72
22:13–14	73
22:15–16	116
22:15	73
22:16	73
22:17	73
22:18	73
22:20–22	73, 75
22:20	71, 73
22:21–22	97
22:21	74
22:21b–27	84
22:22	70, 74, 75
22:23–32	75
22:23–27	13, 74
22:23	74, 76
22:24–32	74
22:24	74
22:25	76
22:26	59
22:27	37, 74
22:28–32	74
22:28	74
22:29	74
23	58
24	13
25	68, 110
25:4–5	68
25:8–10	68
26:4–6	58, 101
26:6	30
26:9–10	30
26:11	30
27:1	21
27:8	68
27:9	31, 98
27:11	68
28:1–2	58, 71

28:1	21	38:4	19
28:2	30	38:5	31
28:8–9	89	38:6–8	116
29	61	38:6	19
29:1	12	38:7	19
30	13, 74	38:8	19
30:1	67	38:9	30
302	59	38:11–15	18–19
30:5	59	38:11	19
31	6, 29, 75	38:18	31
31:2b	31	38:19	58
31:3	97	38:21–22	21
31:8	30	38:21	20
31:14	19	38:22	31
31:16–17	97	39	69
31:16	35	39:13	32
31:18–19	21	40:7	36
31:18	31	40:10	30, 98
31:20–25	76	40:18	36
32	13, 74	41	34, 40, 73
32:4	99	41:2	59
34	69, 110	41:6–11	19
34:5	37	41:10	19, 34
34:11	37	41:14	100
34:18–19	97	42–83	37
35	6, 34, 73, 75	42:4	19
35:1–3	58	42:12	19, 21
35:3	7, 35, 75, 77, 99	42:13–14	19
35:7	58	42:15–16	19
35:11–16	58	42:17–18	19
35:11–15	19	42:21–22	19
35:12	34	43:4	76
35:13–14	32	44	62, 89, 94, 108, 118, 119
35:17	58		
35:18	21	44:11–14	22
35:20–21	58	44:13	94
35:22–24	58	44:23–26	22
35:22	31	44:23	99
35:25	31	44:27	35
35:26–27	21	45	13, 64
35:26	31	46	13, 89
35:27–28	13	48	13, 89
36:11–13	35	49	38, 39, 69
37	38, 39, 40, 69, 110	50	69
38	6, 73	50:7	69
38:2	19, 98	50:8–13	36
38:3–15	58	50:15–18	69
38:4–9	7	50:19	83

Psalms (continued)

50:23	84
51	6, 58, 73
51:5–8	31
51:6a	31
51:9	7
51:10	99
51:18–21	36
52:4	83
52:11	13, 84
53	25
54:3	29
54:8–9	13, 84
55	6, 73, 75, 81–90
55:2–3	83
55:4–9	82
55:4	83
55:4b	83
55:10–16	21
55:10	83
55:10a	82
55:10a–12	82
55:10a–b	82, 83
55:10b–12	83
55:11–12	83
55:14–15	83
55:13ff.	99
55:13–15	82, 83
55:13	83
55:16–20	83
55:16	82, 83
55:17–20	84
55:17–20b	82
55:18	83
55:20–23	82
55:20	83
55:20c–22	82
55:21–22	83
55:22	83
55:23	82, 83
55:24	83, 84
55:24a–d	82, 83
55:24e	82
55:34	19
56:10	58
56:13–14	76, 84
57:5	83
59	6, 73, 75
59:2–5	19
59:2–3	99
59:3	97
59:17–18	84
59:18	76
60	89
61:3	30
61:9	84
62	58
64:4	83
65	13, 61, 89
65:2–4	61
65:5	61
65:6–9	61
65:10–14	61
66	61
66:1b–12	89
67	61, 89
68	13, 62, 118
68:7	31
68:20–21	89
68:22	31
69	3, 6, 27–43, 73, 75
69:2–5	29, 33, 36
69:2	37
69:4–5	29
69:5	19, 30
69:6–14a	30, 33, 37
69:6–7	38
69:6	37, 98
69:6a	31
69:6b	31
69:7b	31
69:8–13	38, 116
69:8–14a	32
69:8	32, 99
69:9	32
69:10	32, 42
69:14–19	58
69:14a	38
69:14b–19	33
69:14b–16	33, 36
69:14b	33, 37
69:15	33
69:17–20	37
69:17–19	33, 38
69:17–18	33

69:17	33	78:1–4	68
69:17a	37	78:56–72	68
69:18a	33	78:67–72	64
69:19	33	79	62, 94
69:19a	33	79:8–13	89
69:19b	33	79:10	22
69:20–29	34	79:12	22
69:20	38	80	62, 89, 94
69:21–27	36	80:7	22
69:21	34	80:53	100
69:23	34	81	69
69:23–26	34	81:2–4	89
69:24	34	81:7–17	69
69:25	35	83	33, 62
69:26	34	83:2	31
69:27	35	85:5–8	89
69:28–29	35, 37, 38	86:1	36
69:30–32	36	86:2	29, 30
69:30	37	86:2a	29
69:30a	36	86:7	68
69:30b	36	86:11	68
69:31	36, 37	87:6	35
69:32	36	88	3, 6, 29, 32, 40, 73
69:33–37	29, 36, 37, 38	88:2–3	71
69:33–34	29, 36	88:3	32
69:33	37	88:7–19	20
69:34	37	88:9	99
69:35–37	29	88:10	30
69:35	36	88:14	32
69:36–37	36	88:18	99
69:36	38	89	22, 64, 108, 118
70:3–4	19	89:2–30	13
70:6	36	89:42	22
71:1–3	21	89:51	99
71:2	97	90	69, 89, 111
71:10–11	19	91	75, 85
72	13, 64	92:5–6	59
72:12–13	97	94	69
72:18	89	95	13, 69, 89, 111
72:19	100	95:7–11	69
73	38, 39, 69, 73	96	13
73:2–3	24	99	13
74	22, 62, 94	99:5	89
74:1–11	89	99:8–9	89
75	69	100	13, 89, 110
75:2	89	102	6, 29, 40, 73, 85
75:3–6	69	102:1	5
78	67	102:2–3	58, 71

Psalms (continued)

102:13–23	66, 88
102:15	89
102:29	89
103:10–12	89
104	61
105	67
105:1–6	29
105:4	37
106	67
106:4	99
106:6–7	89
106:6	111
106:47	89, 111
106:48	100
107	59
107:11	99
108:12–14	89
109	6, 34, 73, 85
109:2–5	19
109:2	83
109:4	32
109:6–20	21, 83
109:16	35
109:22	36
109:30–31	76
109:30	58
110	13, 64
111	110
112	110
115	89
115:2	22
116	74
116:17	59
117	89
118	74
118:1–4	59
118:8–9	59
118:21	59
118:24–27	89
119	68, 69, 110
119:1–2	69
119:111	99
120–134	65
120:2–3	83
120:5	101
123	89
124	13, 61, 89
126	89
127	60
127:3	60
128	60
128:3	60
129	61
129:8	89
130	3, 6
130:1	30
130:2	59
131	58, 60
132	13
132:6	89
133	60
136	67
136:1–26	29
136:14	93
137	89, 118
138:1–2	59
139	69
139:1ff.	98
139:2	30
139:4	30
139:16	35
140	6
140:4	83
141	6
141:2	32
141:5	32
142:2–3	30
142:4	30, 98
143	6
143:3	19
143:11–12	34
144	13
144:3–4	60
144:3	30
145	110
146	40
147:1	89

Proverbs

19:18	19
22:22	30
31:10–31	60

Ecclesiastes

1:9–10	44

Isaiah

4:1	100
4:3	35
5:24	99
6:5	101
10:6	94
12	74
12:1	59
14:4–21	29
21:2	100
21:3–4	100
22:13	99
24:16	101
25:1–5	74
26:1–6	74
26:17	60
28:7–10	32
35:10	99
38:1	7
38:4–8	7
38	57, 59, 75, 85, 89
38:21	7, 57, 73
40–55	51
41:10	97
42:14–17	12
42:22—43:4	94
43:1ff.	97
43:1–7	12
43:1	100
43:7	100
43:3	94
43:10–13	12
43:14–21	12
44:6–8	12
48:4	98
50:1ff.	97
50:1	94
51:3	99
51:11	99
51:19–20	103
63:1–6	118
63:7—64:11	119
63:7–14	119
63:19	119
64:4–11	111
64:7	119

Jeremiah

1:6	97
1:8	97
1:7–8	97
1:17–19	97
1:19	97
2–6	102
2	107
2:1	102
3	114
3:13–31	62
4–6	107
4:1–2	96, 105
4:10	103
4:13–18	100
4:19–20	100
4:31	60, 101
5:13	99
5:19	93
6:10	99
6:28	98
7–10	102
7:1	102
7:5–7	96
7:10	99
7:11	99
7:14	99
7:16	97, 103
7:25–26	98
7:27	98
7:30	99
7:34	99
8–9	107
8:9	99
9:18–20	111
10:17–18	100
10:19–21	100
10:19	101
11–12	102
11:1–8	
11:5	100
11:8	96

Jeremiah (continued)

11:14	97, 103
12:1–6	
12:3	30, 38
12:5	96
13	102
13:8	102
14–15	102, 106–7
14:1—15:9	95
14:1—15:4	100, 102, 103, 104
14	22, 62, 102, 106, 107
14:1ff.	103, 104
14:1	96, 102
14:2—15:9	106
14:2ff.	105
14:2–9	105
14:2–6	102
14:7ff.	100
14:7–9	94, 102, 111
14:9	99
14:10	94, 102, 107
14:11ff.	105, 106
14:11–16	103
14:11	97, 102, 103
14:13	103
14:14	102
14:17–18	102
14:17	102
14:19–22	94, 102, 105
15	93, 94, 98, 101, 102
15:1–4	94, 102, 103
15:1	102, 106
15:2	102
15:3–4	102
15:5–9	100, 103, 104, 107
15:5–6	104
15:5	103, 104
15:5b	103
15:6	104
15:6a	104
15:6b	104
15:7–9	104
15:10ff.	100, 103, 106
15:10–21	91–109
15:10–14	93
15:10–12	100, 101, 104
15:10–11	107
15:10	94, 101, 105
15:10b	100
15:11–12	94, 100, 101
15:11	93, 94, 100
15:12	93
15:13–14	92–95, 100, 107
15:13b	94
15:14	93
15:14a	93–94
15:15–21	100, 101, 104, 107
15:15–18	94, 95, 98, 99, 100, 105
15:15	30, 38, 98, 99
15:15a	98
15:15b	99
15:16	99, 100, 105
15:17	99
15:18	99
15:18b	105
15:19–21	95, 96, 97, 100, 103, 104, 105
15:19	95, 99
15:19a	96, 105
15:19b	97, 105
15:20	97, 99
15:20a	105
16–17	102
16	102
16:1	102
16:9	99
16:13	93
16:21	96
17–22	102
17:1–4	93
17:1–2	93
17:3–4	92–93
17:12	93
17:13–14	93
17:13	35, 93
17:14	96
17:16	30, 38, 101
17:24ff.	96
18–20	102
18:7ff.	96
18:20	101
18:23	30, 38

20:7	96, 109	44	65
20:14–18	20	44:4	98
20:18	109	45:3	101
21–23	102		
22:28	93		
23:17	99	Lamentations	
24	102		
25	102	1	
25:1	102	1:1–9	110
25:3ff.	98	1:3	117
25:3	102	1:4	120
25:10	99	1:5	119
25:11	93	1:6–7	117
25:29	99	1:6	120
26	65, 106	1:8	118, 119
26:3	96	1:9	110, 119
27:17	96	1:11–22	110
28	106	1:12–15	119
28:6	100	1:13	119
28:12	102	1:14	119
29:12–13	96	1:15	117, 119, 120
29:19	98	1:17	110, 119
29:30	102	1:18	117, 119, 120
29:31	96	1:19	120
30–31	95	1:20	118
30:11	97	2:1–10	110
31:7	99	2:1–8	119
31:13	99	2:2–3	117
31:18	96	2:2	115, 119, 120
32:34	99	2:6	115, 119, 120
33:3	96	2:7	119
33:9	99	2:9	115, 119, 120
33:11	99	2:11–16	110
34:15	99	2:14	120
35:15	96, 98	2:17–19	110
36	65	2:17	119
36:3	96	2:20–22	110
37	106	2:20	120
37:3	97	2:21	120
38	106	2:22	119
38:17ff.	96	3–5	111
42:1ff.	102	3	110, 111, 115
42:2ff.	103	3:1–39	110
42:2	97	3:1–18	116
42:10ff.	96	3:1	112
42:11	97	3:4	116
42:20	97	3:14	116
42:21	98	3:37–47	111

Lamentations (continued)

3:40–48	110
3:40–47	111
3:40	111
3:42	118, 119
3:45	119
3:49–66	110
4	110, 111, 112
4:1–6	110
4:1	119
4:5	115
4:7–8	115
4:9	117
4:11	119
4:12	117
4:13	118, 119, 120
4:14–15	119
4:16	120
4:17–20	110, 111, 112
4:20	115
4:21	120
4:22	119
5	112
5:1–22	110
5:1–16	117
5:1	112
5:2	117
5:3	117
5:4	117
5:7	117, 119
5:8	117
5:10	117
5:11	117
5:12	117, 120
5:13	117, 120
5:14	117, 120
5:16	117
5:21–22	112
5:21	112
5:22	114

Ezekiel

1:3	99
2:8ff.	99
3:8–9	98
3:14	99
7:21	94
8:1	120
8:11	120
8:12	120
11:98	98
13:9	39
13:21	97
13:23	97
14:1ff.	102
14:1	120
14:5	93
14:14	102
15:2	102
16	114, 119
20:1ff.	102
20:1	120
23	114, 119
29:19	94
30:12	94
33:30ff.	102
34:10	97
34:11ff.	97
36:26	98
37:3	30
47:3–4	93

Daniel

7:10	35
9:18–19	99
10:21	35
12:1	35

Hosea

1–3	114, 119
1:2ff.	95
6:1–3	62, 111
6:4ff.	103
11:5–7	100
11:8–9	100

Joel

1–2	22, 62
2:17	22
4:8	94

Amos

5:2	103
9:12	99

Jonah

2	29, 59, 75
2:3–7	18

Nahum

3:7	103

Habakkuk

3:16	94

Zechariah

7:2–7	120–21
8:19	120–21

New Testament

Matthew

8:1–4	39
25:40	25
27:46	70

Mark

15:34	70

Luke

18:24	43

John

2:17	42
17:21	41

www.ingramcontent.com/pod-product-compliance
Lightning Source LLC
Chambersburg PA
CBHW022121160426
43197CB00009B/1104